Dentist Goes Animal, copyright © 2014 by David A. Fagan.

All rights reserved. No part of this publication may be reproduced, stored in a retrieval system, or transmitted, in any form or by any means, electronic, mechanical, photo-copying, recording, or otherwise, without the prior written permission of the author, except in the case of brief quotations embodied in critical articles and/or reviews.

Printed by CreateSpace
ISBN 978-1494717544

September 2014

A project of The Colyer Institute
Post Office Box 26118, San Diego, California 92196 USA – Phone: (858) 566-9297 or online at www.colyerinstitute.org

Cover photos and title page photo from the files of David A. Fagan.

Dentist Goes Animal
A Personal History of Modern Veterinary Dentistry

by

David A. Fagan, D.D.S.

with illustrations by John Whalen

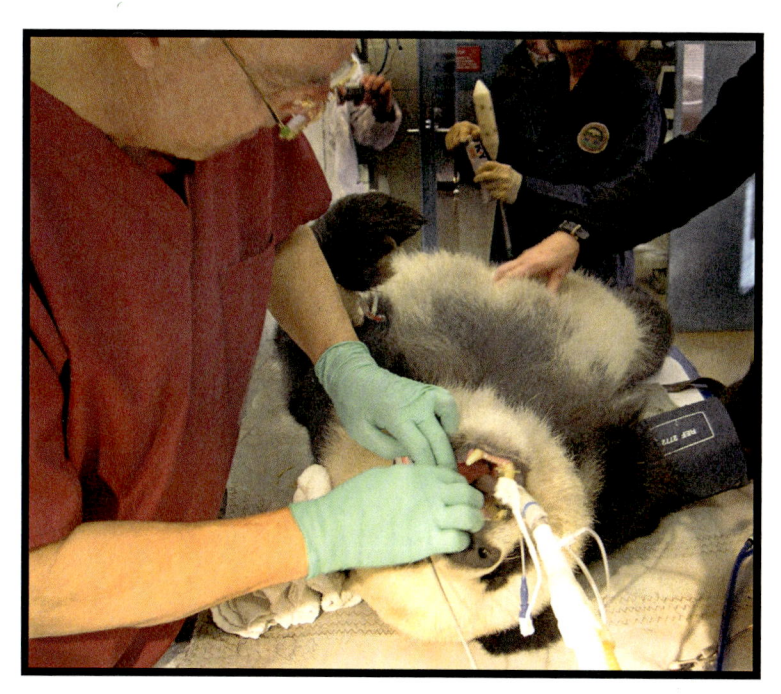

Dr. Fagan with male giant panda Gao-Gao in 2005, when Gao-Gao arrived at the San Diego Zoo

DEDICATION

This book is dedicated to my wife PAULA,
whose gentle and loving ways enabled me to
slow down long enough,
to take a long hard look at my wake, and then,
helped me find the words to describe what I saw.

Introduction by Douglas Myers

David Fagan, D.D.S., is a master storyteller. His tale here begins with his youth and takes you through the steps leading to his success as a world-renowned exotic animal dentist. You will learn of his family, his friends, and how he gained expertise in both his human and animal dental practices.

Enjoy the stories of the many different animals and people Dr. Fagan has helped—and be sure to pay close attention to the incredible innovations he single-handedly created in the field of animal dentistry. David Fagan's dedication to the profession has taken him around the world to improve the welfare of animals and help solve medical problems using his people skills, dental skills, and innovation skills.

Before you read about his adventures, you will most likely picture a dentist and his assistant doing basic dental work with unusual animals. After you read these wonderful stories, you will see that Dr. Fagan is like the conductor of an orchestra, with dozens of people working in unison to solve unique wildlife dental problems.

Douglas G. Myers
CEO/Executive Director
San Diego Zoo Global

Foreword by Kurt Benirschke, MD

When an elephant has a toothache, what do you do? This is not an infrequent question asked in the world of zoos. How do we know whether an elephant even has a toothache? What is it that tells us when any zoo animal has problems with their teeth, or any other physical problem, at all? These are some questions that confronted me when we started CRES, the Center for the Reproduction of Endangered Species, at the San Diego Zoo. I believed then and still do, that with human medicine and its diagnostic tools having made such enormous progress in recent years, many of these advances could and should be shared with the animals under our care. And so, the concept of "one medicine" evolved. Many of the animals we see are mammals just as we are, so why shouldn't they have similar problems?

It was this concern and his experience at the Veterinary Medical Teaching Hospital at UC Davis that brought David Fagan to us in those early days of 1974, asking to be of assistance in the zoo. Thus, a most fruitful collaboration began. Developing special tools and drills to perform root canals on tigers was one challenge. Developing a complete mobile dental unit that could be used anywhere at any time with any animal was another. At the turn of the last century, Sir Frank Colyer, an English dental surgeon, had paved some of the way, but much more was at stake now with medicine having made such enormous strides.

One of the first things David recognized was the abnormalities in the mouths of cheetahs, a condition that had been attributed to inbreeding. David showed it wasn't. Rather, the culprit was too soft a diet, one without the "hassle factor" found in their natural diet, a term he coined and still loves to use. The surveillance of fecal evidence to identify causes of poor nutrition and identifying how discarded elephant molars were being extracted with inadequate tools were two other contributions of David's that still have a major impact on our ability to keep our animals healthier.

Word of his work spread, and many other zoos consulted our veterinary staff to make his expertise available. More recently, he even closed the book on a bit of folklore when he demonstrated that broken, abscessed or bad teeth do not a mean elephant make. The reason: There are no nerves in an elephant's teeth—something that had not been recognized before. Despite his vast experience and the many animals he has helped, David has one major flaw: he hasn't put down on paper most of his findings for publication in the literature.

Thus, I am extremely happy to see that this has come to fruition in this book. We all in the zoological community congratulate him on this important step.

Author's Preface

Shortly before the turn of the last century, a British dental surgeon by the name of Sir Frank Colyer clearly demonstrated the profoundly negative association between oral disease and the overall systemic health of animals—including humans. Based on a wide range of very interesting experiences at the Veterinary Medical Teaching School at the Universit of California at Davis, back in the 1970s, I re-oriented my clinical dental practice to include the clinical care, education and research in the field of oral disease and nutrition of various animals.

This book chronicles a few of the events that have occurred along my path of adventure and discovery, contributing to the birth and development of a new sub-specialty in the field of veterinary medicine, and the panoply of colorful characters, human and animal, that have enlivened the journey.

I suspect all writing with an honest autobiographical perspective rapidly evolves into a difficult task. In my case, this undertaking has consisted of a series of starts and stops for the past eighteen years or so, and has required a great deal of prodding. Dr. Benirschke was the first. Shortly thereafter, Paul Lapolla, formerly senior editor and director of special projects at both Doubleday and Random House, as well as founder and director of Psychology Today Book Club provided focus, help and encouragement. Thankfully, both stayed the course. Fifteen years ago, my good friend Margaret Gordon helped me massage a huge pile of stuff to develop a little character and some flavor for the undertaking. And all the while, I continued to slog slowly forward with an enormous amount of review, introspective reflection, and rewriting.

For reasons I find difficult to explain, I've never spent much, if any, time worrying about yesterday's news. That was then, this is now, and it has always been tomorrow's activities that occupied my attention and focus. Fortunately, however, and also for reasons I'm unable to adequately explain, for years I've kept a daily journal, and filed away my clinical records with thousands of photographic images. So I have a fairly accurate record of past events upon which to call.

What has been much more time consuming and daunting for me, however, has been the task of rehashing, reconstructing, and trying to appreciate the complete context and significance of what occurred.

The final impetus to pull it all together and get it finished was another recent admonition by Kurt Benirschke, when he said, "You know, Fagan, you're going to be dead soon, and it would be nice if your kids knew what you've been doing for the past thirty years."

The fact is, sooner or later, he's going to be correct. Moreover, I never knew just how much of a profoundly influential military career my father had until twenty-plus years after his untimely departure. And, I've always felt badly about that, because there was so little detail.

So finally, here's my story —and I'm sticking to it

DF

CONTENTS

Introduction by Douglas Myers vii
Foreword by Kurt Benirschke, MD vix
Author's Preface xi

Chapter One - HOW IT ALL BEGAN 1
Chaper Two - JUANITA'S MONKEY 16
Chapter Three - FROM HUMANS TO HIPPOS 25
Chapter Four - THE BLACK EAGLE'S STORY 36
Chapter Five - MACGYVER GOES TO THE ZOO 43
Chapter Six - TRIB 55
Chapter Seven - LIONS AND TIGERS AND TEETH 67
Chapter Eight - THE HYENA'S STORY 75
Chapter Nine - ARUSHA LAUNCHES A SEARCH 84
Chapter Ten - BINKY'S LEGACY 94
Chapter Eleven - AN ELEPHANTINE CHALLENGE 101
Chapter Twelve - ELEPHANT DENTAL SCHOOL 118
Chapter Thirteen - A TRIP TO VIENNA - 135
Chapter Fourteen - WHO WAS SIR FRANK COLYER? 143

Acknowledgements 151
Appendix A - List of Clinical Cases in 1980 153
Appendix B - List of Publications 154
Appendix C - List of Protocol Development Cases 158
Appendix D - Some Interesting Reading 159

Chapter One
How It All Began

An Ode to the Elephant
(having taken liberties with a frequently retold Sufi tale)

Wandering near the Taj Mahal
A clutch of blind students is held in thrall
By an elephant met along the way
"What a curious being!" the students say.

"Stop," commands the mahout to his charge.
"These inquiring minds have need to enlarge."

Throughout his more than sixty years
This beast has oft been moved to tears
By the solemn quest of humanity
To untangle his vast complexity

"Let us pause in the shade of this fine tree,
there's plenty to learn here, though we can't see."
... and as the students all gathered near,
They reached out to the elephant to touch, smell and hear.

DENTIST GOES ANIMAL 2

There was a precise moment when I first realized that I shared my life on this planet with a variety of other creatures that deserved admiration, respect, and on occasion, a healthy dose of fear-driven caution.

That moment occurred on the 30th of April in 1950 at about 6:30 in the morning. I was moving slowly along a wet, severely rutted dirt road, deep in the heavily forested rolling hills of central Germany. I was following my father about thirty feet behind him, as quietly as I could. We were stalking a large European wild boar, who had killed and partially eaten a teenage farm girl several days earlier on a nearby farm.

I was immensely proud, but more than a little bit apprehensive to actually be hunting in the woods with my father and older brother. Much as I would have liked to think of myself as a mighty hunter, the reality of the situation was that I was just a fortunate little kid carrying his father's double-barrel shotgun through the dark, early morning woods of occupied West Germany shortly after the end of World War II. My weapon was a rare sixteen-gauge Darne Halifax side-by-side with a unique sliding breech. I was trying really hard to help with the hunt, and learn something about dangerous animals—because hunting and killing stuff was a historical fact of everyday life in this part of the world, and on occasion was an absolute necessity.

Our family lived in the small town of Giessen, about 30 km north of Frankfurt am Main, near Wetzlar, where the Leica camera factory is located. My father was an officer in the U.S. Army Transportation Corps. He was deeply committed to, and heavily involved in, the process of rebuilding Western Europe as envisioned by the Marshall Plan. Every few months or so, someone would get seriously injured or killed uncovering newly discovered unexploded munitions while working their fields, or chasing off a family of hogs, while protecting their developing new food crops.

One of the least reported realities of the rural farm life at the time involved the European wild boar. These omnivorous pigs had been living very well on the abandoned vegetable fields and dead bodies of the soldiers and civilians killed during the previous several years. Large family groups of these intimidating creatures were having a great deal of trouble adjusting to the terms of the newly imposed peace accords enforced upon the locals by the Allied Occupation Forces.

The farmers were doing a wonderful job of replanting their fields to reestablish a reliable source of corn, root vegetables and potatoes for themselves and their livestock. But this process of slowly reintroducing civility to a portion of the world so recently destroyed by such ferocious warring was not going over very well with the carnivorous faction of the local wildlife community. Large mobs of disgruntled wild hogs were randomly creating considerable havoc in the fields. The boar had grown accustomed to all the free, and easily accessible, meat 'n potatoes laid out for them during the war years.

It was the generally unpublicized responsibility of the American army officers like my father to efficiently eliminate the problem when the pigs got out of hand. This was to be done as quickly as circumstances would allow, with the help of the locals, and if at all possible, promoting a little domestic tranquility in the process.

So here we were, my father, my older brother, and me, the youngest, stalking our way along this abandoned and shadowy dirt road through the chilly, mostly silent, early morning woods listening to the sounds of the various animals moving through the underbrush away from the noise of the beaters several hundred meters ahead of us on the other side of the hill to our right. My father was approaching the crest of the ridge. This was in a section of the forest partially cleared of undergrowth, where he could get a fairly clear shot, should the rustling and grunting in the brush on our right turn out to be the killer boar he was looking for.

My father quietly motioned me with a pre-arranged hand signal to get down by the base of a large tree, stay low, out of the way, and remain quiet, which I did. He then signaled my brother to stay low about six feet behind him, to move forward with him, and to watch his left flank, which he did as well. Together they quietly moved into position another forty to fifty meters further up the ridge. In a few moments, I was very much alone, surrounded by, and intently listening to, all of the muffled sounds of the early morning forest.

Then suddenly, surprisingly, and very quietly, the underbrush about ten meters in front of me rustled, parted, and out leaped a huge reddish deer.

This fellow, now directly in front of me, was a very large, very healthy looking stag in the prime of his life with a full rack of very large, pointy antlers. He swiftly materialized out of the underbrush, rapidly heading away from the hunters directly toward me, and skidded to a stop about six feet in front of me. He actually scared the hell out of me, and I turned into an immovable block of rock salt. In fact, we both just froze in our tracks for what seemed like an eternity. With his head lowered, his eyes intently focused on mine, and his weapons ready for use—with the safety off—we stared directly into each other eyes.

Instantly, there was a detailed, in-depth, mutual analysis underway. In the middle of my skull, I could hear him thinking. He was much better at it than I was. But I vividly remember every nerve ending in my body was suddenly on full alert. Paying very close attention to everything he was "saying"—thinking?

Here was a rational, analytical, calculating, enormous life form towering above me, and processing everything about me in a heartbeat. This fellow was alive, worried about his future, and contemplating putting an end to mine. Finally, he must have decided that I didn't look like much of a warrior. In fact, just about as quickly, it seemed, he knew I was nothing to worry about. I knew positively that he had seen a bunch of real mean, bad-ass warriors during the preceding few years. He knew the real thing when he saw it—and it certainly wasn't me. In fact, I was just another harmless little bi-pedal humanoid in the process of trying to comprehend a few lessons about real life out in his world, the heavily wooded forest. Then, just as suddenly as he arrived, he departed. For the next several moments, I watched as this magnificent creature silently bounded down the slope to my left, and slowly disappeared into the undergrowth a hundred meters or so down the hill.

Almost immediately, I heard the sound of my father's German Karabiner model 98K Mauser bolt-action 8mm rifle. By the time I caught sight of him again kneeling beside the base of a large tree, he was signaling me to approach. The hunt was over. It was a success. I joined in, as a 225-pound male boar was field dressed on the spot where he dropped.

This killer boar hung from a tree in our backyard that evening at #3 am der Rodthohl Strasse down the street from the Universität Giessen, where Professor Roentgen had been employed in his early years developing the principles of radiology. Over the next several days

DENTIST GOES ANIMAL 4

the boar was butchered, wrapped and shared with all of the participants in the hunt.

We enjoyed a wonderful pork roast dinner a few days later, at which I told about seeing the deer. But, until now, I have never spoken about our "conversation." It would be many, many years after the fact, before I could find any words, or the occasion, to explain even to myself the truth concerning what I had experienced.

A smaller sow had also been taken at the same time by one of the other hunters, and her six little orphaned piglets were now busy eating themselves closer to adulthood under some branches we had placed on the floor of one of the bomb shelter rooms in the basement of our home. Within a couple of weeks, the piglets all found new homes to be raised and consumed by several of the local farmers, including, I thought fittingly, the family whose daughter had been killed and eaten by their family some months before.

The boar's tusks were mounted on a small plaque by one of the farmers, and together with a small Giessen coat of arms presented to my father in appreciation for his help in making their farm a little safer to work. Today they still hang with some other mementos on the wall in my office with the sow's smaller tusks nearby. They regularly remind me that we do not live alone on this planet. They tell me every day that we are responsible for our decisions and actions, and on occasion we are obligated to employ our talents to help our neighbors, or to defend our families and ourselves.

For me, the red-deer stag experience slowly evolved into a lifetime of helping a host of very interesting captive and free-ranging exotic animals, as well as a bunch of quite bizarre humanoids, in some very strange and unusual circumstances.

From the files of David A. Fagan

The top plaque reads:
Wild Boar 5 jears old 225 Lbs
Shot on 30 April 1950
by CAPT Charles FAGAN
at Lahrbock Hessen Germany

The war had only been "over" for a few brief years. Actually, wars do not suddenly stop as they appear to do in the movies. They wind down slowly, and step back from the brink more slowly still. Eventually—with any luck—back to some kind of normality. During the previous several years the weather in Europe had remained bitterly cold during the long winter months, which didn't leave much time for the removal of all the frozen bodies still entombed in the remaining bomb damage. The local farmers were kept very busy trying to feed their families and rebuild a little infrastructure. It would take another five to ten years to remove the majority of the rubble, properly bury all of the dead, and find and defuse all of the unexploded ordinance still hiding in the fields. It was a similar, but a much larger and more complicated process to what we watched occur at Ground Zero in New York City after the 9/11 incident.

Capt. Charles H. "Hal" Fagan was a transportation logistics specialist at the time, with his office in the Giessen U.S. Army motor pool railroad yard. This is where Mike and I actually learned how to drive—with the help of a variety of partially damaged military vehicles. We quickly learned to recognize an easy repair. As I was to discover much later, our father was also a major player in the war in China, the war reconstruction effort in Europe, and the Berlin

Airlift, as well as having a central involvement in the Korean conflict.

The U.S. military's primary focus at the time was the orderly reconstruction of infrastructure, including the European rail system, in order to re-establish direct, functional, rail access into the major shipping ports at Bremerhaven, Hamburg, Köln, Düsseldorf, etc. My older brother Mike and I attended a small military dependents' school, with all twelve grades in a one-room schoolhouse. We skipped school as often as possible—which was actually quite often—to explore the countryside, and supplement our over-crowded, small-school education with a great deal of wandering about, post-war reality, and black market enterprise.

We learned very quickly that many of the common items found around the kitchen of our American household, which were always there in great abundance, had enormously inflated cash value at the Giessen Bahnhof. In short order, we acquired the necessary elements of a practical street education with the help of our closest German friend, a very experienced local lad, who had nicknamed himself Chicago. His family owned a goat farm just outside of town. With the benefit of his war-tested, street-smart savvy, my older brother and I quickly became experienced, and successful, black-market entrepreneurs.

We regularly slipped a little something extra into our daily school lunch bags. A candy bar, a small bag of chocolate chips, a fresh container of margarine with the dye pouch intact, a sealed one-pound tin of coffee, or if we had something really big planned, like Christmas presents for everyone, or a really long round-trip train ride to one of Germany's more famous

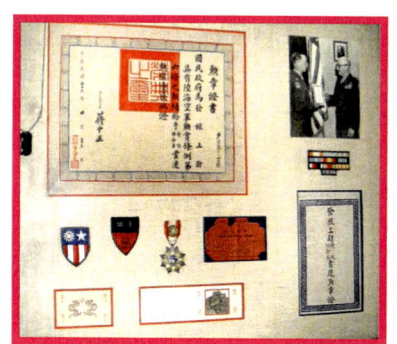

From the files of David A. Fagan

My father's first military assignment took him to Peking (Beijing) in mainland China as part of the China/Burma/India campaign moving men, material and supplies—over the hump of the Himalayan mountains, which spawned the origins of the famous Flying Tigers in the 1940. He received the Clouds and Banner Award from the Nationalist Chinese government for his efforts. I had it framed with his Christmas and New Year Greetings card from General & Mrs. Chiang Kai-Shek.

Following my father's military tour in Europe, our family returned to the States, while my father stayed in France, and then went directly to Korea to participate in the equipment and material logistics raging up and down the Korean peninsula. Among other things, he helped coordinate the infamous body exchange with General Clark at the end of the war at the DMZ in Panmunjeon, where the Korean War Armistice was signed.

Following the death of my mother in the mid 1980s, I discovered a classic military memo in his papers relating to the unpleasant business of returning the bodies of dead soldiers. It was a letter he'd sent to all U.S. military rail station chiefs in Korea noting that there were a hundred-plus rail boxcars of frozen dead bodies going north, but only ten or so boxcars of Allied bodies scheduled to come south. His letter dispassionately asked: Did anyone have anything to ship south to fill up the other ninety-plus rail cars?

My oldest son, Chris, is now the official keeper of many of our family mementos from this period, including my mother's 1948 edition of "The Army Wife," by Nancy Shea, as well as many of my father's maps, photos, and artifacts.

DENTIST GOES ANIMAL 6

From the files of David A. Fagan

The Giessen Bahnhof (railroad station) looked the same in the early 1980s, when I took this photograph, as it did when my brother Mike and I learned the lessons of life and travel in war-devastated Germany after years of conflict. In 1948-9, my mother had a local artist do the drawing of me seen on the right.

castles, a five-pound container of coffee or some cigarettes.

All kinds of American smokes were great bartering chips: a bag of reasonably clean, partially smoked single butts, an opened pack sold as fresh singles, a fresh unopened pack, or to pull out all of the stops, an unopened carton of Lucky Strikes or Camel smokes. It seemed every buyer at the Giessen Bahnhof was willing to walk that extra mile for a Camel. This was because the old Reichsmark was now worthless, and the new Deutschmark had not yet been completely accepted. During this period, and to fill the void, American cigarettes were universally accepted in exchange for many goods and services. In other words, cigarettes functioned as money for many small transactions. My brother Mike and I quickly learned how to conduct an active little business on this fluid playing field.

All of the stuff that we rich Americans took for granted, and generally left lying around unattended, became great fuel for our educational adventures. These things taught me to appreciate, value, take care of, keep an eye on, repair, trade and recycle my belongings. This trait is still with me today, and on occasion still drives my wife a little batty. But as the following chapters will show, it has been immensely valuable in the ad hoc design of a wide variety of dental equipment suitable for use with exotic animals, when no ready-manufactured versions have been at hand.

I spent a great deal of time in the woods in my youth. In fact, it was in the patchwork of quilted dense forests and farmlands surrounding Giessen that I learned the art of classical German equestrian dressage.

Dressage is the fine art of riding in harmony with a horse. Classical dressage evolved from selected offensive and defensive military cavalry movements preparing both horse and rider for a real battlefield encounter. It has since developed into a competitive series of formal movements on horseback involving a series of predetermined patterns. The Olympic Three-day Equestrian Event is considered the ultimate test of this horsemanship, testing both horse and rider to their limits in this classical format.

One of the not-so-well publicized consequences of the Second World War in Europe was the displacement of many of the world's most accomplished Olympic caliber, three-day event, equestrian dressage teams—and their horses.

Of course, the story of General Patton's involvement with the relocation of the world-famous Lipizzaner stallions from the Spanish Riding School in Vienna is fairly well known. What is less well known is all of the other forgotten equestrian units displaced during and after the war. The German army utilized tens of thousands of accomplished equestrians and their horses in various military units during the early war years. There were hundreds of superior-caliber, and thousands of lesser-caliber horses killed and eaten during the lean years throughout the war zone. In fact, horsemeat or "cheval," as the French know it, is still a favored item on many menus even today, and more recently has even included a fair number of American mustangs.

Although I had seen the stallions in the company of my parents, when I was a little kid living in Giessen, it wasn't until many years later that my wife and I really got to know these marvelous animals. It was in 1999 when I was invited to speak at an elephant conference at Tiergarten Schoenbrunn in Wien (Austria). One evening we attended a command performance at the historic Spanish Riding School in downtown Vienna, and then a few days later we drove 143 km south of Vienna through the beautiful Austrian countryside to tour their birthplace at the Piper Stud Farm near Graz. It was here that I was reminded once again that they are all born a very dark black and slowly turn color to white as they grow to maturity. Their mothers are all stabled in large, immaculately clean, communal stalls in compatible mom/baby broodmare bands.

Frau Hanna Voit was one such displaced person or "DP" whose name I remember very well. In addition to his involvement with the logistics of repeatedly relocating the Lipizzaners, or arranging rail transportation for hundreds of liberated Jewish DPs relocating out of the American Occupation Zone, my father had taken the time to help this DP, and her horses, find a place to live and begin the process of recovering their lives. When I met Frau Voit, she lived above her stable of horses in the partially bombed out Verdun Kasernen, or Giessen River Barracks, previously occupied by the German army.

Frau Voit became the focus of my life for the three years we lived in Giessen, before we moved to Paris. Her pride and joy was an accomplished, competition dressage stallion by the name of Perol, as I remember. He was a champion, and she had all of the ribbons to prove it hanging in her tack room. He was also the horse upon which I learned to ride—very correctly.

Frau Voit, a classic German disciplinarian, became my instructor in the empty dirt parade grounds inside the open interior of the crumbled Verdun Kasernen. As I learned how to ride, I became one of her best grooms, and most trusted exercise boys. In exchange for my labor and most of my meager allowance earnings, she taught me how to sit on a horse; to post; to give and take a leg up; to have soft but confident hands; to keep track of what was going on by looking them in the eye; how to muck a stall; to feed and water properly; to clean and hang tack; to get up early in the morning; to get the work done on time; and how to get the stable prepared for a road trip. This was actually one of the best parts. There were no racy trucks or fancy horse trailers to be had at the time. When it was time for a competition, we packed up the gear, loaded it onto the backs of the horses, and rode them across the countryside, around the freshly planted fields, and then through the woods to our destination.

Because I was the smallest and lightest, I rode the big horse. If the trip took more than one day's ride, Frau Voit arranged for all of us to stay with a friend along the way. We put the horses up in her friend's barn, and ate dinner at the farmer's family dinner table that evening. It was at one of these rural German farmhouse dinner tables that I first tasted authentic borscht, a Russian all-root-vegetable soup made with beets, onions, cabbage, carrots, potatoes, garlic and red wine vinegar. I also spent many nights sleeping in the hayloft of another strange barn with our horses. I learned about the old ways of managing a working farm, caring for the families' valuable livestock, and sleeping secure after watching another local farmer turn a large pack of well trained guard dogs loose at dusk to watch over his farm, home, and family. I always slept well in those barns. And the dogs always keep us safe through the night. These trips added another immeasurably valuable ingredient to the mix of my grassroots education, appreciation and understanding of livestock—and my interest in the welfare of animals. I also learned to speak the German language fairly well in the process.

My second favorite activity at the time was our mock "fox hunts" on horseback through the woods to one of the nearby castles. We drew straws to determine who got to be the fox. Then, we tied a real red foxtail onto the back of our mock fox's saddle with a slipknot, and gave the fox a half-hour head start. Crossing the drawbridge into the castle meant the fox had made it safely into his foxhole. The only rule was our equine fox had to drop a handful of paper confetti from his saddlebag at the location of any change in direction, with another handful within fifty meters marking the new direction.

High-spirited, athletically fit horses require a lot of exercise. These mock fox hunts provided that exercise for Frau Voit's horses, as well as a great deal of practical riding and tracking experience for us riders in a secretive, dashing game of hide-and-go-seek through the dark forests and shadows. Each hunt was always a fresh adventure, with new things to see and learn about. I spent many hours exercising horses, or quietly riding on horseback through the forest on the way to the castle a few kilometers out of town. I was taking another few steps closer to becoming immersed in the world of animals.

In due course, the army transferred my father again, this time to Paris. His new office was located at the western end of the Champs Elysée near the Arc de Triomphe, which stands in the centre of the Place de l'Étoile, or Star Square, now known as the Place Charles de Gaulle. His job now involved working with the United Nations to integrate the railroad throughout Europe into a unified rail system with direct access to all of the regional ocean shipping, and air transport terminals in Western Europe. He was an integral player in the farsighted Marshall Plan economic reconstruction program, which not only helped rebuild Europe and Japan after the war, but also laid the foundations for the containerized cargo transport system in worldwide use today.

My brother and I were suddenly out of the woods, and enrolled in the École Saint Louis de Gonzague, a Jesuit boys school in the middle of Paris located on Rue de Franklin near the Trocadero across the Seine River from the Tour Eiffel. We were both intentionally skipped forward many grades to a senior year of high school class, because the Jesuit priests wanted us with a group of boys who were their same height.

During the war years, all Americans kids ate better than most European kids. Therefore, we were generally taller than European kids our same age. We were in school from 6:00 a.m. to 6:00 p.m. This was not a silly, bilingual joke school like we now have in California. We immediately dropped our fluent German, and learned to speak proper, fluent French and Latin in a big hurry.

Actually, we began immediately to learn enough in time to make our first visit to the school's uniquely French toilet. All of our classes were now in French. We were expected to utilize and apply the language in all of our college preparation courses in math, geometry, history, drafting, etc. My brother and I actually began learning college prep algebra in French, after three years of no preparation in their enemy's country. Two years with this bunch of real, tough, no-nonsense Jesuit priests rapidly made up for all of the unsupervised truancy of our three years in a small, over-crowded, under-staffed, military dependents' school in Germany. Getting lost regularly on the Paris Metro to explore the city was an extra carry-over bonus to our more formal education, as we now traveled daily back and forth on the Metro to the Trocadero for athletic field activities. By the end of 1951, the cold war was heating up again, and many of the U.S. military dependents were being sent back to the States. It would be thirty-three years before I would get back to France.

Although I was born in Seattle, home for our family was wherever our father's military career took him and us. By the time he retired, and I finally made it into college, I had had thirteen home addresses. However, at the time we left Paris, we really didn't have a home to go home to. This was because he stayed in France, and then he went directly to Korea. We couldn't live with him in either place. My father was the oldest of ten kids, five boys and five girls. All five of his generation's Fagan boys were in the U.S. military service during World War II. The Seattle newspaper labeled them "the Five Fighting Fagans." So when it was time for us to leave Paris, he arranged for us to stay with one of his sisters, our Aunt Maggie and Uncle Jack at their small lake shore farm home in the logging country northeast of Seattle. Our departure from Paris was very sudden, with no time to pack anything or say any good-byes.

For the entire five years we lived in Germany and France, each member of our family was required to keep their personal run-away bag, packed, and ready to go on twenty minutes notice. One cold winter day in late 1951, we got our notice, and we went. The reason for our sudden departure was several weeks of violent student riots in the streets of Paris originating at the Sorbonne. My father had arranged for us to take the last three seats on a four-engine military air transport aircraft headed back to the States after bringing General Eisenhower and two of his staff to Paris. The plane would not wait for us. So, as soon as he confirmed the flight, we grabbed our bags, said good-bye to our dog Moritz and went to Orly Field. The Eisenhower party got off the plane and we got on. We flew from Paris to London, then Reykjavik in Iceland, to Westover Field near Boston, and then took a train across North America to Seattle. In just a few days, we were out of the big city (Paris), and back in the heavy forest again northeast of Seattle, where our Uncle Jack owned and operated the local auto parts store.

Now, every morning and afternoon, we walked a mile or so each way, back and forth from our lakeshore home, through the heavy woods and occasional fresh snow, to the school bus stop on the closest main road in order to attend another rural country school in a small logging community nearby. Only this time, I was back in grammar school again, trying to learn how to diagram subject/verb/object words in stupid Dick and Jane sentences in English. Interestingly, by this time, English was my fourth language, and the one I knew the least about. I really needed to get a grip on English language grammar. But, it didn't happen there. It wasn't until my last year of undergraduate college work at Long Beach State College, when I took an English phonetics course titled "English for Foreign Speaking Students," that I finally began to understand what in the hell all the talk was about.

In due course, my father returned home from Korea so we moved again, this time to Long Beach, California. I finally stayed put long enough to formally graduate from a good Catholic grammar school under the strict supervision of another no-nonsense teaching order of Catholic nuns, who rapidly filled in the blanks in my very un-orthodox European education to quickly qualify me for an American grammar school diploma. Then I immediately moved into three years of American high school under the sharp eyes of another teaching order—the Franciscan Brothers on this occasion. In the process, I got another heavy dose of Latin with an English chaser this time, instead of French.

At the end of my third year of high school, we moved again to Fort Knox, Kentucky near Louisville, where I finally, formally graduated from high school in another small military dependents' school with only thirty-two students in my class. It was here that my father helped coordinate the first major containerized cargo/troop relocation in history. This time, I participated as one of the smoother movers working for North American Van Lines. I helped move the U.S. Army's entire Third Armored Division, including all of the soldiers, all of their equipment, tanks, ordinance, dependent families, and household goods out of Fort Knox across the North Atlantic Ocean to Germany.

My moving-man experience was just one of the first in a long, string of hard, tough, short-lived jobs that my father helped me find, in order to subtly make sure I learned why I should get a proper education, and stay in college until I finished.

I had a great time, and got a fantastic education as an army brat.

As graduation of my class of seniors from Fort Knox High School approached, my favorite instructors, Mrs. Frances Matarazzo, who taught mathematics and English, and Mr. Salvatore Matarazzo, who taught me more Latin and philosophy, encouraged me to continue in college because I had "what it takes to be a good engineer." However, I had always planned to become a military officer like my father. I had applied for, and managed to secure an appointment to the U.S. Army's Military Academy at West Point. I was on the short list, and thought I knew where I was headed after I graduated. In the end however, fate, or the tooth fairy, or the deus ex machina, had a different plan in mind for me.

A few weeks before graduation, I was involved in an automobile accident, and got smacked in the head. The result was a fractured skull with the loss of depth perception, color vision, and a couple of teeth. I wasn't healed well enough to be able to successfully complete the military's medical and physical exam in time for West Point, so I wasn't going into the army. This turned out to be a fairly good thing I suspect, because many of the West Pointers from this period bit the bullet in Vietnam. The odds were pretty good that I would have been one of them had I attended West Point.

While I continued the process of getting my face and head repaired, and my life back in order, my father retired from the service. He then moved his family back to Long Beach. I attended and graduated from Long Beach State College, got married, went to work for NASA at North American Aviation, and began a family of my own, with the birth of the first of five wonderful kids. I have two girls and three boys. They're a great bunch. We have ten university degrees among the seven of us, and as far as I know, none of them has spent any time in the slammer. They've all grown into productive, self-sufficient, contributing members of our society.

However, I was still having a lot of trouble with the orthodontic work being done as the last phase of recovery from my accident. While on a winter ski trip with the Long Beach State College Ski Club, I met a dentist who was also a member of the ski club. In due course, he took over the task of fixing my dentition. During the process, Dr. Omar Nelson suggested I should think about becoming a dentist. I liked the idea, because the government bureaucracy associated with NASA was beginning to make me a little crazy. I really enjoyed the work, but the politics was quickly becoming more than I wanted to live with.

My undergraduate education qualified me for admission to dental school, so I applied. Shortly thereafter, I was accepted to four different dental schools. I elected to stay in California. So began four intense years at The College of Physicians and Surgeons (P&S), School of Dentistry on 14th Street in San Francisco's old Mission District, now a satellite campus of the University of the Pacific in Stockton. After graduation, I moved north across the Golden Gate Bridge towards the woods again, this time just north of San Rafael in Marin County.

In due course, as my five kids grew, I felt it was time they should learn how to ride a horse. I wanted to offer them an opportunity to enjoy the outdoors on horseback as I had. So now, nearly 5,700-plus miles west of Giessen, and some twenty-five years later, I got back into the horse business with the purchase of a small, jet-black thoroughbred mare by the name of Red Beaver at a livestock dispersal auction near Sacramento.

Although I bought her simply because she looked like a good saddle horse for me and my kids, this tough little lady turned out to have a fine pedigree. Moreover, she had finished 122 races, running with the boys, as sound and solid as could be. Nowadays, a racehorse is lucky to finish a dozen races without suffering a flat tire or worse. I also discovered a little bit later that she had seen enough human testosterone to last her a lifetime. She got along great with women, kids, and dogs, but she didn't like human males at all. A number of years later, a well respected live stockman friend of mine declared her to be "the second-best thoroughbred mare I've ever seen in 60 years of working with the finest equine livestock in the country."

The real reason I purchased this particular animal was that she looked sound, was reasonably priced, and was in foal to a well-respected stallion from Kentucky named Goshen. My plan was to sell the foal before it was born in order to recover my purchase price. Which I did, for more than I paid for the pregnant mare. But I didn't tell anyone about it. I figured my kids would lose interest in caring for the foal, when it got to be a weanling with warts all over its nose. But by then, I'd have a nice riding animal for just the price of her board and care. I was feeling pretty good about it all.

However, my plan rapidly fell apart when my father-in-law, Jack, discovered the foal's pedigree. A total surprise to me, Jack was a confirmed, experienced, relatively successful horse player, with his bookie's runner stopping by the back of his bakery on a daily basis for years to process his wagers. So, two months later, I quietly bought the young colt back for three times what I sold him for. I was now really back in the horse business, and we were on our way to the racetrack.

"Winning Jack" was just that. This little gelding was the first offspring of my first mare, my first foal, my first race horse in training, and he won his first race at Golden Gate Fields Race Track. We were now all hooked on the thoroughbred racing business, big time.

However, since Red was in foal again, I still didn't have a horse to ride in the beautiful Marin

County countryside. So, I bought another one, this time, a strong, green-broke, four-year-old, racetrack reject thoroughbred by the name of Blue Mora. She tore away from a flimsy cross-tie five minutes after she was delivered to the stable, and ran loose around Marin County for nearly three months before trapping her right fetlock in a loop of barbed wire. She nearly amputated her right front foot trying to escape. I finally brought her back home. Over the next nine months we saved her foot, and got her on the mend. She turned out to be a nice ride for me, but a very strong, bull-headed filly. Altogether too much trouble, and unsafe for my kids to ride. So, I sold her, and bought another one.

This one was a beautiful five-year-old thoroughbred filly named Rocket Sis. She was a wonderfully agile saddle horse, but skittish as a loon. She had spent her entire life inside a small box stall around various racetracks, and found the great outdoors altogether too scary to comprehend. She was even afraid of birds and butterflies. I decided to have her bred to try to settle her down a bit, and perhaps she would mature into a dependable saddle animal. So, we found a fine local stallion for her, and she settled on her first cover. It was time to find a more racetrack-oriented home for our growing stable of two pregnant mares, and a yearling colt ready to begin training for the racetrack.

The process of finding a suitable home for my rapidly growing equine family involved inspecting all of the boarding facilities in that portion of Northern California, which was great fun in itself. Two events in the process turned out to be very memorable, and most significant to my continuing animal education.

The first occurred at a beautiful farm in Marin County. Early one Saturday morning, we were inspecting another upscale equine boarding facility. While walking through a fancy barn of box stalls, I noticed Blue Mora's name on one of the stall doors. I had sold the filly to a young girl as a show horse prospect. So, I asked if the owner was around. The reply was that the filly belonged to the old lady who lived in the house on the hill in back of the stable. I thought it would be interesting to learn how Blue Mora's foot was holding up, so I went up to the small house, and knocked on the door. A voice replied that I should come in, that she was in the kitchen getting a cup of coffee, and would I like a cup.

I opened the door, and spoke to the bodiless voice as I approached the kitchen replying that I would, with a little cream in it, please. As I came into the kitchen, the old woman's voice was mumbling under her breath in German, saying "Nur Kinder trinken Milch in ihrem verdammten Kaffee." And, then, in English demanded, "What do you want?"

I asked about Blue Mora, and learned that her foot was fine, and that she was on her way to Argentina as an Olympic Three Day Equestrian Event trainee. Seems although she couldn't run fast enough for the racetrack, she was tough as nails, could jump like she had wings, and was a strong, sure-footed, promising dressage prospect.

I told the old lady, "I'm surprised that she ever walked again, let along turned out to be any good as a dressage prospect."

The old women looked me directly in the eye again, and asked, "What do you know about dressage?"

I replied, "I learned to ride a little a few years back in Germany."

"Where?" she asked, looking at me closer.

Slowly I replied in German, "In Giessen, mit einem Dressurkonkurrenten hat Frau Voit genannt."

It was Frau Hanna Voit all right; I could see it in her eyes, and she remembered everything.

She had purchased my filly after she proved to be too much of an athlete for the little girl who bought her from me. I introduced her to my family, and we spoke for an hour or two, while my kids looked at the horses outside.

Hanna was now teaching spoiled rich kids how to ride fancy show horses, and collect blue ribbons. She still followed the dressage circuit, and bought and sold a few good horses when she ran across them. But, essentially she was retired from competition, and enjoying a taste of the good life in California. We stayed in touch sharing horse stories until she passed away a few years later. My father had always told me "it's a small world we live in." He was absolutely correct.

The second major event of importance that came out of the search for a home for my mares was meeting Richard E. "Dick" Lynch on the roof of a shade cover over a feed station he was constructing for his brood mare band at the Green Oaks Stud Farm in the heart of Napa Valley.

This beautiful stud farm is gone now, replaced by more grape vines. But in 1969, it was the functional 65-acre home of Mr. Kjell Qvale, one of the directors of Golden Gate Field Race Track, owner of the British Motor Car Dealership in San Francisco, and "father" of the Jensen automobile. Located at the north end of "Money Road" in Rutherford, it was within walking distance of Robert Mondavi's brand new controversial winery, right smack in the middle of Napa Valley's finest wine growing district. Even though Kjell was in the process of getting out of the boarding business, he still boarded a couple of horses for Bing Crosby. Green Oaks Stud Farm was also the home of Silky Sullivan, the famous "Heart Attack" racehorse. Silky stood at stud there. Dick was general manager of Kjell's ranch.

Dick and I hit it off right away, and he took us in. My mares had found a real fine home for gals of their caliber. Little, hard as iron, born blind in his left eye, and color blind in his good

---

Dick Lynch had a most interesting life. He was born in Chicago in 1915, and raised in the horse business around the Chicago stockyards. His father owned and operated 140-plus teams of working draft horses, some American saddlebreds, his mother's hackney ponies, and a few harness-class racehorses. In 1933, Dick rode his horse west from Chicago to Miles City, Montana, where he wrangled horses for the U.S. Army's Re-mount Service, and then trained saddle horses in the early thirties. By 1936 he had a big Harley-Davidson flathead, and by 1939 he was the Harley-Davidson Utah District's Hill Climbing Champ.

Alaska was his next stop. He owned and operated a small commercial halibut fishing boat, the Molly out of Seldovia. He caught a 561-pound world-record halibut in May of 1942 not too far outside of Icy Straits west of Juneau. The official rain-soaked photo taken that day on the dock still hangs in my office.

In 1944, he returned to the lower 48 to raise and train harness horses for Clay Hash on the Harness Horse Grand Circuit, with some of his animals winning all three of harness racing's big triple crown events. In 1947, he moved to Hearst's Pico Creek Arab Ranch at San Simeon on the California coast, where he managed the entire equine division of the famous 82,000-acre Hearst Ranch. It was here that he helped establish a foundation for the American Arab Horse breeding program out of the dispersal of King Farouk's band of Egyptian Arabs. Dick is credited by some to be the father of the Arab horse industry in the United States. When Mr. Hearst died in 1951, Dick was in charge of the dispersal of all of the equine and exotic livestock on the San Simeon Ranch.

one, Dick had forgotten more than most cowboys or livestockmen ever learn. Dick Lynch was one of the most knowledgeable, experienced, innovative live stockmen and stud managers in the world. And, he was about to become my mentor.

What began that hot summer afternoon in the Napa Valley over my first glass of really good red wine from Robert Mondavi's place down the road, developed into a tight, long lasting, thirty-plus years of close friendship.

Dick and I hit it off from the day we met. When Red Beaver's colt was old enough to wean, he arranged for Winning Jack to be properly trained for the racetrack, and he taught me the fine art of preparing an animal for racing. Because of her dependable reproductive history, Dick selected Red Beaver to test breed an unproven stallion who was the offspring of the great Bold Ruler and the fine English mare Aunt Edith. Predictably, Red delivered a beautiful, healthy filly, and the Traditionalist was a proven sire.

In the beginning, Dick insisted that if I really wanted to learn anything about the livestock business, I needed to go to the vet school at University of California at Davis, get to know the vets, and then get a handle on the medical aspects of the game.

So, I did.

I spent five years at UC Davis in one capacity or another. I attended rounds, audited classes, and lectured with some regularity on the subject of veterinary dentistry in Dr. J. D. Wheat's large animal surgery program. On a weekly basis, I participated in treatments, and followed various cases in all three of the hospital's principal disciplines—small animal, large animal, and exotic animal medicine.

In due course, I also became licensed by the California Thoroughbred Horse Racing Board as an owner/trainer of thoroughbreds. All the while, with Dick cutting trail, we bred, raised, and trained thoroughbred flat-track runners for seven years.

Dick and I shared a great adventure traveling together down stream on the riverboat of life. Our friendship finally ended a few years back, when I helped lay my old friend to rest on the side of a hill just north of Morro Bay overlooking the beautiful California coast he knew so well, and loved so much.

What happened unexpectedly along the way was that I became completely infected with the life and times of all of the other warm-blooded species living among us, and sharing their space with us. I met Dr. Murray Fowler. I watched his first M-99 elephant immobilization procedure in the parking lot west of the UC Davis Veterinary Medicine Teaching Hospital. I developed an equine sinus surgery protocol with Dr. Wheat. And I was introduced to the world of primate research and zoo animal medicine by Dr. Roy Hendrickson, and on, and on, and on.

The seed that had been planted in the mind of that little kid in the dark forests of Germany so many years before, had finally found a place to germinate and develop into something. The combination of a great deal of practical hands-on animal experience; a whole lot of grass-root, broad-based, and strictly formal education in dressage, science, medicine, and dentistry; and a burning intellectual curiosity, had finally found a worthwhile focus—and that was addressing the heretofore poorly recognized maxillo-facial, oral, and dental problems of all sorts of animals.

I knew for sure that I'd never find the time to learn how to play golf or tennis. I wouldn't be joining a fancy country club any time soon. I even dropped out of ground-school training for my private pilot's license. I began assisting various clinicians in a wonderful hospital full of some of the world's finest veterinarians with the diagnosis and treatment of all sorts of unusual and previously unsuspected oral problems.

Simultaneously, I was owner/director/clinician running a large multi-location, multi-specialty dental group practice for humans in the San Francisco Bay area. I was also becoming very comfortable associating with all the rail-birds hanging along the back-stretch gap of the Pleasanton Fair Grounds, Golden Gate Fields, Santa Anita, Bay Meadows race tracks, as well as the San Luis Rey Downs training facility just north of San Diego.

What begun at the veterinary medical teaching hospital at the University of California in Davis in the summer of '69 is forever etched in the memory bank of my mind as a virtual file cabinet full of great stories, including my first rabies suspect case, involving a feisty little primate belonging to one of Northern California's legendary locals, known to all simply as "Juanita."

Chapter Two
Juanita's Monkey

"These small naked apes may have noble intent,"
Thought this regal and wise old elephant.
"But they forge ahead so imprudently.
I see here an ideal opportunity.
to learn why they oft act so foolishly."

Though the groping students were indeed confused,
Bewildered, astounded, or even amused
Their collective psyche was clearly hounded
by this massive presence, which so confounded.

Wrapped in one of her trademark brightly colored Hawaiian muumuus, Juanita Musson, a wonderfully eccentric, 340-pound waterfront character, and one of San Francisco's legendary restaurateurs, lounged on a heavy, ruby-red love seat in the entry foyer of her latest hotel-restaurant in Boyes Hot Springs. With the air of a massive queen of the islands, she rose and greeted me as our group came through the front door of her hotel.

"Show these folks to the banquet room upstairs, Jenny," she instructed the attractive young waitress waiting at her elbow. "They'll need the privacy." She then quickly turned in one fluid movement, winked at me, and gracefully glided back onto her loveseat to assume command of her notorious domain.

Juanita—known as an extremely generous and outrageously controversial woman—shared the spotlight during the 1950s and hippie-dominated 1960s with her good friend Sally Sanford, who was San Francisco's most notorious nocturnal queen. Sally was eventually elected to the office of vice-mayor of Sausalito in the late 1970s, and no doubt died laughing. Sally did vice and money very well. Juanita collected strays of all species, was always "in the wrong place at the right time," and for years created mountains of excellent food in a number of different, wildly eclectic locations, but always north of "the City".

Currently aging rapidly, and still generating lots of good copy, Juanita was once again battling with the local health department. Her constantly evolving, free-roaming menagerie, which now consisted of chickens; a rooster named Mr. C. S. Smith; game hens; rabbits; ducks; several squirrel monkeys; a pig named Erica; the little red fox Sally gave her (she called it Rommel); and Beauregard, her alcoholic South American woolly monkey, were all causing trouble—again.

Beauregard was under house arrest for a second time in two years. The first time the Sonoma County Health department locked him up in the rabies isolation ward upstairs in the small animal clinic at the vet school hospital in Davis. I had met him there as a rabies suspect with a court order to have all four of his canine teeth removed for biting another one of her dinner guests—or be euthanized.

Not surprisingly, there had not been a lot of volunteers for the task. When a woolly monkey attacks, he uses his canine teeth like a woodpecker uses its beak. Tilting his head back, and drawing his upper lip back to expose his large canine teeth, the woolly prefers to attack from up above his target, striking downward with his mouth wide open. His purpose is to strike at his target's skull and/or eyes with his protruding canine teeth. An aggravated woolly monkey is capable of driving his maxillary canine teeth completely through the bones of a skull into the brain. Provoked, this is his objective.

Thus, it was with caution, and a good-sized audience of interested small animal surgery student observers, that I attended to my first exotic animal patient. Since I was the only dentist in the group, and since no one else wanted to volunteer, I was asked by Dr. Jerry Ling to assist one of his senior surgery residents in the capacity of consulting specialist in oral surgery. The oral surgery procedure prescribed by the court was completed in a timely manner with a minimum of stress on both our patient and me. My reputation as a capable oral surgeon spread quickly with each re-telling of Beauregard's story.

This time, for Beau's second offense, Juanita had talked the health department into leaving him locked up in his "bedroom" on the second floor of her rambling restaurant-hotel. Beau wasn't happy about it, and neither was Juanita, which usually meant "there be trouble brewin'."

Having met her the previous year at the University of California at Davis Veterinary Medical Teaching Hospital, I was invited by Juanita to bring a team of qualified clinicians to her place, examine Beau again, and discuss the problems she was having with the health department. As both an inducement to make a house call, and as compensation for our efforts, she suggested we invite along our technicians, assistants, girlfriends or wives to enjoy a free prime rib dinner at her infamous Fetter Hot Springs Restaurant-Hotel, known far and wide simply as "Juanita's Place," near the heart of the Napa/Sonoma Valley in California's finest wine country.

This was not hard for me to arrange, as everyone knew the legendary temptations of Juanita's sequential series of fabled "Galley Restaurants."

Two of the equine surgery residents with whom I had been working at the vet school immediately volunteered to bone up on primates, and become instant "primate consultants" for the occasion.

I accepted, and we thought we were ready.

Our group was promptly shown to an imposing, private dining room upstairs, where we were seated at a stunningly large antique oak dinner table elegantly set for eight—with none of the mismatched tableware and mason jars routinely used downstairs.

As our dining experience began to unfold, I could tell we were on our way to having a meal we'd never forget. I watched spellbound as two large silver platters were placed on the table. Several magnums of champagne in a silver bucket stood surrounded by generous plates of fancy appetizers, deviled eggs, and several of Juanita's fancy fruit salads with a bowl of her notorious blue cheese dressin' on the side. We dove right in, and made quick work of this first course, then sipped the last drops of champagne, while we waited for the main event. It had been another long, hard day at the hospital. We were all running on empty, and ready to put on the feedbag. Appetites properly teased, we were helping ourselves to little nibbles of the crispy mixed salads, when in came eight large dinner platters with Juanita's notoriously huge two-and-a-half pound slabs of perfect prime rib draped over the sides of our plates, each with its rib bone still attached, and caressing a large baked potato steaming under piles of butter, sour cream, fresh bacon bits and chives. Several more bottles of red wine and

Juanita's infamous Fetter Hot Springs Restaurant-Hotel

From the files of David A. Fagan

Dr. Fagan circa 1970
From the files of David A. Fagan

"*Juanita is a person one will never forget in their lifetime. There are hundreds of stories about her, but the one that I find quite funny was her 'Juanita Boob Muffin Wrap.'*

"*Juanita would sneak up from behind one of her male restaurant customers, grab her - ahem - boobs and wrap them completely around his head leaving each victim gasping for air. There were lots of laughs, of course, but the loudest laugher was Juanita, herself. It was an "honor" to get "boobed" by Juanita. At her restaurant you dined from mismatched dishes, drank from Mason jars and served yourself at the salad bar where the vege's were placed in hospital bedpans. Last, was her famous prime rib... so thick that she wouldn't allow anyone to order just for themselves. It had to be for two. It came (if you weren't ordered to get it yourself) to the table with a super-sharp butcher knife in which one would cut it into two, 2-inch thick pieces. Good!*"

—*from C.M.Herman Blog - 9 Nov 2001*

serving bowls of fresh seasoned green beans were added to the table. A platter of homegrown, sliced heirloom beefsteak tomatoes rounded out an overwhelming spread.

Throughout the duration of our lengthy feast, an attractive folk singer wearing a tight, low-cut evening dress entertained us. Shimmering sky blue, the dress was daringly slit up one side candidly revealing the woman's shapely figure as she strolled around our table teasing us with a memorable assortment of humorously obscene folk songs, ribald jokes, enticing gestures, and a medley of lovely melodies played on her magnificent assortment of string instruments, including a chorded zither and a beautiful antique mandolin—all accompanied by a most lovely, melodiously clear voice.

Relaxed by her performance, we consumed every generous ounce of the fine Napa Valley red wine, and most of the prime rib set before us. We were thoroughly enjoying every sensual moment of her infamous "Galley revelry." We were all so thoroughly immersed in the evening that no one gave a second thought to the task facing us—to examine Beauregard, Juanita's pet woolly monkey, and recommend a plan to resolve the current conflict with the health department.

Finally, dessert arrived. That would be a large bowl of nut-stuffed dates mixed with a pile of the after-dinner mints she kept in an antique urinal on the bar downstairs. Her bartender Everett dispensed the mints to spoil her two little marmosets rotten. Our mints and dates were served with steaming cups of fresh, rich aromatic coffee with fresh heavy cream and sugar, to be quickly followed by our choice of a good cognac, or a Christian Brothers brandy. While we were still lingering over our drinks enjoying every aspect of the good life, the door suddenly burst open, and in whirled Juanita, startling the hell out of all of us. She made a noisy, dramatic entrance with two little monkeys, one sitting on each shoulder, clutching onto her mantilla-quaffed hairdo. Her immense presence stopped directly behind me, situated at the head of the table with my back to the door. She began stroking my crew-cut hair-do with what felt like the gentle paw of a huge bear, while placing her other hand heavily on my right shoulder.

Pinioned in the soft, vice-like grip of her two enormous breasts, I tried moving sideways to loosen their hold on me. "Relax, kid," Juanita said wickedly, "you've got strong shoulders, and I've been hauln' these jugs around for a long time looking for a place to rest 'em."

I sucked in my breath, and glanced around the table for visual indications of impending disaster, while the two little, unseen monkeys continued chattering, screeching and hopping around somewhere just above me—too damn close to my eyes for comfort. So, I just sat as still as possible, hoping the other shoe wouldn't drop, and I'd have one of the little buggers clawing its way across my face.

Still doing my best to breathe calmly, I waited for Juanita to let go of my head. My predicament seemed to entertain my companions as much as it did Juanita.

"Are your ears burning?" someone quipped from across the table. Doctor Bob Norris, our recently drafted equine surgery resident—turned Old World Primate Specialist for the evening—grinned wickedly, and raised his glass toward me in a toast accompanied by a devilish wink. There was more table chat.

Then suddenly Juanita stepped back and announced: "All right, you guys, its time to go to work, and pay for this spread." The party was instantly over. We needed to get our act together, and get to work. Excusing ourselves to the restroom, we splashed cold water in our faces preparing for the impending task.

Prior to this occasion, I had only known monkeys from afar in the zoo visitor setting of my childhood, and they had always looked small, weak, not very clean, and rather defenseless to me. However, this woolly monkey, *Lagothrix lagotricha*, was one of the largest of the Brazilian primates, weighing between 35 to 45 pounds. They are related to the slender, long-armed spider monkeys, the booming-voiced howlers, and the little capuchin known for their intelligence in learning to help quadriplegic humans.

Woollies live in the South American jungle treetops, 100 to 150 feet in the air above the dense Amazon River rain forests. They are very agile, and very strong. Their long, unusually agile prehensile tails, each with its unique "fingerprint," provides them with a fifth hand. Most pet male monkeys eventually become increasingly sexually frustrated as they reach adulthood without access to an interested female. When limited to an unnatural lifestyle of captivity, without a mate, even with the luxury of easy access to a fancy restaurant bar supply of gin martinis with several maraschino cherries, they are often subject to fits of rage and depression, not unlike some of their distant sexually deprived human cousins. It was actually not too surprising that Beauregard demanded, got, and thoroughly enjoyed his daily martini—or two.

After refreshing ourselves in the restroom, we all gathered again downstairs around Juanita, where she was once again perched on her loveseat, while another one of her strangely uniformed valets brought Beauregard downstairs from his private bedroom-turned-jailhouse. He obviously remembered me, and our last encounter—even though it was pushing two years ago. Glueing his piercing little eyes onto me like burning lasers, it seemed to me that he didn't interrupt his glare, even to blink.

Dr. John McKee, my second large-animal surgery resident recruit, and our New World Monkey Expert, had more animal experience than any of us. Stepping forward with an air of authority, which made us all think he knew what he was doing, John announced with a strong, steady voice:

"I'll hold him still, Dave, while you take a look at his mouth."

Beauregard didn't think much of John's plan—no more than he liked the crowd of restaurant patrons gathering to watch the commotion we were creating. I realized immediately that we should have done the exam in an upstairs room, undisturbed by curious onlookers, but by this time it was too late.

Agitated, Beau suddenly jumped onto John's right shoulder. He swung around into a seated position grasping his neck and shoulder firmly with each foot, grabbed a handful of John's hair with his left hand, and John's right ear with his right hand, while simultaneously wrapping his strong, prehensile tail securely around John's neck. Without any doubt, the monkey now had John completely under control. John knew enough to just stand still, and he didn't move a muscle—he'd been had—just like I'd been had at the dinner table.

Beau sat there looking at us, calming a little, to John's relief, while Anna, my assistant, and I took advantage of the opportunity to proceed with a quick exam.

I stealthfully raised my left hand up to the back of the monkey's head without touching him, while I distracted him by wiggling my right hand a foot or so in front of John's face. Then I suddenly grabbed Beau by the back of his head with my left hand, and around the front of his neck with the fingers of my right hand firmly in control of his mandible, restricting any sudden movements of his jaw. We now had Beau nearly as securely as Beau had John. Thus the three of us were mutually restrained, and tied in a nice Gordian knot of our own making.

At this point, Anna was able to safely retract his lips without any difficulty, so I could have a look at his teeth. Amazingly, during the year or so since I had removed his canine teeth, Beau's first pre-molars had all drifted forward into the space left by the missing canine tooth, rotated about 45 degrees, and now functioned perfectly as a set of double-tipped, new and improved canine teeth. Immediately trying to demonstrate their proficiency on my hand, he proved them extremely effective, and almost managed to get a good bite out of my right thumb.

It was instantly obvious to me: these shifting teeth could not be removed without causing excessive debilitation to the animal's masticatory apparatus, and seriously limiting his ability to eat. The only logical solution was to reshape them a bit, eliminating their sharpness by rounding off their sharp pointed cusp tips, and thereby removing most of the hazard from his bite. This procedure would render him able to eat normally, but unable to easily lacerate Juanita's restaurant patrons on the fly, while he snatched another maraschino cherry out of someone's gin martini at the bar. Beau liked gin martinis.

Planning to put a quick end to the siege on John's head, I gently began moving forward, guiding John's head toward Juanita. Beau was still firmly attached to his head and shoulder, while trying to keep a nervous eye on me. The plan was to gently transfer him to the care of his loving mother.

"Damn it!" she exploded. "Don't give him to me. You guys have scared the hell outta him. Take him upstairs, and lock him in his room! He'll swing for a while on his rope, and then settle down for the night."

No dice. Beau knew before Juanita got the words out of her mouth that he had to act now, if he was going to have a chance in hell of getting away from us before we got him back to his jail cell.

Free-spirited, wound up as tight as a drum, and in a mood to get social, Beau had no intention of going to bed yet. His prehensile tail still secured around John's neck, still holding onto John's hair, he became more and more agitated at the thought of going back into solitary lock-down for the night. Dangerously close to John's eyes, his clawing little fingers could move with unbelievable speed. There was no really good way for John and me to control him for much longer. So, with Anna running interference parting the crowd in front of us, I followed behind, restraining Beau, while John and I crept up the grand staircase toward Beau's prison cell.

"You keep a tight hold of his head 'n neck, so he can't bite anything," relayed John. "I've got both of his hands now, and his feet don't seem to be moving much. Let's just keep going up the stairs. This damn tail of his is killing me."

Masters of leverage and balance, these natural-born acrobats perform daily miracles in the canopies of their South American rain forest habitat. They regularly leap up to sixty feet through the air when they're on the move. Provoked, they are capable of driving their long maxillary canine teeth, in this case Beau's double-tipped pre-molars, through an adversary's skull into their brain. Provoked indeed, Beau was now in his own territory, with every item familiar, and a potential tool. Hoping to be able to restrain him long enough to safely free John, we planned to leave him on his rope in solitary confinement.

Anna grabbed for his feet again, and missed one. Anna was now holding the tip of his strong, sinewy tail, preventing it from choking John too much, and then managed to catch hold of Beau's left foot. I now had him by the back of his neck and his right leg. John somehow had now restrained both of Beau's feet. But Beau stayed locked onto a handful of his hair and right ear as we entered his bedroom. We slowly began disengaging John from the now outraged monkey's grip.

Beau finally weakened, his efforts matched by our growing strength and determination, born from our collective pumping adrenalin. Then came the piercing scream,

"Mamma, Mamma, look at the monkey!"

Without anyone noticing, a small boy had followed us upstairs. Panicked again, Beau instantly lunged for his rope, while still clenching John's wrinkled, and now bleeding, ear.

He pulled savagely at the ear, while trying to firm up his partial left-handed grasp onto his familiar rope swing hanging in the middle of the room. John stumbled to his hands and knees trying to get back out of the door. Nostrils flaring, patience waning, John gritted his teeth. "Keep at it," he bellowed, "and try to salvage a few pieces of my damn ear if you can!" I was thinking we could sew an ear back on, but we couldn't replace an eye. And Beau's sharp, gouging little fingers seemed to be trying to go everywhere at the same time.

We were slowly inching the collective mass of us backward again closer to the partially opened door, when I suddenly realized Beau was now intently focused not on us, but on his familiar rope swing. He was preparing to trade in John's flimsy ear for the rope, in order to get free—and attack us frontally with the help of a launch on his return swing—totally giving him the upper hand. We were clearly sliding off the losing end of our present standoff. I figured if we could manage a little re-positioning, and if we could all just let go of him at the same instant; and if I could push him away in the direction he wanted to go without getting bitten, it would probably take him a moment to swing across the room and regroup before he could attack us again. But, if he got too much of a push, and if he could swing faster than we could move out the door, then we'd all be in trouble. Those were a lot of "ifs." However, the reality was we were already in big trouble—and well on our way to getting more than we might be able to handle.

I managed to free John's ear, and on my command, we all just let go, while I gave Beau a firm push forward. Beau immediately swung away from us on his rope swing, like Tarzan. As John and Anna tumbled backwards through the door, Bob kept me from falling, while I pulled the door closed behind us. Within seconds, Beau pushed off from the other side of the room, and began his power swing back towards us. Hurling himself through the air with the momentum of the rope, he hit the barely closing screen door like a cruise missile right at my face level, and gave us all kinds of "& ! % ! $ @ # ?" in monkey language.

"He almost won that round," I said softly, as I sank to the floor with my right hand firmly holding the door shut, and my right foot wedged against the door jam, while Bob secured the lock setting us free.

We all felt damned lucky to have escaped without serious injury.

John's damaged ear wasn't as bad as it looked, and would heal. As would the small scratch wound on my right thumb. Our collective experience of quick thinking and fast reactions, prerequisite for working with any animal, including humans, saved us from sure disaster.

Though pale and shaken, we were all laughing as we reached the bottom of the stairway. "I'll find an antiseptic to cleanse your wounds," Bob Norris, our "Old World Monkey Expert" called over his shoulder as he disappeared into the cavernous bar. We strung along after him, still jumpy and pumped full of adrenalin, as though we had been fused inseparably together during the struggle.

Anna sterilized our wounds from a fresh shot glass of Christian Brothers brandy, while John began expounding on the virtues of "Old World treatments as opposed to modern day aseptic cures." Truly effective, our Old World remedy, a series of palm-warmed Christian Brothers snifters, brought us down gently from a very accelerated metabolic state. Shattered nerves quickly regenerated, while we enjoyed our new found kinship, trust and camaraderie.

While the group recovered and reconnoitered, I found Juanita, and gave her my diagnosis with a suggested treatment plan.

"It would be a wise to keep him out of the restaurant until we get him fixed. He clearly has no more regard or respect for humans," I concluded.

"I'll do as I damn well please," she snapped.

"And I want you to work on him here, as soon as possible. Beau doesn't like going to that damn hospital of yours any more than I do," she barked. "But, if he doesn't stop biting people, I'll go broke with all these damned lawsuits and medical bills."

"It ain't gonna happen here, Juanita. Your place doesn't lend itself to the procedure," I answered, suddenly irritated with the direction our conversation had headed.

"It can't be that complicated,." she snorted, puffed up like an insulted hen.

"Complication isn't the issue, Juanita," I snapped back. "There's too much equipment necessary, and you don't have the proper support facilities. I can't bring a mountain of medicine in here. There is no way I'll do it here. Either bring Beau to the hospital or forget it." And I began to turn away from her. "All right, gauddamnit," she conceded. "I'll phone the hospital tomorrow, and set up a time." She did, and within a few days Beau's bite was safely rendered relatively harmless, although still intact. The next day, Beau went back home to his favorite bar for another round of post-operative gin martinis.

Less than a year after this incident, a fire swept through Juanita's restaurant early one morning, and left everything in ashes, including Beauregard, and one of her waitresses, who'd spent the night on the veranda upstairs sleeping off another late-night party. Even though I was the enemy from Beau's perspective, and his is the only bite injury I've ever received from one of my animal patients, I felt like I'd lost an old friend. The little scar on my right thumb is a constant reminder of him, as well as of my first case of exotic animal veterinary dental care.

My experience with Juanita and Beauregard had helped give birth to a thirty-plus year career of creating, assembling, and moving a virtual mountain of highly specialized dental equipment to wherever it was needed to join with other veterinarians to solve more unique oral problems in many other unusual locations and surprising circumstances.

Little did I realize at the time how this undertaking would slowly unfold, and evolve like the proverbial blind man trying to discover the true nature of some enormous unseen elephant. I had just taken another giant step forward into the captivating world of animals.

I was now completely hooked on the clinical practice of veterinary dentistry. And it was beginning to transport me, and my chosen profession of dentistry, into a whole new, unknown dimension. In reality, the process of clinical creativity is in itself an act of transformation. I had no way to comprehend at the time just how much change, discovery, and adventure lay ahead. Not only had the practice of veterinary medicine taken it's first few steps forward along the path toward toward becoming an entirely new medical sub-specialty, but we were all rapidly moving toward the technological developments that would carry all of us into the 21st century faster than any of us realized in the late 1960s.

American Veterinary Dental Society (AVDS) was founded in 1976 for the purpose of creating a forum for the scientific advancement and professional understanding of the knowledge of animal dentistry (www.avds-online.org/). The AVDS publishes a very nice, full color, quarterly **Journal of Veterinary Dentistry.**

By 2008 this fine international journal of veterinary dentistry has grown to become the official journal of the AVDS, the Academy of Veterinary Dentistry, the American Veterinary Dental College, the Academy of Veterinary Dental Technicians, the Australian Veterinary Dental Society, the Brazilian Veterinary Dental Association, the British Veterinary Dental Association, the Canadian Veterinary Dental Society, the European Veterinary Dental College, the European Veterinary Dental Society, and the Japanese Small Animal Dental Society, and is still growing.

The Veterinary Dental Forum was founded in 1987 for the purpose of advancing the knowledge, education, awareness and skills involved in the practice of veterinary dentistry among veterinarians, veterinary technicians, veterinary students, veterinary staff, and anyone else with an interest in veterinary dentistry. The Veterinary Dental Forum is hosted by a combination of the American Veterinary Dental Society, the Academy of Veterinary Dentistry and the American Veterinary Dental College. The Veterinary Dental Forum is not only the largest veterinary dental conference, but is also the longest continually running meeting of its type.

Chapter Three
From Humans
to Hippos

"Ouch, a smooth, heavy… BONE??
 has accosted me."
The first student stammers with urgency.

"How can it remain outside of its skin?
Could it be a horse with a horn on its chin?
What's this thing for? What's the intent?
Inside or out— it's a puzzlement!!

How it all works is a mystery
But that is something I won't let be!
I will study this thing, and in time understand.
Orthopedics will be where I'll lend my hand."

DENTIST GOES ANIMAL 26

Although Beauregard was my first exotic animal encounter, Buster, a dromedary camel at the Sacramento Zoo, provided my first actual zoo animal experience. It was another major step forward in the formulation of my career as a veterinary dentist—during which I have methodically worked my way through a veritable alphabet soup of fascinating creatures. In fact, at one time or another during the past thirty-plus years, I've treated nearly everything from aardvark to zebra, ranging in size from a few ounces of pygmy marmoset to a 15,000-pound African bull elephant. That any of this occurred at all was the direct result of my friend Dick Lynch's encouragement to spend some time at the vet school in Davis.

Dick and I shared a compulsive need to know concerning nearly everything involving our training program for thoroughbred flat-track racehorses. As a consequence, on a regular weekly basis for five years during the late 1960s and early 1970s, I found myself associating with all sorts of very well educated veterinarians, addressing every conceivable topic and type of equine training problem at the University of California Veterinary Medical Teaching Hospital and Regional Primate Research Center in Davis.

The city of Davis is a small, self-contained, rural, academic community located on the fertile flood plain of California's bread-basket central valley farmland. It's located a few miles west of Sacramento, the state's capital along Highway 80, which is the second-longest interstate highway in the United States, connecting San Francisco on the West Coast to the suburbs of New York City on the East Coast.

In fact, like most small university communities, the pulse of Davis gallops hard and fast all during the week, and except for the intensive study sessions associated with final exam periods, it suddenly lapses into a restful, introspective quiet on the weekends and during the summer vacation periods. The hospital facility, however, operates 24 hours a day, 365 days a year with a very heavy flow of referral patients from all over the country. The medical drama resulting from this diversity of patient problems rivals the best of the human hospital soap operas.

It was in the middle of this kaleidoscope of medical activity that I learned to appreciate and admire the education and skill of the veterinarian—as a true, profoundly well educated.medical professional.

Over the years, I also discovered that the practice of medicine is always a complex undertaking, but the successful practice of veterinary medicine is much more complicated than most specialties of human medicine. This is because of the diversity of the animal patient population, i.e.: large animals, farm animals, small domestic pets involving a rich assortment of dogs and cats, various small pocket pets (mostly rodents of one sort or another), and a multitude of diverse avian species from hummingbird to ostrich. Moreover, the practice of exotic animal veterinary medicine by a board certified clinical specialist is absolutely the most demanding, exacting and complicated clinical practice of them all. What works like a miracle with one species, as often as not is lethal to another. My own broad-based professional education, diverse clinical and practical experience, and a solid research-orientated perspective had created a one-of-a-kind combination. It enabled me to function in this demanding field in the capacity of a resource consultant, capable of providing a unique assortment of skills and information with practical clinical solutions, not readily available in the average clinical setting of the veterinarian. Essentially, I functioned as a special arrow in the quiver of the veterinary medical specialist. This unique role and relationship evolved quite naturally over time, as I slowly became a technology transfer specialist. It wasn't planned, and for many years I was not fully aware of exactly what was happening. However, from the beginning, we were selectively applying methods, materials, and techniques from the fields of human dentistry, medicine and biotechnology to address unresolved clinical problems in veterinary medicine.

My first trip to the vet school equine hospital in Davis involved bringing one of my own thoroughbred racehorses, named Partygoer, to the radiology clinic to have his legs X-rayed and evaluated. He was intermittently lame on his left front leg, but we could find no specific clinical cause for the problem. After repeated radiographic investigations, we finally discovered a traumatic, sub-clinical, stellar fracture in his right knee, which caused him to favor his right leg, while putting inordinate stress on his left fetlock when training. While we were waiting to have the first of several radiographic series read by Dr. Tim O'Brien, then chairman of the department of large-animal radiology, one of the large-animal surgery residents, Dr. John McKee, who, a year or so later, nearly had his ear ripped off at Juanita's, noticed from my horse's medical record that I was a dentist. As we discussed my horse's case, John casually asked if I knew anything about sinus problems. As it turned out, I was not only very well educated on the subject, I had had a personal encounter with a very nasty sinus infection during my senior year of dental school, and I knew a whole lot more than I wanted to about it from painful first-hand experience.

So while we waited for Dr. O'Brien, McKee and I walked out to the B barn to take a look at one of his patients. As we walked along, we discussed the various difficulties and treatment options available to deal with a case of chronic allergic sinusitis in a valuable thoroughbred racehorse. What began quite casually as a discussion between two diversely educated clinicians quickly developed into a multi-year experimental surgery research project approved by Dr. J. D. Wheat, then chairman of the school's large-animal surgery department. Our plan was to modify and adapt one of the common human sinus surgical procedures (Cauldwell-Luk), developed to enter the human's sinus from the front of the patient's face under their upper lip, into an equine procedure, which creates a "trap door" on the lateral side of the horse's face large enough to get the surgeon's entire hand into the horses sinus cavity. It was during this period of clinical research that I worked very closely on a weekly basis with doctors McKee and Norris. For several years during development, our equine sinus flap surgeries were simply referred to as "Fagan's Flap." Subsequently, however, it quickly evolved to become one of the standard care procedures to address various equine sinus problems.

It was during this early equine research period that I acquired, along with Dr. McKee, my first dubious record for the longest stay by an equine patient at the UC Davis large-animal hospital. I don't know if our record has subsequently been broken. But, in the early 1970s, it was fourteen months in the hospital.

Just recently, Dr. Jim Oosterhuis and I matched the fourteen-month record working on a gazelle known as Addra-290, at the San Diego Wild Animal Park, but that's another story altogether. The first record holder was a fine thoroughbred stallion by the name of Summer Vacation belonging to Mrs. Connie Ring, the gracious owner of the Three Rings Thoroughbred Ranch in Banning, California.

It was Mrs. Ring's primary concern to provide the best possible husbandry care for her animals. Fortunately, her desires were combined with the financial ability to pay the bills to ensure that it really happens. This fundamental fact of life—desire backed with money—one way or another, ultimately fuels the research and development engine in nearly all aspects of clinical medicine. This has been true from the time of the Temple of Aesculapius on the Tiber Island in early Rome, and it is still true today, despite the many self-indulgent declarations of ill-informed politicians to the contrary. All of us owe a huge debt of gratitude to the Mrs. Connie Rings of the world for encouraging the continued development of clinical research to find a host of new clinical treatment alternatives. It is narrow-minded to declare this a selfish motive. It may well be personally motivated, but it eventually is definitely of great benefit to the public at large.

Each week during my five-year stay at Davis, I would attend morning rounds, which is the walk-through review of all of the in-house cases conducted by the individual clinicians responsible for the cases in each section. This always proved to be a real eye-opener for me. In fact, it was during one of these morning rituals that I first heard about Juanita's Beauregard.

The process of learning about woolly monkeys had led me to the Regional Primate Research Center located down the road a mile or so west of the teaching hospital. I had arranged to meet with and discuss Beau's case with Dr. Roy Hendrickson, the veterinarian responsible for the health and well being of several hundred rhesus, green, macaque monkeys and numerous Hamadrayas baboons living at the facility. Roy was also the veterinarian responsible for the animals at the nearby Sacramento Zoo. In due course, I developed a working relationship with Roy, which resulted in a trip to the zoo one afternoon to meet Buster, their new dromedary camel, who was destined to become my first zoo animal patient.

The curators at the zoo had acquired this healthy, robust male camel with the hopes of developing a breeding group of camels to provide surplus animals to sell to other zoos. Their plan was not working. Camels are unique animals in a variety of ways. To begin with, they copulate with the female resting on the ground in what's known as "sternal recumbency." The male encourages the females to get interested, and to assume the position by nibbling her fanny or hindquarters.

Buster turned out to be a biter, not a nibbler.

As a consequence, none of his females ever got pregnant, because none of them would tolerate his foreplay. As a result, the zoo didn't get babies; they got an abundance of substantial veterinary medical bills, while Roy repeatedly sutured up a series of serious rump lacerations—ergo my visit. I was asked to apply my reputed canine-removal capabilities to Buster's situation, in order to eliminate the slash from his bite. The idea was to convert him from a biter into a nibbler, and hopefully a better lover and father.

This looked like a very tall order to me. And, before I committed to the task, I wanted time to go to the Museum of Natural History in San Francisco to look at a couple of camel skulls in order to get a better grip on the size of the task I was being invited to attempt. Thus began one of my most valuable pre-operative rituals—before each new exotic animal undertaking, I always arrange a get-acquainted research session at my local university library, and/or nearest natural history museum. Nowadays, much of this can be accomplished via the Internet.

My preparations for Buster revealed that the canine teeth within a camel's jaw represented approximately 80% of the structural or architectural support of the front end of their jawbones. Remove these teeth, and the front end of his jaws and face would be severely weakened to such an extent that the next time he bit anything, Buster would most likely fracture his maxilla or mandible—or both. The requested cure was in fact worse than the illness it was supposed to fix. Buster needed to keep his teeth, but the ladies would be a whole lot happier if he had them all shortened, and blunted to eliminate the slash from his bite. This was a reasonably straightforward, common clinical dental procedure. And it could be accomplished with a relatively minor set of occlusal adjustments, a partial pulpotomy or two (more about this procedure later), and topped off with a small composite restoration.

Not at all a big deal for a human patient, and I'd done each of these procedures multiple times. So, I'd still be treading on relatively familiar ground. However, for the camel, this procedure would require a general anesthetic immobilization with an expensive new narcotic drug known as "M-99"—which Roy had never used before on a camel.

This lack of familiarity issue with the immobilization drug developed into a bit of a project for us. Roy's first immobilization attempt failed because the manufacturer's recommended dosage did not adequately immobilize our camel. It was a reasonable educated guess or guesstimate, but it didn't work out as they suggested, or as we had planned. Their recommended dose of the drug turned Buster into a cranky, slobbering, wobbly, drunk. And Roy didn't have enough of the drug left to safely top it off with any predictability. Consequently, we rescheduled the procedure for a couple of weeks later, while Roy arranged to get more of the very expensive new anesthetic drug. For our second try, he had a better idea of an effective dose, and Roy got the job done.

That was the good news. The bad news was that Buster's dental procedure nearly became both my first—and—my last—exotic animal dental procedure.

By the time we managed to get everything rescheduled and ready, it was the middle of August. It can be hotter than hell in the Sacramento Valley that time of year, and it was. In addition, we didn't have an accurate indication of Buster's exact body weight, so once again the induction was difficult, and a little dicey. When he finally did hit the ground, Buster was right out in the middle of a hot, dusty paddock in the 120-degree sunshine adjacent to the back of the zoo's elephant house. It is always a very difficult if not impossibly time-consuming task to move 1200 to 1500 pounds of immobilized, inert animal flesh. Rather than waste more time trying, we elected to work on him where he landed.

Camels, I suddenly learned, also can have very dirty mouths. As a consequence, every available fly within several hundred meters of us immediately heard about the easily obtainable free lunch, and showed up to help themselves to their portion of his copious, stringy, dirty, drooling saliva.

As I remember, we ended up reducing six or eight of his teeth—including all of his canines and several adjacent and opposing pre-molars—and it took several hours. The blistering heat and gravel under my knees were killing me. The flies were all over my face—in between visits into Buster's bazaar looking oral cavity.

For me, the take-home message from Jeff Goldbloom's movie *The Fly* was that flies regurgitate their digestive stomach acids onto the surface upon which they land in order to prepare the food thereon for consumption. Ever since I saw this Hollywood masterpiece, I have been decidedly opposed to having flies land on me. And I especially don't like the idea of them parking all over my face. Nevertheless, I was coping fairly well until my heavy breathing resulted in repeatedly sucking the little bastards into my open mouth and nose. To their credit, one of

From the files of Dr. David A. Fagan
Dr. Roy Hendrickson has successfully secured rope around both of Buster's back legs prior to the operation.

the more sympathetic members of the zoo's support crew noticed what was happening, finally took mercy on me, and with the help of a large umbrella, provided me with a little shade. Then, someone else used up several cans of toxic fly spray to reduce the buzzing body count around my face.

The problem was that I was inhaling as much of the toxic fly spray as the flies, which combined with the oppressive heat quickly give me a raging headache. In spite of it all, we finally got Buster's dental work completed, and our patient recovered and got back up on his feet.

In due course, Buster settled down a bit. I heard later he also fathered some kids. So everyone was pleased. The director of the Sacramento Zoo gave me an intact ostrich egg shell for my efforts. It still has a prominent spot on the bookshelf in my office. By the time we got Buster finished, I felt like something the cat drug in, and I didn't improve for about three weeks thereafter. I knew instinctively that if the practice of veterinary dentistry was ever to succeed in the zoo environment, the first rule must be that you must not kill the dentist during the procedure. Sooner or later, someone would notice. I needed to get a whole lot better organized, and I needed better equipment.

One of the most significant events to occur in the practice of veterinary medicine during this period was the availability of new anesthetic drugs. Prior to 1970, the drug choices were few, and the patient's risk of dying from an anesthetic complication was, at best, as good as your average coin flip. On occasion the odds were greater than the risk of death from the illness for which the procedure was prescribed. This fact had a chilling effect upon the decision-making process of many owners of sick animals, which also had a retarding effect upon the growth and development of the field of veterinary medical care in general. After all, what difference did it make to be better able to diagnose an ailment, if the process of applying the cure killed the patient with an unpredictable anesthetic complication?

This same situation has existed for centuries in human medicine as well. Recall the opening scene of the movie *Dances with Wolves*, and remember that the cure for Kevin Costner's bullet-induced leg injury was to have his leg amputated without an anesthetic, while he bit the bullet, or a wooden stick.

It was during the drug-appreciation frenzy of this period that M-99, a derivative of morphine, was discovered. It is nearly ten thousand times stronger than morphine, and when used in small doses works very effectively and relatively quickly to produce an effective narcotic sedative effect. Better still, it could be completely reversed in a matter of moments with an antagonistic drug, known as "M-50/50."

This combination of drugs proved to be an extremely effective anesthetic combination with application to a whole spectrum of animal species. These narcotic chemicals turned out to be one of the major keys to opening the door to the creative and innovative transfer of technology and information from the field of human medicine to the field of veterinary medicine. In fact, with the 20/20 clarity of hindsight vision, it can be said that the ongoing discovery of many new practical, safe chemical solutions to the anesthetic problems of exotic animals has resulted in a dramatic increase in the perception that many of the most trusted, proven medical procedures, which work well on one species of mammal, function just as well on many other species of mammal. Of course, in other respects this is not always true, but then neither does everything that applies medically to an adult member of a species apply equally well to a juvenile member of the same species.

Essentially there are only minor differences between a surgical procedure in the mouth of a human, called human dentistry; a surgical procedure in the abdomen of a child, called human medicine; and a surgical procedure on the leg of a monkey, called veterinary medicine. My point is that with relatively minor, yet critical and sophisticated variations, the practice of all three of these different medicines is essentially just different forms of the practice of mammalian medicine. When it is all said and done, we are after all just a bunch of mammals. The clinical reality of all this is that there is just one medicine.

During this same time period, I also owned and operated a very busy multi-specialty, multi-location, human dental group practice with our main office near the geographic center of San Francisco on the corner of Castro and Market. All during the late 1960s and early 1970s, the San Francisco Bay area was the heart and soul of everything the Age of Aquarius had to offer. My clinical dental practice maintained a 24-hour emergency, on-call service, 365 days a year. This meant we kept our offices open for business seven days a week all year long—including holidays. All of us worked long, hard hours dealing with the seedy under-belly of San Francisco's chapter of the '60s hippie movement.

I got to know many of the Bay area's developing musical groups—Country Joe & the Fish, Big Brother and the Holding Company, Quicksilver Messenger Service, Mother Earth, CCR, Jefferson Airplane, as well as many of the flash-in-the-pan groups like Capt. Beefheart & His Magic Band, Moby Grape, and the soon-to-be-famous Warlocks. The Diggers and Family Dog sent us a lot of business. When any of their people had an emergency dental problem of one sort or another, we as often as not were the ones they finally contacted to get it resolved. I distinctly remember treating one of O.C. Smith's drummers, and vividly recall one of Janis Joplin's backup singers who ODed one night in our parking lot after self-medicating a nagging toothache from someone's personal stash of street drugs.

Wherever there is a profusion of sex, drugs, free love and loud music, there will also be an abundance of drunks, sleeplessness, lots of unappreciated sexual advances, facial trauma, broken teeth, unbrushed dirty mouths, and a plethora of head and neck injury, disease and infection.

My dental practice regularly dealt with the results of all sorts of vehicular accidents, drunken brawls over the hill in Golden Gate Park, on the beaches, and in Haight-Ashbury. Hard-core, get-down, uninhibited chicks and dudes with drugs and booze on their minds are always a marvelous resource for any growing medical or dental emergency business. In fact, it's almost too damn good for business, because it never slows down. However, I had a growing family to support, so we stayed the course, and built a fine clinical practice.

It is generally accepted that the locus of a person's identity and personality resides in their face. Dealing with facial trauma is a stressful endeavor under the best of circumstances, but dealing with repeated episodes of uncalled-for, drug-induced head and neck trauma intentionally or unintentionally inflected upon innocent bystanders in the name of having a "good time" can get to be a little much

In 1967, the Human Be-In in San Francisco popularized hippie culture, leading to the legendary Summer of Love on the West Coast of the United States, and the 1969 Woodstock

Festival on the East Coast. In time, the clinician gets to the point that anything short of arterial blood pulsing from the eyeball or ears just isn't a real emergency, and it becomes time for a change. Military medics and field hospital nurses in Vietnam often experienced this same sort of burnout. I was overdosing on the underbelly of San Francisco's Hippy-hood. As one of my drug-addicted patients told me late one night, "I ain't found much God and love in Sodom and Gomorrah, Doc."

It never ceases to amaze me how few individuals are adequately taught the fundamentals of good oral care, and then take personal responsibility for their own dental health. It is actually not that complicated an issue, and should be a mandatory ingredient in the universal Mother Manual. The essential facts, which apply to humans, basically apply to all of the other species of animal as well. Oral disease and tooth decay, correctly referred to as caries, are not foregone conclusions destined to take your teeth because you had immoral thoughts in your youth, or something of the sort. Oral health is a simple cause-and-effect issue with a few little twists to keep it interesting. It is not necessarily true that if your mother or father lost their teeth, you're sure to lose yours. You may in fact lose all of your teeth, but it will generally be your own fault, not always the fault of some long-gone ancestor.

It is also true that mothers give their babies all of the necessary oral organisms to cause tooth decay between the ages of six to eighteen months by the simple act of kissing them—but only if they have the pathogenic organisms to give. Mothers can also give their babies a lot of other good things as well, like antibodies to help develop a strong immune system, good nutrition, a strong sense of cultural values, etc. It is also true that every human being carries in their saliva the microbial fingerprint of every other human being they have ever kissed. So it is a very good idea to know something about the care and maintenance of your mouth or oral cavity. This is especially true if you do a lot of late-night pub crawl'n swapping spit with a bunch of strangers.

The mouth is just the top end of a long soft pipe, which runs through the mammalian body from top to bottom. It is the garage door into your digestive system. The same mob of microorganisms found in your stomach, which digests that ham sandwich and beer you had for lunch, actually begins its work in your mouth or oral cavity. Your digestive tract is in reality just a long, tubular, specialized eco-system full of microbes designed to convert edible stuff into usable amino acid units in a complex process referred to as "digestion."

In order to maintain a normal, healthy environment, all mouths must maintain a balanced population of some forty to fifty microorganisms, e.g. bacteria, viruses and yeast, referred to as the "indigenous biota" of the oral cavity. If you were suddenly given a perfectly clean, organism-free mouth or oral cavity, say by your friendly neighborhood dental office, it would actually last only until you took your next bite of food, breath of air, or hiccup. The microbes in your nose, throat, and digestive tract immediately begin the process of re-establishing their oral eco-system as they double every twenty or thirty minutes. Within three days or so, the environment of your mouth has been repopulated with the entire range of organisms appropriate for your particular oral cavity and digestive system. The secret to the rapid success of these microbes is that saliva—spit—is good food, as well as the fact that the mouth is a great habitat for microbes to live. Your mouth has a constant temperature, stable climate, lots of food, and no rent to pay. Humans produce and swallow their own saliva three to four thousand

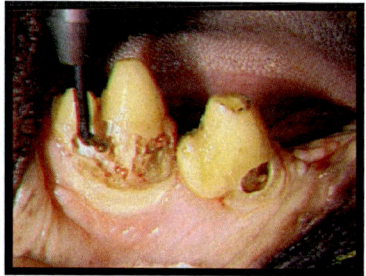

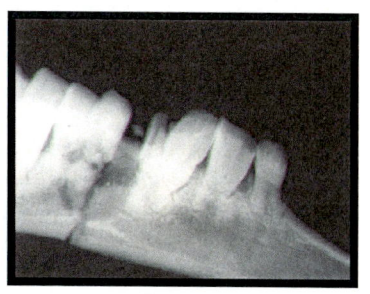

From the files of David A. Fagan

Animals have all of the 28 categories of oral, dental, and maxillo-facial diseases and disorders commonly identified in humans. The view on the left is a severe congenital cleft palate in a common chimpanzee (Pan troglodytes); the middle is classic tooth decay (caries) in a spotted hyena (Crocuta crocuta), and on the right is a pathologic fracture of the mandible of a pronghorn antelope (Antilocapra americana).

times a day. If immediately after your mouth got cleaned, you did nothing but sit in the corner and meditate on world peace, or an end to global climate change, your teeth would begin to decay and rot out of your mouth within a reasonably short period of time.

Moreover we humans, like all of the other animals, were designed to eat a specific assortment of raw, unprocessed foods. Most wild animals do just that. Most zoo animals, and we humans, actually eat mostly cooked and processed stuff. Its like burning diesel fuel in a gasoline engine. Sooner or later something bad is going to happen to your engine—or your teeth.

As a rule, a healthy animal has a healthy mouth, in spite of the fact that it never brushes its teeth. So, how does this work? Why don't they have all of the dental, oral and maxillo-facial problems that we humans have. What happens in the wild? The answer to these questions was the first big issue we faced when attempting to determine exactly what was the cause of the oral problems we were identifying in the animals we examined.

The answer is: animals do have all of the same problems we have.

However, in the wild, if a dental or oral problem gets out of hand, the animal dies, and generally nobody worries about it. The good news is that someone else gets a free meal. The sick animal's body gets eaten, re-cycled, and all of the evidence disappears.

But whether in captivity, or among humans, or in the wild, one of the major causes of oral disease in animals is the impact the food we eat has upon the indigenous biota of the oral cavity. This has been known and reported in the scientific literature for over 100 years for both humans and animals.

This does not mean that you shouldn't eat. Or eat only green leafy stuff. Or become a vegan. Humans and many other mammals, like pigs for example, are classified as omnivores, which means that they (we) are designed to eat lots of different stuff. What it does mean is that all mammals have a recurrent oral bacterial management problem to deal with. Each species has evolved with a specifically designed oral cavity to capture, process and consume a very specific diet of foodstuffs. As long as they stick to eating what they were designed to eat, the difficulties are kept to a minimum. The problems get interesting when animals eat too much of the other stuff. Humans and zoo animals do a lot of this. Therefore, humans and zoo animals tend to have more oral and dental problems than free-ranging animals.

There is a very big difference between brushing your teeth and cleaning your mouth. Just as there is a big difference between brushing your hair and cleaning your head: it is impossible to brush lice out of your hair, or to brush all of the microbes out of your mouth.

The mouth is actually not a very big object, so logically it should not take a lot of time, or be too much trouble, to keep it cleaned properly. However, it is important to understand that the maintenance of a healthy mouth is a bacterial management issue—not necessarily just a mechanical brushing or scrubbing issue.

By the time the Flower Children started to drift out of the San Francisco Bay area, I had seen and treated enough self-inflicted, severe human dental disease to last me a lifetime. For me, it was time for a change of pace. And coincidentally, a close friend in the insurance business, who knew of my research background, asked me to help him evaluate several research projects underway at Stanford Research Institute. I had directed a number of research projects over the years, and the task was well within my capabilities. I was thoroughly reinvigorated discussing issues and debating rational circumstances with an assortment of dedicated, hard-core research scientists at Stanford Research Institute and NASA's Ames Research Center at Moffett Field south of San Francisco near Mountain View. The experience reminded me of the work I had done on the Apollo project. I completed the final report for my friend, and within a few months was offered the position of director of research for a start-up lumber company with offices in San Diego and Eugene, Oregon.

After some lengthy soul-searching discussions with my family and business associates, I arranged to sell my remaining interest in our San Francisco group dental practice to my partners, and retire from the practice of dentistry on humans—for the first time. I continued my association with the vet school in Davis, but soon I was commuting between San Diego and Oregon on a regular basis. My mother and brother liked this because they lived in San Diego. So after discussing the matter with my family, we decided to relocate to the southland. Initially, I was not too excited about this move because the San Diego climate is a coastal marine desert without much in the way of natural forests.

I was talking about the move with Roy Hendrickson at the Primate Center one day when he said, "If you move to San Diego, you must go to the zoo and meet Dr. Kurt Benirschke, the director of the Center for the Reproduction of Endangered Species at the Zoological Society of San Diego." I thought this would help keep things interesting, so I did.

I phoned, made an appointment to meet Dr. B at his office in the historic Helen Browning Scripps Research building—built in 1926 behind the Old Globe Theater in Balboa Park. We spoke about what I had been doing at Davis, and he invited me to come on in, take a look at some of their animals, and see what was to be discovered.

Dr. Benirschke introduced me to Dr. Phil Robinson, the zoo's director of veterinary services, who was intently focused on building the zoo a functional new hospital. Phil was charged with the responsibility of establishing a new level of clinical excellence for the roughly three thousand animals in the zoo's extensive collection.

What followed was my next giant leap forward in the care and understanding of oral disease and its relationships to the systemic health of exotic animals. By January of 1978, Phil had his new hospital ready to accept patients, and he selected a dental surgery case involving a northern chinese mountain leopard to be subject of the new facility's first clinical procedure. The San Diego Zoo's official *ZOONOOZ Magazine* publication proclaimed the dedication of its new hospital—known as the Jennings Center for Zoological Medicine—with an article focusing attention on the dedication ceremony, and veterinary dentistry.

Phil and I immediately became thoroughly involved in developing and implementing a

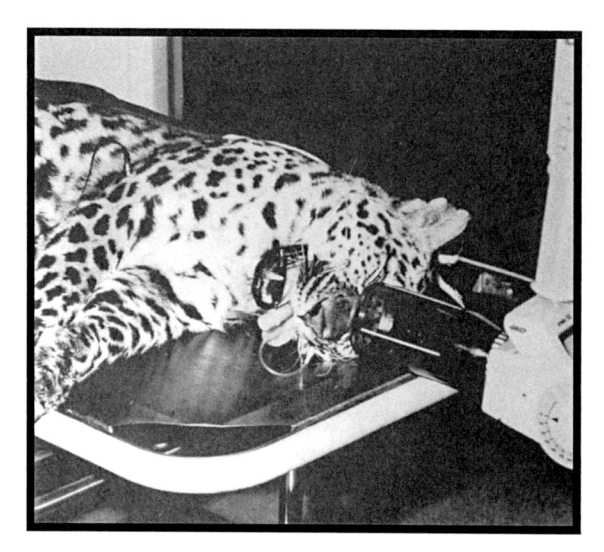

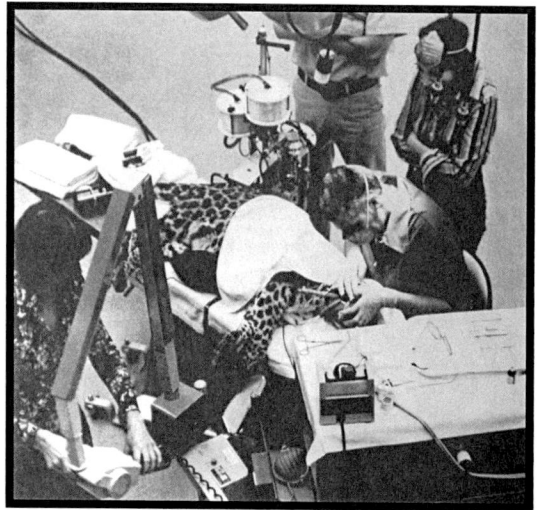

From the files of David A. Fagan

The image on the left shows a north Chinese mountain leopard (Panthera pardus japonensis) from Manchuria immobilized, and in the process of being radiographed in preparation for his first complete oral/dental examination. The image on the right shows Dr. Fagan conducting the examination, while his dental assistant, Joyce Schlachter, is repositioning their first semi-portable dental x-ray machine. This image shows the view from the observer's window in the library room overlooking the new hospital's operating room. The operation was the cover story for the January, 1978 **ZOONOOZ Magazine,** *San Diego Zoo's official newsletter.*

program to methodically examine the zoo's extensive collection of exotic animals in order to identify and understand the extent and causes of the oral disease we were systematically uncovering. I worked with and participated in the education of others concerning the nature of the problems, and in the process we all discovered that the impact of watching the animals you love go see the dentist you hate is a surprisingly powerful public relations tool.

But more importantly for me, I had been invited to participate in the care and treatment of a wide variety of very rare and special animals, from mountain leopards like the one in the photos above, to a hippo with a herpetic lesion (cold sore) the size of a dinner plate, encountered early in my zoo career, and cured with the help of Du Pont's slogan "better living through chemistry."

I worked side by side with some of the most talented and most diversely educated group of veterinarians, medical clinicians, researchers, animal health technicians, keepers, photographers and assorted exotic animal specialists in the world. I had found my calling, and I was lovin' every minute of it. We did our job, published some papers, and had a great time. The problems were always fresh and tough, but the satisfaction that came with each success was—and has been ever since—absolutely delicious.

Chapter Four
The Black Eagle's Story

Little biped, your brain is under duress!!
Rely on all senses in times of stress
to apprehend what your eyes can't see
You must seek to learn comprehensively!!

So now, put an end to all those blind mumblings.
But continue on with your physical fumblings.
On the edge of discovery you teeter and flail.
Reach out with more senses, and you'll not fail!!

More than half her beak and part of her nose were missing; she was hemorrhaging freely and in shock when she arrived at the zoo hospital. Apparently this south Asian black eagle had flown full speed into one of the steel upright support poles in her large flight enclosure. It was approaching four in the afternoon, Tuesday, May 27, 1980, when Dr. Don Janssen called me back into the treatment room.

Walking into the small crowded room I smelled halothane, a pungent, gaseous anesthetic leaking from around the plastic nose cone covering the bird's face. She was actually in the process of waking up again following a second attempt at placing a secure endotracheal breathing tube in her throat necessary to connect her directly to the gas anesthetic machine. Vigorously flopping about, talons flexing searchingly, she was struggling again to get away from the hands holding her down on the examination table. She was a determined fighter. My first impression was that if there was any hope of treating her injury successfully, her admirable spirit was more than willing to meet us halfway.

"We're having trouble getting her intubated," Don reported as I moved closer to take a better look over his shoulder.

"As soon as we pull the mask off, she rapidly blows off the gas and starts waking up again before we can get the tube in and secured," he added, giving her more of the anesthetic gas. "The underlying vascular bed of her beak is badly torn up, and we haven't quite managed to get all the bleeding stopped yet either."

Finally intubated, and looking more like a bloody feather duster attached to a pound of raw hamburger than a bird, the eagle seemed to be more dead than alive. She appeared to be convulsing again—or was it a last ditch attempt to fight her way back as death tried to squeeze the life from her? With a gauze pressure pack taped over the artery to temporarily stop the bleeding from her broken beak, we took the time to grossly clean and examine her injured face, revealing the torn mid-sagittal artery trying to pulse away the last of her vital juices. Fortunately her heart was still beating, but we had no idea how much blood she had left, or just how long she'd be able to last.

A concerned and worried staff encircled the table. Without a lot of quick focused help, this was rapidly turning into just another dying-bird dance. With bloody fingers, Don and I finally looked each other in the eye. He knew we had no other choice but to hold her on the anesthetic until we could figure out a way to patch her face together well enough for it to heal.

"Got any ideas, Dave?"

"Ahhh... yeah," I finally mumbled, lost in a flood of thoughts. "Let's give it a try... "

All of my equipment had been dismantled and packed for shipment to Las Vegas, where I was scheduled to spend the next week working on Siegfried and Roy's animals with Dr. Marty Dennis. Everything had already been loaded into my vehicle ready for the trip to the airport's freight office. Valuable time would be consumed going to the parking lot, unpacking and setting up my equipment and instruments again.

Four p.m. was not a good time either, with staff changes underway. People were leaving for the day, and the night crew had not all arrived yet, with the potential of creating an intermittent staff vacuum during the switch.

DENTIST GOES ANIMAL 38

"I'll get her set up and stable in the surgery prep room," Don volunteered, "while you get your gear ready." He rattled off the names of the surgical team and instructed them to get an assortment of necessary monitoring equipment assembled and hooked up.

"OK," I said, "but I'd like to take another quick look at her first. It'll give me something to think about while I get my gear."

I wanted a second look to make sure that this effort was justifiable. Examining the wound for a second time, I saw she had detached the entire beak structure breaking off approximately 70% of the beak itself. Both of the side walls of the remaining beak were very loose, and had less than a square centimeter of undamaged vascular bed substance between them, and just above the opening into her nose a good deal of the specialized soft yellow facial tissue, or ceres, had been damaged, torn away, or badly bruised.

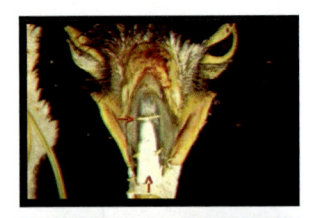

"We just might be able to do it," I mumbled again, with the makings of the rough outline of a plan now beginning to form in my mind—knowing this would be a step-by-step procedure of finding the right answers as we proceeded.

Quickly finding several familiar faces in the audience eager to help me, I headed for the parking lot, retrieved my equipment, and hurried back to the larger surgery treatment room, where Don had the bird fully anesthetized and stabilized on an adjustable stainless surgery table.

From the files of Dr. David A. Fagan
A bird's beak has the structure, layers and texture similar to that of a human's fingernail. When it is traumatically injured, it represents a very serious problem for both its owner, and the clinicians attempting to repair it. At the time these photographs were taken, 70% to 80% of the remaining "beak" structure was very loose, and very poorly attached to the underlying connective tissue.

With an intravenous drip now slowly replacing her lost fluids, a vital sign monitor announced each strong and steady beat of her heart, she looked as ready as she was likely to get. Though stable for the moment, she had lost so much blood Don was still justifiably worried her heart might stop, or that she didn't have enough red blood cells left to get the job done. She was far from safe, so he continued to keep her under close and intense supervision.

With the first three steps of trauma control completed, Don had a clear airway, dependable breathing and verifiable circulation with IV access to replace fluids and administer medications as necessary. The next step was to thoroughly and vigorously clean the entire wound. It was now my turn to get to work.

"I'll use the electrocautery unit to stop the bleeding," I said, holding my finger on the large sagittal artery running down the middle of the forehead and nose. Dividing into several channels at that juncture, this artery also provides the blood supply to the beak.

Slowed but not stopped, the missing channels were still leaking away the bird's precious blood. Her blood pressure was slowly climbing back to normal, but the bleeding had to be stopped. My eyes scanned for the solution.

As I applied the electrocautery tip to the wound, burning flesh sent a characteristic foul-smelling white smoke up toward the ceiling. With my face directly over the bird, feeling for debris and searching for bleeders in the wound, I moved slightly to one side, trying to avoid the pungency, and noticed one of her eyes was half open. It was as though she was watching me, certainly not trusting, but aware her life was in our hands now, and we were there to help.

As usual, Don was walking that razor-thin line of the skilled anesthesiologist, keeping her just deep enough to hold her still, but not too deep to unduly depress her respiration. This meant that occasionally she would lighten up enough to see through the anesthetic fog. Continuing to thoroughly clean the wounded tissues, I felt the slippery, bloody mass of her face slowly become sticky and firm as the bleeding decreased and finally stopped.

"Be careful not to tear the connective tissues under the remaining beak parts," I whispered as Don slowly rotated her head for me. "She'll need to keep every fiber she's got left to hold these broken pieces of beak onto her face."

Finally, we covered the remaining soft tissue formerly buried within the beak with a quick-setting zinc oxide and eugenol endodontic medicament commonly used to seal and protect exposed dental pulp/nerve tissues in root canal therapy. Applying it over the entire wound area, I ended up using a whole year's supply of the material to create an adequate hermetic seal. This was intended to protect the delicate underlying soft tissues from the harsher chemicals in the final beak reconstruction phase of the repair process.

"Next, we've got to establish some sort of retention and anchorage to hold a fixation prosthesis onto her face," I mumbled quietly to no one in particular.

Everyone was functioning in high gear now, according to expertise, checking the bird's vitals and assisting Don and/or me wherever possible. Placing a series of small threaded brass pins through the remaining beak walls and rigid portion of the roof of her mouth, we then bonded them to the outside of the beak. Using a coarse grinding stone, I gently cleaned and roughened the outer surfaces of the remaining fragile beak parts to facilitate and maximize both the mechanical and chemical bonding of the epoxy-like restorative materials I was planning to use.

Molding the soft, putty-like, self-curing composite resin material into an artificial prosthesis, I covered the remaining beak parts and remaining palatal tissue, which formed the roof of her mouth. We constructed a "nose bandage," much like repairing a torn fingernail with a fingernail repair kit. When it hardened, the composite resin material held the retention pins in symmetrical positions around the remains of the traumatized beak parts, ensuring good mechanical support, as well as complete chemical bonding.

Pinching, glueing, adding ingredients in small amounts, step by step we covered the injuries, and created a new beak prosthesis. I knew if she elected to remove our "work of art" from her face, she could do so with her talons, as quickly as she could kill a monkey. With no idea how it would all turn out, we applied our procedures and chemicals to this torn and helpless bird with absolutely no guarantee our efforts would transform it back into a healthy, functional eagle.

Our last major unresolved problem area was just above the air exchange holes of her nose. Because so much of the tissue was missing, there wasn't much we could do with the actual abrasion other than to gently clean and disinfect this specialized yellow skin. Hoping it would granulate in and heal, we couldn't be sure it would happen that way. Possible gross facial deformity loomed consistently over our efforts. Restructuring the palate, we left a small channel for fluid drainage, and contoured and trimmed the composite beak prosthesis so that the lower portion of her beak could close somewhere near properly.

"I sure hope this contraption works," I whispered.

Its purpose was to provide adequate protection for the underlying soft tissues during the early regeneration phase of the beak growth, and required minimal manipulation while facilitating the natural regeneration of a somewhat normal looking beak. A state-of-the-art dental composite bonding material now solidly held both lateral walls of her broken beak together,

Views of the slowly growing beak taken over the next twelve to fourteen months show the results of repeated filings, trimmings, and reshaping of the eagle's beak to stimulate growth and gently encourage growth to resemble a normal, functional eagle beak.

From the files of Dr. David A. Fagan

with the solid portion anchored to the roof of her mouth. Only time would show us it would function as planned.

"She's got the best we have to offer," Don responded as we finished up.

"Looks like a boxer out for the count to me," I responded.

"Would be nice if she decides to leave your art work alone," someone said.

She could bang into something and break it off again in a New York second. We all knew that. We also all knew that this bird must now actively and consciously decide to cooperate with her new prosthesis, if she wanted it to heal and get her face back. Other accidents could occur; she could wedge food underneath it, creating a nasty infection, or a zillion other things could happen.

"We'll just have to watch her closely and make adjustments as we go," I said.

The unanswered questions in my mind were overpowered by my confidence in our team. We would solve the problems together as they occurred.

Still under close observation at the hospital on Wednesday, June 16, when I checked on her, the eagle was on her feet and moving freely around her enclosure still wearing her nose bandage. Don's zoo hospital internship took him to the hospital at the Wild Animal Park soon after the date of the accident, and shortly thereafter he moved on to become an associate veterinarian at the National Zoo in Washington, D.C., where he first became involved with the giant pandas. In time, he would return to San Diego in the capacity of director of the zoo hospital, all the while serving his profession as he methodically rose up through the ranks to become president of the American Association of Zoo Veterinarians, and then Director of Veterinary Services for both the zoo and the Wild Animal Park. The eagle moved on as well—back out into her unusually large flight enclosure.

It was all up to her now.

A few weeks later, from the back of her large flight enclosure, Dr. Tim Reichard, the new zoo hospital intern, and I observed the eagle through high-powered binoculars.

"She still seems to be holding together," I said. "We'll know more when her beak starts to show signs of regeneration."

"Or sooner," Tim responded, "if something goes wrong."

"True, oh so true", I smiled and nodded, but inside I remained confident that everything was on the mend—for the moment.

We parted after setting a tentative date to meet and re-examine our patient again. I was now headed for San Francisco to work on some lions at the old Marine World-Africa USA Park, and wouldn't return for a week or so. That would give the eagle enough time for any post-surgical problems to surface. We were prepared to address them immediately, hoping to keep them at bay long enough for her face to heal.

Pondering this case and its unique aspects, I theorized that since birds do not have real teeth, many individuals believe they don't merit consideration from a dental point of view. Ratites, eagles, owls, hawks and other birds of prey, are known to have a variety of maxillo-facial problems, often further complicated with secondary bacterial, fungal or viral infective agents.

Head and neck soft-tissue trauma and other avian disorders are more common than one would think, and include injuries such as bill or beak fractures, dislocations, and malformations resulting from trauma or improper diet.

The oral cavity is the natural entry mechanism into an animal's digestive system, and it contains a triad of interlocking components, which make up a functional entry mechanism known as a masticatory apparatus to process food. Dentistry applies to the care and repair of this entire apparatus; so avian species do indeed have "dental" problems. More accurately, they have a whole host of oral disorders and diseases.

Dentures are a generally accepted prosthetic replacement device for human teeth. As wheelchairs substitute for legs, dentures are a modest substitute for teeth, and our eagle's nose bandage would function like a temporary denture or prosthesis to enable her to eat while she healed herself—if she chose to cooperate.

Tim and I documented our patient's progress during regular weekly visits, observing her with high-powered binoculars or a telephoto lens on a camera. Every month or two, we would have to capture and immobilize her to trim, adjust and modify the irregularities in growth as they occurred. She didn't like this.

An assortment of views of the slowly growing beak taken over the next twelve to fourteen months showing the results of repeated filings, trimmings, and reshaping of her beak to stimulate growth and gently encourage growth to resemble a normal, functional eagle beak.

The new intern was an excellent, creative and dextrous clinician. He had lost his left hand just below the wrist in a childhood accident, which gave me a bit of a surprise the first time he pulled on a freshly sterilized prosthesis to help me with another surgical procedure. He was so skilled surgically however, that his "impairment" was irrelevant. Often he would be able to outmaneuver me with his hooked device, long before I could reach for and pick up a hemostat to do the same task. In due course, Tim also moved on to assume the position of director of veterinary services of the hospital at the Toledo Zoo in Ohio. I always thought it was interesting that we used Tim's prosthesis to maintain and repair the eagle's prosthesis.

Our patient grew out of her prosthesis about ninety days later. At first, the minimally damaged lower jaw beak grew much faster than the more traumatized upper jaw beak, so on occasion it was necessary to shorten the lower in order to prevent an irreparable bulldog-like Class III malocclusion from developing. Thereafter, we routinely trimmed the lower beak to match the slower growing and shorter maxillary or upper beak.

Eventually, however, the now rapidly growing upper beak grew into a deformed, curved encasement growing over her lower beak, almost preventing her from opening her mouth. With our help, after nearly two years of regular immobilizations, each one resulting in minor cuts and/or scratches on her prominent eyebrows, a fairly traditional looking hook slowly returned to the front of her face, enabling her to thrive on a normal captive diet without our intervention.

Finally we were able to discharge the eagle—healthy and fully functional with a normal-looking face. On the last immobilization, however, she managed to run one of her talons through the forearm of one of the keepers. Her beak may have been broken, but clearly her fighting spirit was intact and never in doubt.

All of our blended energy and resources were responsible for healing this bird. Specific knowledge and skills applied with confidence and faith, personal egos sublimated for the benefit of the patient, and her strong will to survive—all contributed to the success of this case.

These long, intense treatment procedures are quite often very physically draining. Whenever I'm asked to consider the uniqueness of my clinical practice of veterinary dentistry, I initially describe the differing degree of personal satisfaction I derive from treating both animals and humans. Working with exotic animals is therapeutic for me. Treating humans is occupational. Without a doubt, the reason is that animals more actively invest their internal energy into the clinical process to influence the outcome. Much more passive about it all, humans do not seem to connect with their inner self-healing role in the same manner as animals.

Our patient some twenty-four months later —looking fully recovered and bristling with attitude . . .

In the words of an older Chinese friend of mine, "Animals pay their bills immediately. As treatment begins, the chi begins to flow, and their yin meets, mixes with and balances with your yang."

The encounter then becomes equally satisfying, therapeutic and restful for patient and clinician alike. Born of this union, occupational gestalt renders both participants renewed by the process. Refreshed and feeling restored after each session with the black eagle, I was always ready to face another challenge, whatever it might be. Her spirit was her energy, and she shared it freely to the benefit of those who helped her.

Chapter Five
MacGyver Goes to the Zoo

The next student grasps a large fan-shaped ear.
Between her palms she feels the beat clear
And cheek to cheek, they both quietly listen,
And after a moment, her eyes start to glisten.

"Why is it that front and back do not match??
What causes this drumbeat I cannot catch??
What's passing within these soft velvety hoses??
Their study may answer the secret life poses.

In order to learn more about this process.
Cardiology's where I will aim for success."

Within a matter of weeks after my initial conversation with Dr. Phil Robinson, it became abundantly clear that his primary responsibilities had him deeply involved with the design, planning and construction for the zoo's new hospital. The urgent necessity for the new building was directly related to the fact that up until the time it opened for business in 1978, the "hospital" at the world-famous San Diego Zoo was in reality nothing more than a single, small, sixteen-by-twenty-foot, one-room building located twenty feet due north of the old Helen Browning Scripps C.R.E.S. Research Building. The old one-room hospital is still there today, but now the room has been remodeled to function as the hospital staff's locker and lunch break room located between the two buildings. It was indeed just the same small space in the old days, but a great deal of quality medical care occurred inside and passed through that narrow little door on the south wall of the room—which is no longer there. The door is now on the west wall of the structure facing the newer two-story cinder block hospital building.

In very short order, with Dr. Benirschke's unceasing encouragement, and working closely with Dr. Robinson, I became a regular participant in the diagnosis and treatment of the dental disease identified in the animals within the zoo's extensive collection. Dr. Robinson was anxious to include dental X-rays and oral evaluation with each routine physical examination. Our primary difficulty at the time was their old, large, medical X-ray machine. It was designed to take very good full body and skull images, but it was not very good at localizing small lesions of developing oral infection and dental disease. In spite of these difficulties, we identified a broad range of oral problems with surprising regularity. Of course, the next big question to follow was what exactly were we planning to do about all this oral disease. With each new case, this issue gained in importance.

With the experience of Buster still fresh in my mind, my first order of business was to focus attention on the design and assembly of a dependable, versatile, mobile dental unit. With each new case, I thought of something else to be added to my evolving specialized dental equipment design. It must be movable. It must be limited to just a few manageable pieces. It must be "something" capable of supporting comprehensive veterinary dental care, regardless of the species, large or small, as I would be working on nearly everything. And finally, it must be sturdy enough to not fail me during translocation to one of the unusual locations where I'd be working. Fortunately for both me, and our patients, the individuals capable of helping me realize these objectives were close at hand.

Wayne Black was the physical plant manager for the hospital buildings at the zoo, and Earl Thrailkill was the general manager of the S.S. White dental supply house in downtown San Diego on 6th Avenue. Both of these two individuals had an extraordinary large network of resources available to them, and both responded positively to our discussions regarding my requirements for a mobile veterinary dental unit. Before long, the fabrication process got underway.

I wanted to be able to quickly assemble and/or disassemble my entire office package of typical dental office equipment and instrumentation, and then easily and safely transport it to a new location. To start the process, Wayne contacted a friend of his at the Navy military surplus supply facility downtown, and managed to secure a matching pair of wooden WWII Marine Corps foot-lockers and a relatively unused, but very rare medicvac unit's airborne anesthesia instrument cabinet, made of light-weight aluminum with a locking front cover, which also functioned as an expanded table-top working surface. It was perfect, and it has been the object of serious male tool-box lust ever since, everywhere it travels.

From the files of David A. Fagan

This small plastic suitcase also contains a complete dental hand-piece controller panel. The extra brass plumbing items on the outside support an extra pneumatic assembly of valves, gauges, and quick connectors to expand the capability of this small unit to power an assortment of our elephant dental tools—making this unit very light, easy to transport, and very efficient.

We had two narrow angle-iron cradles welded onto the frame of a medivac stretcher carrier with eight-inch pneumatic tires. These held the two rectangular footlockers in an easily accessible position. Then we installed a simple brake system, and applied a fresh coat of hospital green paint. While all of this was underway, Earl assembled the necessary dental hand-pieces with a small air/water controller box, a lightweight, semi-portable, Phillips dental X-ray machine, a Cavitron tooth-scaling unit, an electro-scalpel unit, and a compressed-air-operated vacuum system. Soon, all was ready to be installed within one of the freshly painted footlockers.

I decided early on to use compressed nitrogen, and not compressed air to operate the system, in order to eliminate the oil droplet contamination problem universally associated with compressed air in dental offices. With many years of hindsight, it has proven to be a very cost-effective decision. Finally, with lots of creativity, one of Earl's service repairmen, a fellow by the name of Jack Huntimer, neatly installed everything into one of the footlockers. With a little bit of fine-tuning, I finally had a fully functional, two piece, completely portable, entirely mobile, veterinary dental cart operational and ready to go to work.

With only minor modifications over the years, and with some fresh paint from time to time, this original unit has traveled and functioned very well for more than thirty-five years. It is still in use today (see photo next page)—although it did require a nice new hospital blue paint job in 2002 in order to qualify for the "very rigorous esthetic standards" established by Jeanette Fuller, RVT at the Wild Animal Park's new Harter Veterinary Medical Center.

Periodically, as I come across something new in my travels, I'll add another useful item or two to the mix. Now, my equipment stash is easily divided into one of three individual arrangements depending upon what I'm trying to do. There is a small suitcase arrangement to use in tight spaces; a medium-sized foot locker on an instrument case system for more flexibility in the smaller spaces; and the full package of goodies, which tops out at nearly 2000 pounds of uniquely specific mobile, dental office equipment prepared to tackle any new surprise encounter with comprehensive capability.

I have the ability to work anywhere, anytime, and do any procedure, on any size animal. Everything has been used often, routinely functions very well, and on occasion has been badly abused

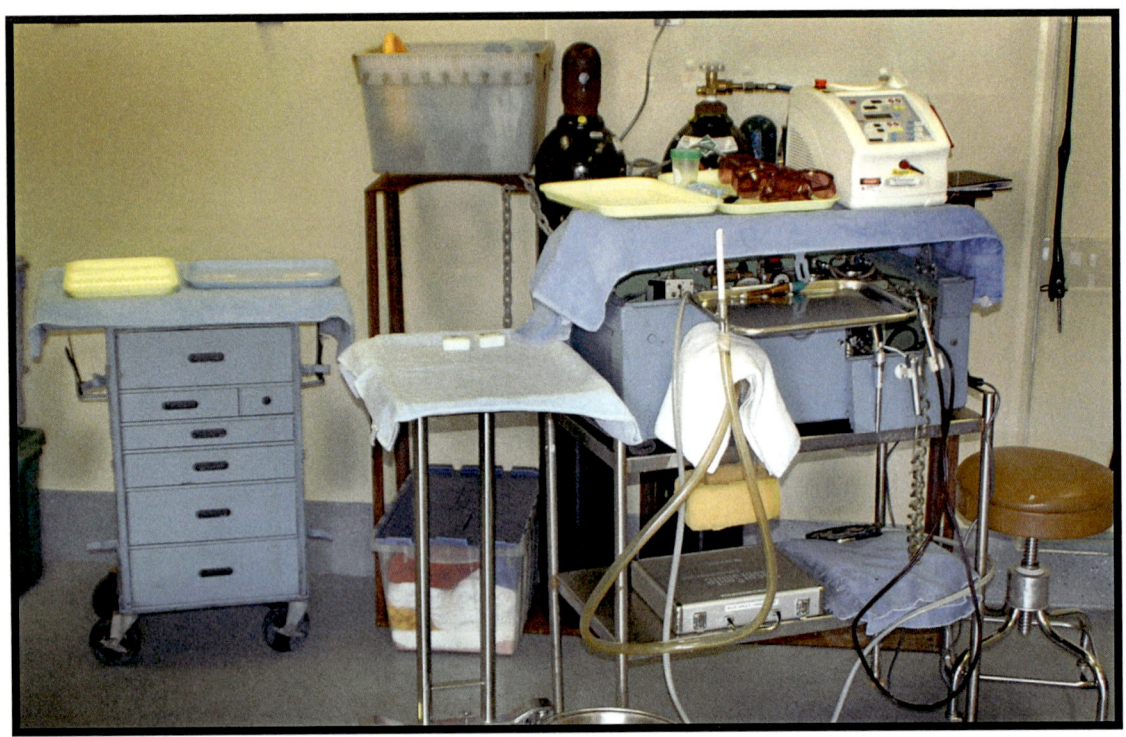

From the files of David A. Fagan

This is our medium mobile dental unit set up circa 2008—with the now blue footlocker controller box and suction system positioned on top of a small metal stand with a Mayo stand to its left, and my instrument case near the back wall. The brown stool, metal waste can, and small white diode laser all fit into the several plastic shipping cases of instruments, materials, etc. stacked in the left background. The dark green box on the bottom left holds my x-ray film developer tank. The black N2 tank against the wall powers the dental drills, etc.

by the rigors of some strange location or airport travel—just like your personal luggage.

In one form or another, my assembled comprehensive dental office equipment stash has traveled all over the country from Texas to Alaska, Chicago to Las Vegas, and into the mountains of Utah. Just about the time I begin to have doubts about the sanity of lugging 2000 pounds of luggage around the countryside, it was time get it all ready for another road trip. Each time I lighten the load, I end up needing the instruments or equipment I'd left behind. Currently, we're slowly assembling a new veterinary dental unit using a set of six matching instrument carts to incorporate the latest instrument packages to make it a little more travel friendly. Hopefully, our new modular concept will prove to be easier to transport, provide more clinical flexibility, and require less setup and break down time. The completed assembly will include both our hard- and soft-tissue lasers, a very flexible intra-oral multi-camera cart system, our NOMAD-75kvp portable dental X-ray machine, a thermograph camera, a digital radiography sensor and software system, as well as all of our assembled instruments, materials, assorted drills and dental hand-piece sets including our new pulp insert surgery kit.

During this same period, in the other aspect of my professional life, I managed to complete the lumber company research project after several years of very interesting work, and was reluctant to get back into clinical human dentistry on a full-time basis. So instead, I established a clinical research dental group practice management consulting business to support the family, as they all worked their way through high school and college. Not too many years later, I am very proud to report, we finally ended up with ten solid academic college degrees among the seven of us.

The view on the left looks into one of the 50,000-gallon dolphin pools at Sea World San Diego—after many hours of preparation. The yellow crane supports our small stretcher/operating table for a neonatal dolphin. I have a very expensive diode laser unit with a 110 volt power line secured inside a water tight gray trash can tied to the pool's railing above. On the right, I am working with Dr.Todd Schmitt, associate marine mammal veterinarian in the red shirt, and two of the park's dolphin training staff to bio-stimulate this young animal's dorsal musculature in an attempt to help resolve what initially appeared to be a muscle cramp following an injection of antibiotics in this two-day-old animal. We treated this little fellow twice a day for week with some signs of success until x-rays and further diagnostics confirmed an underlying fatal genetic problem. It took fifteen to twenty people several hours to safely provide each treatment. Sea World spares no expense to insure each and every one of their animals receives the very best of available clinical care.

During the process, I meticulously developed, focused and expanded my primary interest—a comprehensive veterinary dental, oral medicine and oral surgery consulting service. While maintaining this dual-track professional life, I soon discovered that it was easier to stay current with the latest clinical equipment and product developments in the human dental care arena if I were to participate actively in a part-time human dental practice. So, for several very practical continuing education reasons, I dropped the practice management work, and have continued over the years to maintain this dual-focused clinical balancing act. Although I still continue to practice all aspects of clinical dentistry with humans on a very limited part-time bases, for many years most of my clinical work has involved animals. I enjoy oral surgery and prosthetics the most.

I have found that only about one third of the instruments and methods I use in a human dental practice have direct application to a comprehensive exotic animal veterinary dental practice. One of the most surprising revelations for me is that many of the discarded older orthodox dental techniques, materials and procedures, which are no longer used in human practice, have unique, practical and sometimes very functional—yet quite unorthodox—applications in various exotic animal circumstances generally involving birds and/or reptiles. The remainder of the necessary instruments and equipment has undergone a slow but steady process of redesign, research and development by a whole host of creative veterinary clinicians all around the world. Now that veterinary dentistry is a recognized specialty practice of veterinary medicine, new items are developed with regularity and become available every month to fill in the missing gaps.

Another important but often less well-managed aspect of any medical practice is the busi-

DENTIST GOES ANIMAL 48

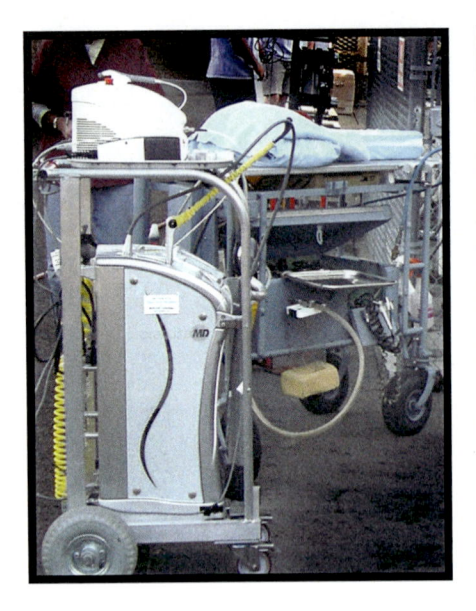

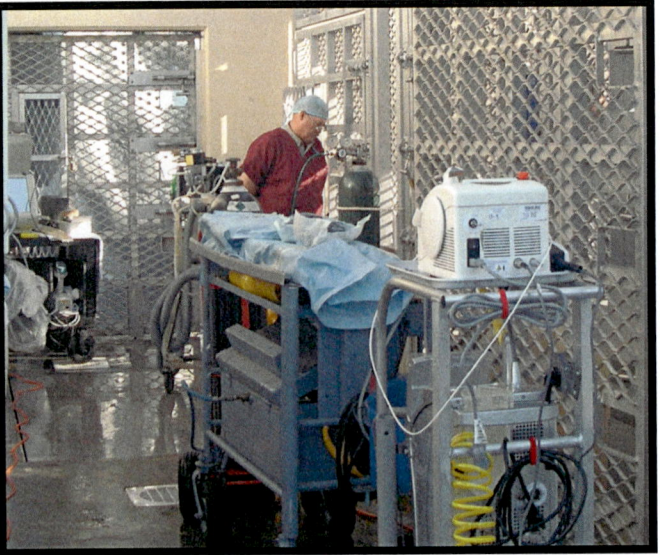

From the files of David A. Fagan

On the left above, my hard tissue water laser with the smaller diode laser on top; the original mobile dental unit with surgical suction hose and a new three-by-five-foot aluminum counter top are next to my original World War II medivac instrument cabinet. All are ready to be moved into a walrus enclosure immediately following chemical immobilization of our patient. The mobile dental cart loaded like a pack mule with our sterile surgical instruments ready for an apicoectomy procedure on the animal's right tusk. The view to the right shows the assembled equipment moved to the front of the walrus bedroom enclosure.

ness of accurate and complete record keeping. This is true in all human medical/dental practices as well, but it is especially true with an exotic animal practice in a zoo or spread all over the countryside like mine. Adequate clinical record keeping for exotic animals involves the necessity of keeping track of patients that live within a herd of very similar looking individuals. There are a multitude of methods to address this issue, and many have been in use for years: ear tags, ear notches, freeze or hot brands, tattoos, and an assortment of high-tech electronic identification systems including surgically implanted transponders.

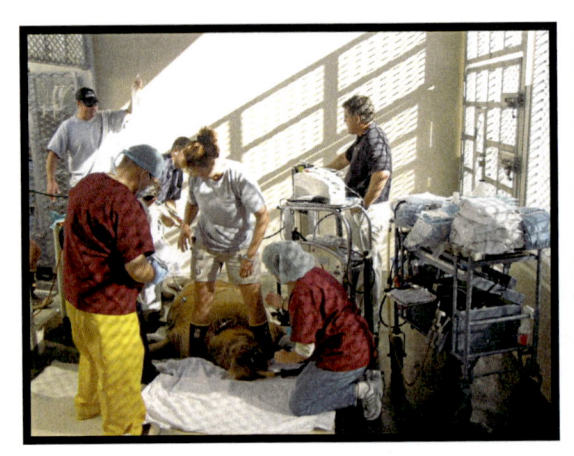

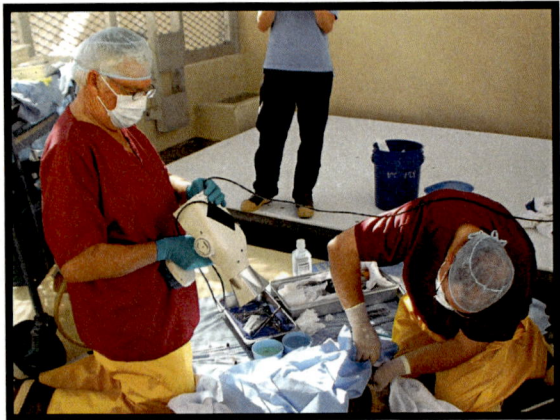

From the files of David A. Fagan

Above left, our equipment surrounds our patient with Dr. Oosterhuis (left), aka Dr. O, and PK (kneeling) in red scrub tops, Dr. Tom Reidarson in the background is monitoring the anesthesia, while Mitzy, one of the park's walrus trainers, is standing over our patient assisting with the procedure setup. The view on the right above shows Drs. O and Fagan preparing to take a digital radiographic image with the little Nomad hand-held X-ray machine. Dr. O is positioning a metal catheter tip into the access hole in the walrus's skull in front of the Eklin sensor plate under the white towels. A small portion of the walrus can be seen below Dr. O's left hand.

Efficient record keeping is absolutely necessary in order to provide the medical history essential for breeding purposes, etc. An efficient, economical, internationally accepted identification system enables and facilitates accurate record keeping. Successful reproduction also depends upon knowing and using the animals' and institutions' correct "zip code" on all of the patients' records. Although it is not uncommon for some of the animals to have names, most are known by a simple alpha-numeric designation such as "Notch 37," or "BK-15," "male lion-WAP 18," or something similar. These identification systems greatly facilitate the essential distribution of accurate clinical information. The details of an animal's medical record treatments are often published in the veterinary reference literature, and the sharing of unique clinical information is an important objective in exotic animal veterinary medicine.

Dr. Oosterhuis and I began working together in the late 1970s. We have treated a great deal of dental disease, written, taught and spoken a fair amount about it all, and in the process have developed a number of new clinical protocols. The two views above were taken in front of the old hospital building at the San Diego Zoo's Wild Animal Park next to Jim's vet truck.

The San Diego Wild Animal Park uses the identification code "WAP" for its animals. The park is located in the San Pasqual Valley agricultural preserve east of Escondido, about thirty-five miles north of downtown San Diego and the San Diego Zoo. I have been staff dental consultant there since 1976, when Dr. James E. Oosterhuis, known affectionately as "Dr. O" to his staff, began the process of assuming clinical care responsibilities for the 3000-plus exotic animals that reside there. These animals now represent roughly one half of the Zoological Society of San Diego's collection of approximately 6000 animals. Dr. O graduated from the University of Minnesota's School of Veterinary Medicine. He spent his first year in private practice, and then completed the one-year exotic animal internship at the San Diego Zoo hospital in 1973. He spent the next year at the Brownsville Zoo in southern Texas, and has been at the WAP since August of 1975. In 1982, Dr. Les Nelson retired, and Dr. O assumed the position of director of veterinary services for the park. Along with all of his other responsibilities, he supervised the design and construction of the park's new 60,000-plus-square-foot hospital, known as the Harter Veterinary Medical Center (HVMC), which is the largest and most complete zoo animal veterinary hospital in the world.

The WAP-HVMC is a clear equal to any human medical facility in terms of quality and quantity of care delivered. exotic animal veterinarians and their registered animal health technicians (RVTs) at the park routinely deal with five to six times the medical complications as do their human counterparts on a daily basis. It is similar to caring for all of the different species of creatures found in the bar lounge at a Star Trek fueling station. These veterinarians have a very complex and demanding specialty medical practice.

The WAP was opened in 1970. One of Dr. O's initial objectives was to establish the baseline medical and health histories for all of the animals in residence. This included a group of about a dozen lions, both males and females. They occupied a fairly large canyon exhibit with a bedroom/den facility tucked into the north face of the south ridge of their enclosure. An equally large tiger exhibit with bedroom area shares the lower end of the canyon on the east side of the park's old Mombassa Monorail Line. Over the years, my mobile unit has spent many weeks within both large-cat facilities during the process of annual examinations, and when dental need was diagnosed and treatment required.

It is a generally accepted practice to feed large carnivores in separate, secure, bedroom enclosures each evening. This enables each animal to consume a specifically prepared individual daily ration and/or medication without interference from any of the other animals. They are then routinely inspected and released back into their large outside enclosure each morning. This morning routine enables the keepers to easily hold back any individual that may require further care or attention. This practice is not as unnatural as it may seem at first, if one remembers that the Tasavo man-eating lions often slept in a cave at night. As is the case with all large cats, those at the park do not like the intrusion of any stranger into their personal territory, let alone a large medical team with immobilization on their mind. All predators are in constant touch, and well connected with their environment. Consequently, these cats know before the door is opened who is coming and why, and they're not at all shy about letting their opinions be known concerning the intruders' predatory intent.

On one of our earliest encounters, Dr. O had arranged to have all eleven of the park's lions locked in their individual bedrooms inside the enclosure's long, narrow, underground, cinder-block den. This was necessary, because once the examinations began, if any lion was not inside, they would not come in for any reason until long after all the bipeds had departed. As a result, and in order to ensure that each individual cat was examined each year, they were all locked in overnight for this annual occasion.

In the lion's den, my equipment was routinely set up at the west end by the inside door of a large "sun room," designed as a bedroom for animals requiring confinement for some medical reason or another. The water and sink we used to clean our instruments between patients was down a narrow access passageway, which extended along the front of each of the individual bedrooms. Every time any one of us approached the sink for any reason, one of the cats along the way would start to roar to protest our repeated invasion of its territory, and soon the entire structure reverberated with the powerful sound of these awesome predators. We did a lot of dental work in the west end of that confined hallway.

My daughter Janet worked as my dental assistant for a number of years, and routinely helped us with the lions. I have always admired her grit, which was periodically stretched to the limit by the WAP lions. All animals can tell the difference between a clinician with predatory intent on their mind, and a little chunk of sweet girly meat trying to get her job done without

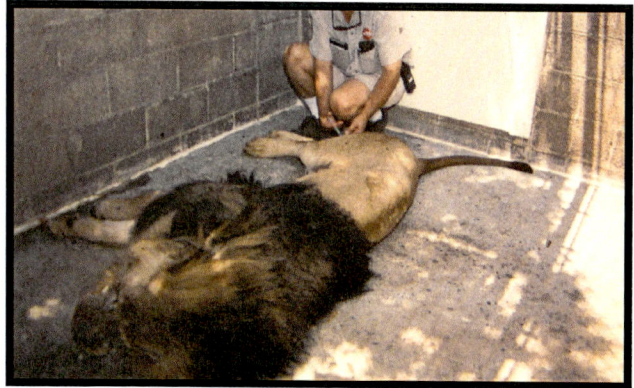

Access to the lion's den or bedroom area is down a very steep driveway, and into the dark, narrow passageway, seen behind the truck. The other side of the wall is the west end sun room covered with an open chain link ceiling. The view on the right shows Dr. O in this west sunroom with one of the large male lions during immobilization.

bothering the locals.

For some unexplained reason, one of the aggressive young males found this whole idea of a "visiting the doctor with a mobile slab of sweet girly meat for a nurse" completely unacceptable. He vented his frustration by giving Janet a particularly noisy reception each and every time she made a trip down the hallway to clean another stack of instruments at our only available source of running water.

The time finally arrived when he was next in line to be immobilized, and he began getting worked up about it. Janet was just ready to return from the sink, as I was approaching to wash my hands. We passed in front of this male's door with Janet closest to the cat. He charged with a very furious "I've got you this time girly" roar, and crashed into the bars on the door about eighteen inches from Janet's right shoulder. My back was to him about two feet away, and in

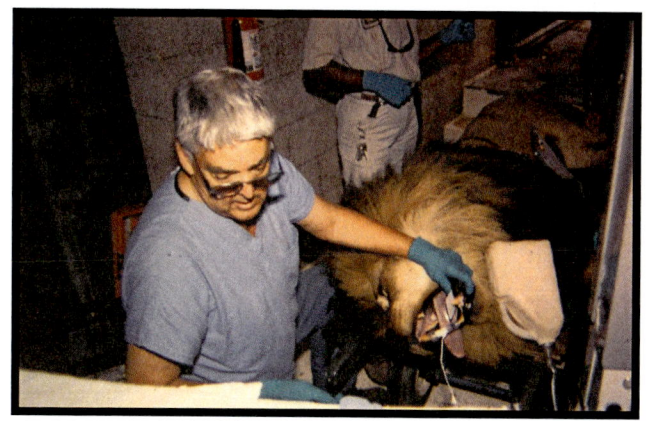

The hallway inside the lion's den was poorly lit with only two or three bare incandescent light bulbs in the ceiling providing all the inside light. We moved the cats onto a rolling stretcher table after Dr. O had them safely immobilized, then we moved them to the west end of the hallway, which had the best light from outside. But all through the procedure, the remaining cats would peer at us thruough the bars of their individual bedroom enclosures with danger in their eyes and mayhem on their minds. The doors along the left side wall provided access to the remainder of the individual "bedrooms." For me, it was an interesting introduction to the world of the big cats. Depending upon how much dental work was required, it was not uncommon to spend three or four successive days sharing space with the remaining disgruntled animals, while we completed their annual exams and necessary dental work. On the right is a typical dentist's view of the lion's large oral cavity and very functional masticatory apparatus.

DENTIST GOES ANIMAL 52

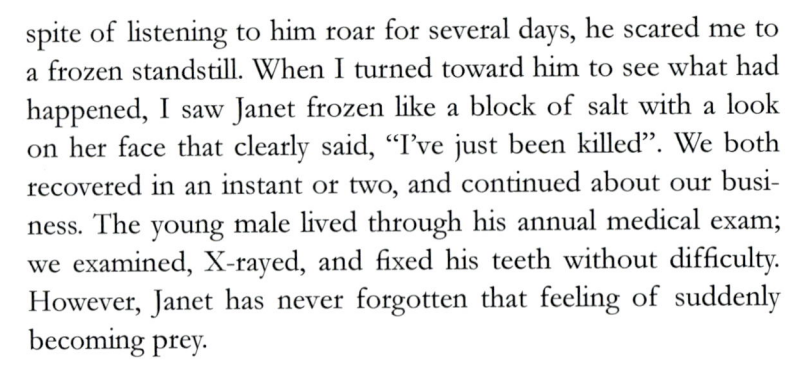

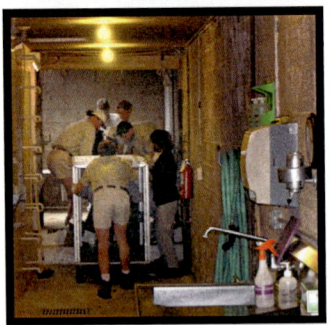

spite of listening to him roar for several days, he scared me to a frozen standstill. When I turned toward him to see what had happened, I saw Janet frozen like a block of salt with a look on her face that clearly said, "I've just been killed". We both recovered in an instant or two, and continued about our business. The young male lived through his annual medical exam; we examined, X-rayed, and fixed his teeth without difficulty. However, Janet has never forgotten that feeling of suddenly becoming prey.

The WAP has a fair number of big cats, including rare Sumatran tigers, African Transvaal lions, a substantial off-exhibit breeding group of cheetahs, and a very nice group of cheetahs living in their new Heart of Africa area within walking distance from the village.

As noted in previous chapters, animals in both free-ranging and captive environments have the entire range of problems with their teeth as do humans, for many of the same reasons. The dentition of all mammals has a great deal in common. Teeth are "outside" body structures like hairs and fingernails. Imagine that a single tooth is like a Coke bottle. You eat with the bottom of the bottle, and the hole in the "neck" of the bottle is buried deep down into the jawbone. This hole is called the "apex" of the tooth, and is where the nerve, or neuro-vascular bundle, enters the tooth. This "bottle" or tooth is held in its position in the jawbone by a complex system of ligaments, just like your knee is held together. Thus a tooth is actually a joint, and has more in common with your knee or elbow than with your hairs or fingernails. The nerve and blood supply to the tooth comes from within the bone and goes through the neck of the bottle into the tooth's pulp chamber space inside. Together, all of these teeth make up a picket fence of teeth, and each mammal inherits a specific length of fence, size and shape of pickets, and how the two fences fit together. If and/or when the bottle breaks, the fluid within the pulp chamber goes

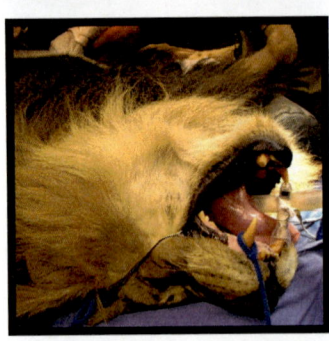

Photos from the file of David A. Fagan

Here we are during one of our long treatment sessions doing a classic root canal job on a lower left canine tooth in the mouth of one of the large males in the den. At the top, Dr. O and I are talking about "Him"—the same lion who took such an antipathy toward my daughter and assistant Janet—while he's looking at us, with malice on his mind. In the next two photos down, he's on his way to our mobile dental office. In the next photo his tooth is restored, and as soon as I confirm that all is well in the final radiograph for his medical record, at our unique, on-site, X-ray viewer located at the end of the exit hallway, shown in the bottom photo, our patient went back to his bedroom to recover.

Dr. O in the lion's den with one of the big males, circa 1979
From the files of David A. Fagan

bad. If it is not fixed right away, the inside/outside barrier of the animal's body is breached, and the bacteria from the outside can now get inside by going through the broken bottom of the bottle into the now empty space inside the bottle. A root canal job is essentially a plumbing job, which sterilizes, seals, fills and obliterates the inside space in the bottle. The bottom, or biting surface, of the "bottle" must then be restored with a glass-like material hard enough to chew on. This can be a filling or a cap, or crown, but is more correctly referred to as a "restoration."

All animals can have problems with their teeth sooner or later. This is often just the consequence of normal wear and tear associated with aging. Unfortunately, there is more steel and concrete in the human-controlled habitats than in natural environments. So generally, in captivity, the animal's dental mechanism tends to get as much use and abuse than their free-ranging relatives, but for slightly different reasons. Another important point is that in captivity, animals tend to live much longer than their free-ranging cousins, because they do not have to avoid their specific mob of natural predators. This results in the occurrence of an entirely new set of geriatric medical and dental issues not normally seen in their free-ranging counterparts. Dr. Andrew Kitchener from Edinburgh, Scotland has recently written about this issue in great detail, and his work is well worth reading.

A broken tooth, then, is essentially an open wound. If it is not repaired, sooner or later the bacteria from without, get pushed within the broken "bottle/tooth," and will get into the animal's bloodstream, causing great systemic difficulty. Before the development of antibiotics—noting that penicillin was the first, and only became available between 1938 to 1942—bad teeth killed a lot of people, as well as many animals. In fact, this is still very true today among human populations without access to the range of antibiotic therapies, which many of us take for granted and consider normally available.

"Broken teeth gone bad" is one of the factors that helped kill off the saber-toothed tiger. Animals in zoos and wild animal parks are generally there to help preserve, and/or help rescue their species from destruction or loss of their home range. Zoo animals do not have the usual predation problems plaguing their free-ranging brethren, so naturally they tend to live longer. Also, older folks tend to have a greater potential for having trouble with their teeth than do younger folks. It is just like the tires on your car: the more you drive, the more wear and tear on the tires. That's why animals in captivity require veterinary medical and dental care, and get annual physical examinations and attention. Like humans, if they live long enough, the odds increase that some dental dysfunction or disease will befall them sooner or later.

Veterinary dentistry is very interesting work. It is safe to say that in thirty-five-plus years, I have never repeated the exact same procedure twice. I've done a fair number of similar procedures on similar animals, but its always a new unpredictable and fresh undertaking. I have also been fortunate enough to be able to work with several hundred exotic cats, both captive and free ranging—and with exotic-animal veterinarians from all over the world. These dedicated and very talented men and women are the real behind-the-scenes guardians of our wildlife. They work hard, and they put in long hours in locations not generally open for public viewing. They are usually so busy working that nobody notices what they are doing. We owe all of them our profound thanks, gratitude, and assistance, when the occasion presents. To this end in 1986, in an effort to promote greater awareness and understanding of oral and dental issues in exotic animals, I published an article titled "Diagnosis and Treatment Planning," in the Veterinary Clinics of North America series. (See item # 16 in Appendix B.)

Over the years, I have been fortunate enough to have seen and treated a very large and diverse patient population. My patient log records document many hundreds of zoo animals including camels like Buster; monkeys like Beauregard; a boa constrictor named Julius Squeezer; several hundred gazelles like Addra-290; an assortment of birds; a variety of movie animals like Midnight Sun, who was the leader of the Doberman Gang, and the dog who kills the evil Nazi death camp physician Dr. Mengle in the movie *Boys from Brazil*; and the little Benji dog of movie and TV fame (see Item #17 in Appendix B).

However, one of my most memorable cases involved the protracted treatment lasting over a twenty-year period, working with Dr. O to diagnose and resolve a complex triad of oral problems in a lowland gorilla named "Trib." We published Trib's story in 1979 in the American Association of Zoo Veterinarians *Journal of Zoo and Wildlife Medicine* under the title "Gingival Hyperplasia Induced by Diphenylhydantoin in a Gorilla" (see Item 7 in Appendix B). But that totally scientific sounding story line barely scratched the surface of what really transpired with this magnificent animal.

Chapter Six
Trib

*A gentle touch, but oh such a tickling!!
She doesn't appear to have much of an inkling
of the disturbances caused by her stroking.
But to help her keep learning, I'll let her keep poking.*

Trib was obviously in trouble from his veterinarian's point of view, but looking across the thirty-foot-wide moat separating us from the nineteen-year-old male gorilla, I didn't know enough about gorillas at the time to be able to understand the subtle signs he was referring to.

"I don't think he is going to last much longer at this rate, Dave," Jim said. "He hasn't eaten anything at all for the last three days, and he's starting to show signs of it."

Photo by Scott Amsel

Trib was the dominant male silverback gorilla at the San Diego Wild Animal Park from 1970 until his death in 1993. Gorillas have very distinctive and individual personalities. I've worked closely with nearly a dozen over the years, and have learned to recognize each of them as unique. Trib was my first gorilla, and he has remained my favorite. This photo was taken in 1981 by a park monorail drive by the name of Scott Amsel, who is now a veterinarian. He gave a framed version to Dr. Oosterhuis as a wedding present, and it has hung in Dr. O's office at the Wild Animal Park ever since.

Though still quite majestic and dignified to my eyes, he was sitting quietly in his favorite spot on the slope under a tree in his large grassy gorilla enclosure at the San Diego Wild Animal Park. This prized silverback lowland gorilla was listless and dull-eyed to the knowing eyes of his keepers, and nothing ever remained hidden for very long from the all-seeing eyes of his veterinarian, Dr. Oosterhuis. Trib even lacked the energy to play with his faithful troop as they moved around nearby, while the youngsters of the group took turns darting behind him. They too seemed aware of his discomfort, and to some observers appeared as though they were trying to console him.

"You still comfortable with the schedule to immobilize him for the exam?" I asked, wondering if I should be asking if he still thought Trib was strong enough to live through an immobilization procedure.

"We'll go as scheduled in the morning," he answered confidently.

It was after 8:30 a.m. by the time the team had finished setting up all of the necessary equipment, and Dr. O was ready to begin. We were all assembled outside the back door of the gorilla enclosure on the black topped service road leading into their bedroom area, for what was to become a pre-anesthetic tradition for the San Diego Wild Animal Park's future director of veterinary services. Dr. O's "Final Instructions with Q&A" assembly was always the last step before he moved off to begin the immobilization of his patient.

This was going to be another very long day.

Even early in the morning, the blistering Santa Ana wind pouring in from the desert to the east was warming up our group of gorilla keepers, the animal management team, and Jim's combined medical/surgical team, including animal health technicians—fourteen people in all, including the society's still and video photographers. We were dressed in the usual assortment of work clothing from the society's basic tan shorts and matching shirts with the park's logo, to green scrub tops with jeans, to just plain "civies."

Peering into Trib's cavernous mouth for the first time, his 432-pound, six-foot-one-inch frame lying sedated on the wooden makeshift stretcher in front of me, I was immediately impressed by the enormous size of it all. This was my first gorilla oral exam, and his mouth was clearly three to four times the size of an adult human mouth. Looking closer, I noticed the magenta-colored margins on the compressed cauliflower-like growths all around his gingiva, on both the medial and lateral aspects of his half-buried teeth. Then I smelled the characteristic foul odor from the small patches of dying gingival tissue. Trib's entire mouth was acutely inflamed, badly infected, and in the process of rapidly becoming a full blown clinical case of acute necrotic ulcerative gingivitis, or ANUG—but there was something else: cauliflower-like growths. There was now no doubt about it in my mind; the problem in his mouth was related to the medication he was taking for his epilepsy problem.

Then, Jim told me their physical exam was completed, and the rest of the exam team had

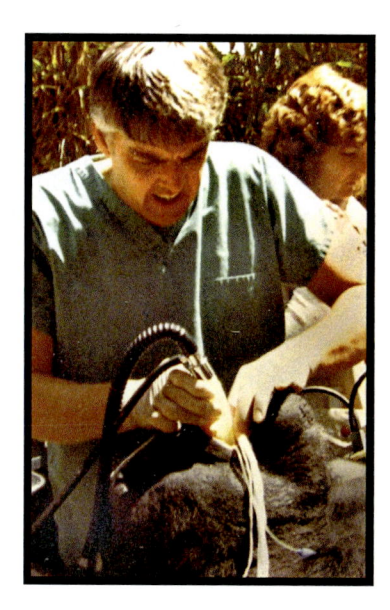

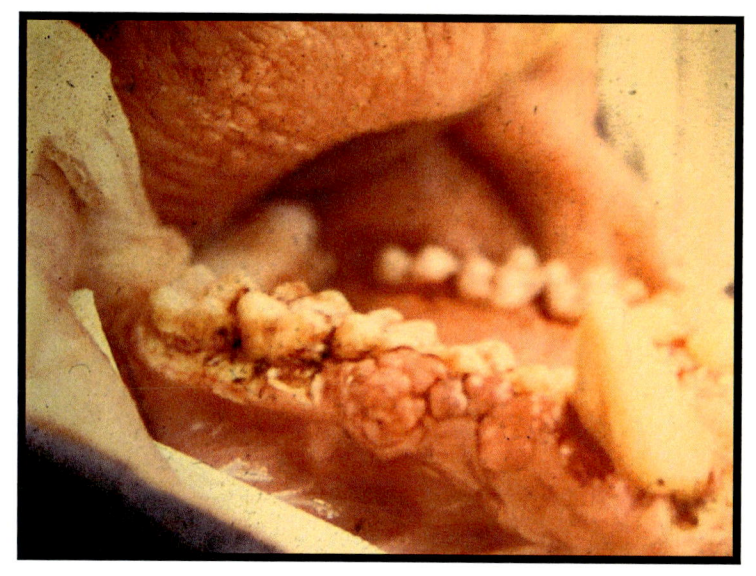

From the files of David A. Fagan

On the left, I am securing Trib's endotracheal tube to an individually fitted syringe casing mouth prop in order to ensure that neither become accidentally dislodged during the procedure. The relatively massive size of Trib's head is also very obvious in this view. My assistant Janet is behind my left shoulder. Notice that, at that time, we did not customarily utilize latex exam gloves, or the typical primate protocol protective suits, which are now mandatory. The view on the right clearly shows the extent of the partially removed hyperplastic gingival tissue overgrowth. I cut it all off with an electro-scalpel, which my human patients tell me is a very unpleasant experience.

found nothing of clinical significance. I was now positive that I knew the primary contributing factor for his current inability to eat.

My clinical experience with human dental patients over the years had included the treatment of a wide variety of developmentally disabled and mentally retarded individuals of all ages. Many were taking the medication Dilantin, which is routinely prescribed by their physicians for clinical cases with epileptic seizures and/or Down syndrome. Dilantin is well documented to predispose these patients to develop an inflammatory, cauliflower-like growth of the gingival tissue in their mouths. When left untreated, these gingival growths routinely develop into a severely painful acute, necrotic, ulcerative gingivitis known as ANUG. A similar, acutely painful, oral infection was referred to as "trench mouth" during World War One. Both disorders were well known to me, and unfortunately are a fairly common human dental problem, particularly among hippie drug addicts. In fact, so common that Trib's problem was described in the medical literature as a syndrome with the common name "Dilantin Induced Gingival Hyperplasia." There was absolutely no reason why this common human clinical syndrome could not occur in gorillas, although it had never been reported in the literature. For that matter, it could occur in any primate taking the same medication—Dilantin—to treat a similar clinical problem, such as epileptic seizures.

I had re-read Trib's medical record and case history a few days earlier in preparation for his procedure, and clearly recalled that Trib began taking a prescribed daily dose of the medication diphenylhydantoin, following a recurrent series of convulsive seizures. "Dilantin" is the common prescription name for the chemical diphenylhydantoin.

Although a definitive cause was never established to explain exactly why Trib had the seizures, he had sufficient opportunity to have sustained a head injury as a baby in the wilderness of Zaire (formerly known as the Republic of Congo) before or during his capture as a youngster, or at the Brazzaville Zoo anytime during his brief year there preceding his arrival in San Diego on July 30, 1960. He was the third young gorilla donated to the zoo by James Copley and the Union-Tribune Publishing Company. His name, "Trib," commemorated the gift.

"No wonder he stopped eating," I muttered to Jim. "The pain potential of this mess in his mouth has got to be overwhelming."

Wondering how he could have tolerated it all, we later theorized that Trib's leadership role with his troupe, and his well established personal "concept of self," left no circumstances for him to acknowledge pain of any sort in front of his troupe. In Trib's world, he either led or he didn't. And he just wasn't the kind of individual to crawl to the back of the line and whine about something like a sore mouth or a toothache. It wasn't in his script to act ill, so he chose to ignore it—until the advancing oral infection finally took control of his options, and revealed itself to the careful observation of his keepers through his inability to eat his daily rations.

Under the bright sun, Jim and I conferred over the implications of the intra-oral X-rays that had just finished developing. Trib's mouth was ablaze with three separate, distinct, and severely painful oral disorders. The most severe was the localized dying tissue over his third molars or "wisdom teeth," properly known as "pericronitis." The second was the Dilantin-induced gingival hyperplasia, and the third was a developing bony infection surrounding two extra fourth molars buried deep inside the bone of his lower jaw. Any one of these regularly sends the toughest of human patients to their dentist with tears in their eyes, and a whimper on their lips.

Dr. O decided we should immediately start him on antibiotic therapy, and begin the stan-

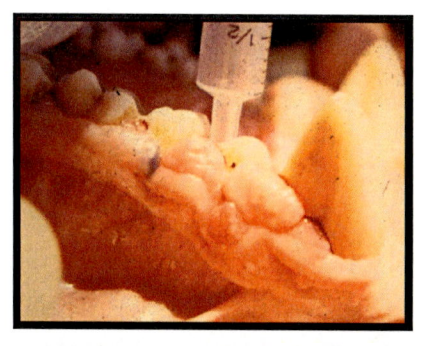

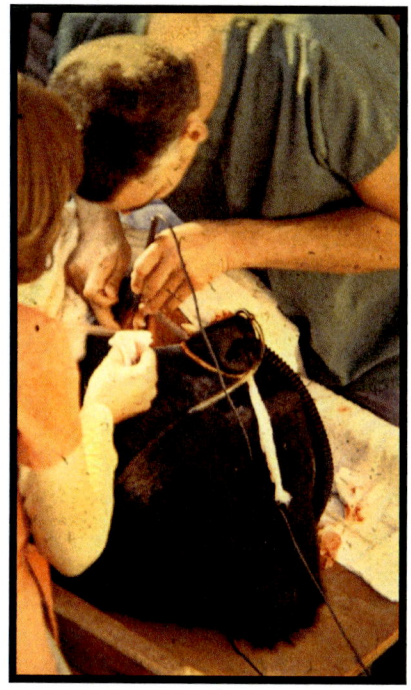

The view on the top shows the extent of the hyperplasti gingival tissue, which nearly completely covers the first pre-molar tooth behind the large canine tooth. The view at the bottom shows very dramatically the relative size of Trib's head compared to mine, as well as the fact that this procedure obviously occurred before the Occupational Safety and Health Administration (OSHA) expressed concerns about contamination following the outbreak of the AIDS epidemic issue. At that time, we typically practiced all dentistry and medicine without gloves, except in sterile surgical procedures. Actually, a healthy hand with intact skin and no open cuts or wounds is one of the body's best natural protections against infection. Humans haave lived, functioned, and evolved in a multitude of very dirty, microbial infested environments, and our skin has evolved to effectively protect our insides from all of this contamination from without.

dard dental treatment for the gingival hyperplasia—clean his teeth, and then proceed with a full mouth gingivectomy. This is the painful "cutting of the gums" procedure for which human periodontists are so infamously notorious. Heavy antibiotic therapy would be able to control and eliminate the infection, while holding the impacted molars at bay until later, after the generalized infection had been eliminated. Without immediate treatment however, this out-of-control oral infection was well on the way to becoming what is known as Ludwig's Angina, another oral syndrome, which could easily and quickly claim the gorilla's life.

Trib's sedated and vulnerable frame lay in front of us on the examination table. Cavernous mouth propped wide open, giant arms strapped to his side, his impressive presence seemed lifeless. It was up to us, and we set about our work determined to help this magnificent animal.

Nine to fifteen millimeters deep, the oppressive-looking proliferative gingival growth was relatively easily removed with my electrocautery scalpel, although it was a uniquely odoriferous undertaking. X-rays had revealed that the infection involved both of the full bony impacted supernumerary fourth molars, as well as the partially buried third molars with chronic pericronitis necessitating the removal of these deeply buried and inaccessible teeth.

"We'll remove the extra molars another day," Dr. O said quietly, in his characteristic director's stance at my elbow looking over my shoulder.

"He's had enough for one day."

I nodded and grunted my agreement. I also needed time to assemble the specialized surgical instruments necessary to be able to do the required magnitude of osseous surgery. Although I had a significant amount of oral and general surgery experience from my emergency work in San Francisco, and time at the vet school in Davis, I had never before attempted to remove a tooth so deeply imbedded beneath such a thick mass of hard, cortical bone. My surgical instrumentation available on this exam day was not adequate for this larger task. In any event, Trib was an easy keeper when it came to taking his daily medications with a cup of orange juice each morning, so the delay would not be a clinical problem, and it would give the soft tissues time to heal before the next procedure.

The next morning, Trib immediately began eating only citrus fruit—lemons and oranges. This was less than twenty-four hours following a full mouth gingivectomy. And then, he immediately resumed his normal, alert, active leadership behavior. It was very clear. We had underestimated the depth of his stoic nature and unemotional indifference to pain. He selected only fresh-cut citric acid mouthwash to help his mouth heal. Eating citrus was an act that would drop any human post-gum-surgery patient to their knees in excruciating pain within seconds. I wouldn't have been so worried about the extent of his surgery if I had known about this earlier. There was, however, no way to know any of it beforehand. After Trib had gained back some of his lost weight, we removed both of the impacted molars uneventfully with my new Stryker orthopedic/oral surgery hand piece specifically designed for this sort of surgical task.

We had lucked out that my prior clinical experiences had kicked in with such a speedy diagnosis. And fortunately, with my fully equipped dental unit nearby, we were prepared to immediately treat his problem without a lot of extra setup or assemble time. My freshly painted and still evolving mobile veterinary dental cart had proved to be an absolutely dependable, very versatile field instrument package. It was a lofty time in my developing, not yet ten-year-old exotic animal veterinary dental career. I was high on the learning curve, gaining a whole new perspective on my chosen profession, and absolutely enjoying every moment of it. I was also pleased that my daughter Janet was there to help us learn from the experience, and able to share in all of the excitement.

Trib's prospects were not as rosy. He enjoyed nearly fifteen more years as the patriarchal role model for the lowland gorilla troupe at the park. His primary job was to father his eventual successor, and to teach him by example how to take over his own position as leader of the troupe. It is quite possible that the necessity of learning how to assert himself dominantly in his early years was one of the contributory factors resulting in his first epileptic seizure in November of 1977. Seizures were possibly triggered by the stress of developing a new leadership style all his own, which required constant vigil against possible transgressions, invasion or usurpations by any one of the other adult male gorillas in the troupe. It had been possible to reduce the dose of the medication over time as his leadership role fell into a less challenging mode of general acceptance by the rest of the troupe.

Field procedures like this gorilla's oral surgery are actually massive, well choreographed events requiring the help of a skilled team of professional and para-professional personnel. Success in the field, with the ability to produce dependable diagnostic information, requires the skillful management of a qualified team by an equally skillful conductor.

Dr. O knows how to conduct this sort of field operation.

His regularly scheduled annual exams provided the occasion for me to visit Trib in the gorilla bedroom area at the park, and brought us into periodic conscious interaction characterized by mutual interest, and what I can only call respect. Naturally curious, humans and gorillas share common traits such as observing and mimicking. Over the years, many hours passed as I watched Trib going about his normal behavior, and he taught me many lessons outside the realm of medicine.

Careful not to upset him by openly staring at him, which is a threatening gesture to gorillas, whenever I was passing his enclosure, I would pause, sit and casually glance sideways at him, when it seemed he wasn't looking. He followed the same procedure observing me. Gentle and un-aggressive, Trib gradually came to accept my visits, and over time slowly stopped moving his sitting position away from the bars of his bedroom enclosure when I approached until on occasion his broad shoulder rested against them during one of our visits.

"You've got an aura about you, old friend," I murmured one day, so close I could smell his gorilla pungency, like ammonia in my nostrils. He looked at me in his usual all-knowing manner, and I could feel his peace and strength around me.

A few moments later one of the vets entered the room, and Trib's eyes turned into narrow slits on full alert. This fellow was one of those humans responsible for shooting the tranquilizing dart whenever it was necessary for him to be immobilized for examinations. It was clear Trib knew the routine, and didn't like it. The changing eye expression and the slight pursing tension of his lips were the only outward indication of past traumas by human hand.

Controlled, dignified, but clearly irritated, Trib stoically met his fate without an untoward show of excessive aggression. Displaying love and care for troupe members and keepers alike, it was as though he understood compassion better than any of us. He always showed more concern for others than for himself.

One of the lead gorilla keepers told me a story one day of Trib's reaction when she accidentally banged her finger with a hammer while hanging a calendar over the desk. She cried out in pain, and Trib came over to the bars of the enclosure to investigate. Drawn by his concern, she moved closer and extended her hand for him to see.

He extended one of his fingers through the bars, and softly stroked her injury. She told me the tenderness she felt from him surpassed anything she had ever experienced from a human. Unconditional and free spirited, it was without expectation of any reward, a gift she accepted graciously from this beautiful creature and still carries with her.

"He's lookin' pretty good these days, eh, Doc?" Ernie said to me as he walked over to the other side of the room where the daily logs were kept.

Removing one of the notebooks from the shelf, he sat down at the desk close by, and began slowly turning pages and reading the notes from our last visit up to the current date.

"Trib has been eating normally and doesn't show any sign of discomfort," he reported. I could see Trib's coat was well groomed and shiny, and his sharp, clear eyes projected well-being. By this time, I had learned more about what my equine instructors, Hanna Voit and Dick Lynch, had been talking about. Eye contact was a very effective form of communication.

"That's what we like to hear," I responded, standing up from the chair where I had been sitting. Glancing at my old friend, our brief eye contact said "so long" better than words. Leaving the enclosure, I headed back to the hospital.

Fourteen years after our first encounter, the stress of finally being forced to share his role as dominant silverback male with Winston, the current rising star of the second troupe, caused Trib's seizures to return. Behind those confident good looks and well-disciplined behavior, his picturesque and majestic appearance easily concealed the extent of his inner turmoil. His medication was adjusted, increased, and finally changed to another drug.

As anticipated however, in due course, his annual physical examination revealed the return of the gingival hyperplasia. This time it was not as badly infected, although he did require another "manicure of the mouth." Human patients on similar medications typically require follow-up periodontal surgery every year or so.

In mid 1992, Dr. O reassembled his formidable team of consultants. This time all of the veterinarians, technicians and the surgical team wore blinding white surgical coveralls, hair covers, gloves and masks, the new protocol required attire for working on primates, carriers of a number of serious diseases, some lethal to humans. However outside in the sun, these new primate protocol uniforms reflected and intensified the sun's glaring rays, making life difficult for the photographers, while our bodies felt like we were operating in a pressure cooker. I remember at one point during the procedure asking someone to please dim the light shining into my eyes.

"It's the sun, Dave," a voice responded. "Adjust. We don't have time to fool with Mother Nature."

Following analysis of a complete electroencephalogram in July of 1992, and with the capable help of thirty-seven dedicated and skilled professionals, on the fourth of November, Trib had his second gingival manicure. In the intervening years, of course, dental instrumentation and technology had evolved to the point that the state of the art in oral surgery was now the ND/YAG LASER scalpel recently approved by the FDA for soft tissue surgery. We managed to secure a twenty-watt, water-cooled masterpiece of a unit, and Trib got the royal manicure this time without any of the postoperative bleeding, pain or swelling I'd been so worried about years earlier.

As before, his recovery was quick and sure. A tendency toward a minor postoperative gingival inflammation was managed by his keepers with a spray bottle of antimicrobial mouth wash—directly into his mouth voluntarily through the bars of his bedroom enclosure, two or three times a day for a couple of weeks. All appeared to be back to normal for an old friend of twenty years.

One afternoon early in 1993, I was en route home from a friend's dental office, where I had been helping him with a human dental prosthetics case, when an announcement on the radio in my van blurted out that Trib had died. I had just checked him a couple of weeks prior, and he had appeared fine. Surprised, my first thought when I reached home was to call Dr. O to confirm Trib's death.

"Yes, it's true, Trib died yesterday afternoon," came Jim's sure voice over the phone. "He seemed to be sleeping in his favorite spot on the grass. Resting there in the afternoon shade, no one noticed anything unusual, until the others moved in for their afternoon meal. Trib never woke up."

"Has the necropsy been done yet?" I asked.

"Yes, he instantly bled to death in his sleep following a ruptured aortic aneurysm." Jim answered.

"Did we get some tissue samples from his mouth for the histology study on the laser wound healing?" I added.

"I'll check it out, but it's been a long tough day, so don't bank on it," he concluded.

"Yeah," I choked, managed a quick "goodbye," hung up and tried to busy myself with some paperwork.

It was impossible. Sitting back in my favorite living room chair that evening, I looked around the walls of the room. A variety of photographs and artifacts occupy the bookshelves and wall space. They remind me of various exotic animal patients I've worked on over the years. Each represented a medical problem I helped solve, bestowing extra time and quality to another animal's life. Trib's portrait hung in the brightest corner, looking out at me from under the branches of a large indoor ficus tree. Studying the image of an old friend, I was overcome with a sense of loss, and there wasn't much relief to be had.

Trib's untimely departure left me feeling empty for several months. One day I got in my van, and drove up to my father's gravesite at the Fort Rosecrans National Cemetery high atop the Point Loma peninsula. As I sat on the grassy hillside overlooking the Pacific Ocean site of the America's Cup competition, everything slowly fell into perspective. Considering that a gorilla's life span is only around forty years, I finally had to acknowledge the fact that it was just his time to split. Trib had simply moved on. There was no way he could have outlived me, or even come close to it. The issue of death and dying is dealt with by veterinarians much differently and much more honestly than by most human clinicians.

Within twenty-four hours following his death, Trib's body was shipped to a natural history museum, where as far as I know, he is stored in a freezer still awaiting the allocation of funds sufficient to process his remains with those of some other long-deceased gorillas into a naturalistic diorama exhibit of some sort.

To this day, I still feel like Charleston Heston in the first "Planet of the Apes" movie, when he discovers his two astronaut companions dead, mounted and displayed as trophies in the apes' local Natural History Museum. I don't look forward to the day I find my old friend like that.

From time to time, early mornings still find me passing the gorilla enclosure at the Wild Animal Park. I spent many hours there over a twenty-year period observing Trib's behavior and interaction with the growing family members of his troop. I would automatically check to see if he was eating normally. The enclosure is a cool, quiet, place in the early mornings, sometimes with wispy fingers of fog drifting through the bamboo or amid the eucalyptus trees overhead. It's almost like being in another world, even mystical at these quite times. On occasion during those brief, early morning visits, I would be fortunate enough to have something trigger a flash of recalled memory of Trib's strength and majesty. I am thankful for those small fleeting gifts. On other occasions, while attending to other animals, I am reminded of Trib's considerable contribution to my growing assembly of dental laser equipment.

One of the most unique and lasting aspects of treating Trib's oral health problems was the early utilization of the dental laser technology developed for human application. The concept of lasers (the word was originally an acronym for "light amplification by stimulated emission of radiation") in dentistry was initially very heavily marketed to the human dental community. Unfortunately, they oversold the concept before their R&D people could deliver a dependable unit. I had been bombarded with propaganda at the annual dental association meetings for several years, so I was very familiar with the concept. My concern about Trib's problem prompted me to contact some of my old aerospace buddies to get the latest, real R&D lowdown. Rather quickly I learned that the proper single-spectrum frequency of light could dramatically provide the tissue cutting capability I needed for such a large animal, and the laser beam would accomplish this without any of the usual pain, bleeding, and postoperative complications. I was very familiar with the issue of postoperative pain, having done a great deal of periodontal surgery on humans. The early laser equipment was nothing more than a very expensive electrical scalpel, which still burnt tissue and precipitated a strong inflammatory reaction within that tissue. These early lasers just burnt the tissue away with light rather than electricity. My R&D friends sent me to Biolase Technology, Inc. to look at their new ND-YAG unit, which had just been approved by the FDA for soft-tissue surgery.

I met Dr. Guy Levi, who invented their special water mediated dental laser, and arranged to borrow one of their ND-YAG LASER units to use on Trib's second periodontal surgery procedure. It worked quite well, and we made a short video clip of the procedure. I was able to do a

DENTIST GOES ANIMAL 64

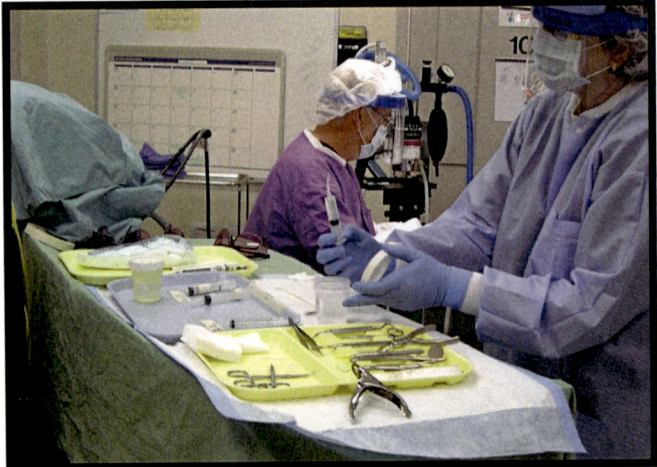

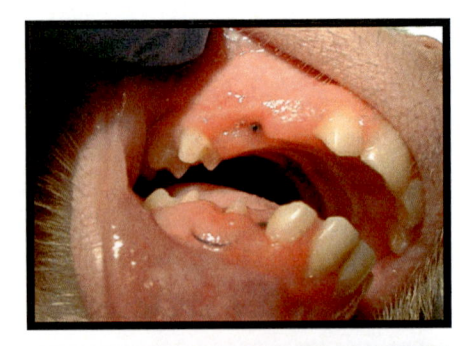

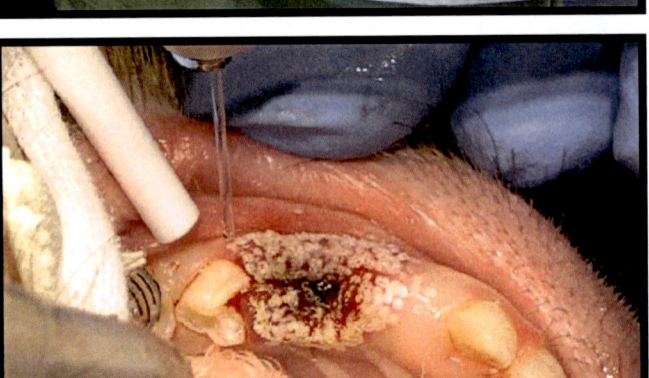

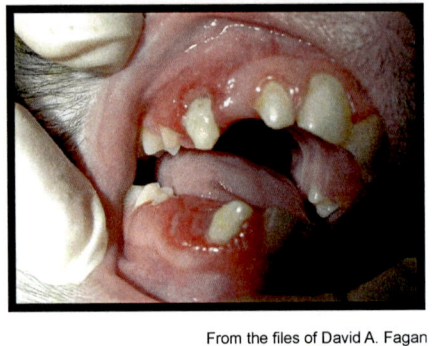

From the files of David A. Fagan

This young animal is a Rhesus Macaque living in a substantial, certified primate facility associated with NASA's Apollo/Spacelab research effort. He presented (see bottom right) with a chronic, non-responsive, localized marginal gingivitis involving all four of his primary canine teeth, which had failed to resolve following more than six months of traditional, human-equivalent, dental treatment and medication. With the able help of my assistant PK, we treated this animal with the YSGG Water-Laser, while buried within our full primate protocol coveralls (see top left). The lower left image shows the laser "painting" the infected area with a single spectrum of 2780nm light energy. The upper right image was taken seven days later, before the sutures were removed, and clearly shows nearly 100% healing, healthy gingival tissue, which completely healed within another week. The mechanisms associated with laser-mediated hard- and soft-tissue surgery—tissue bio-stimulation, disinfection, and sterilization—are all well described in the literature. And each year brings more new applications and interesting solutions.

---

full-mouth gingivectomy in a minimal amount of time with almost no postoperative complications. From that moment on, I was hooked on laser assisted surgery. I really like the concept.

Shortly thereafter, I met the scientist who directed the laser weapon development program for McDonald-Douglas during the Reagan-era Star Wars period. Dr. Larry DeShazer knew all there was to know about lasers. We discussed Trib's clinical problem, and what was coming down the pipeline in the way of next-generation hard-tissue laser surgery instruments. It took another ten years of intensive R&D, but in the early 2000s the same Biolase people in San Clemente released a marvelous YSGG-WaterLaser certified for both hard- and soft-tissue dental applications. This dental laser system works extremely well. I quickly learned that the era of pain-free clinical dentistry was actually upon us.

I went back to work in a human dental clinic to specifically learn how to use this piece of equipment. To this day, I remain astonished every time I recall my first occasion using this laser unit. I surgically exposed a retained maxillary right central incisor on a ten-year-old little girl—without any pain, or any bleeding, or any post-operative complication or medications—and I didn't even use any injectable dental anesthetic. Not only that, but I explained to her what I was going to do before we started, and she looked me in the eye during the entire procedure waiting for it to hurt. Finally, she raised her hand, and politely asked me "Can we begin now?" I told her we could do better than that. "We can end now, because I'm all finished!"

In effect, for many years I've practiced clinical dentistry on the bipeds for the benefit of my quadruped patients. In 2006 the Biolase folks custom-modified one of their computer-programmed 2780 nm M.D. laser units for me with large wheels and a protective roll-bar framework. Dr. O and I—working with their director of engineering, Dr. Dmitri Bouserouf, and the department head laser engineer, Ron Mckee—added a few modifications to turn what Ron calls our "otter laser" into a dream machine.

We also have one of the Biolase 810nm diode lasers developed specifically to treat periodontal disease, and to whiten the teeth of humans. We use this incredible instrument for tissue decontamination and bio-stimulation to promote wound healing. Dr. O and I have used both lasers on a variety of clinical cases with some amazing results. One of the first clinical veterinary applications for this unit was to treat a muscle spasm in a neo-natal Pacific bottle-nosed dolphin.

At the San Diego Zoo WAP, the male addra gazelle #290 holds the Harter Veterinary Medical Center's record for longest patient stay in the hospital. Much to my surprise it is also fourteen months, which matches the equine record I set with Dr. McKee at U.C.-Davis over thirty-five years ago in the early 1970s. In early March of 2006, this handsome male gazelle was introduced to the park's group of addra gazelles as the females new breeding herd-sire. Apparently, the other males in the group took exception to his introduction, and within a week of his arrival, Addra-290 showed up at the hospital with a severe traumatic injury to his left jaw including an apparent "karate chop" to his neck. Clinically, he had a trauma-induced mandibular left jaw abscess involving his last molar tooth, which was draining into his

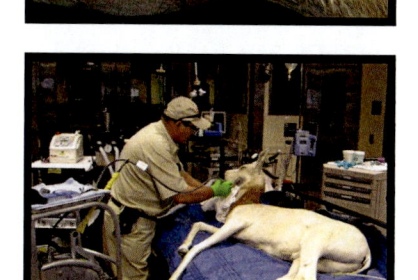

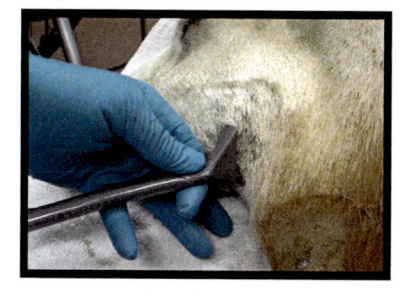

Photos from the files of David A. Fagan

This male Addra Gazelle #290 presented at the WAP's Harter Veterinary Medical Center with a severe traumatic injury to his left mandible, including a fractured hyoid bone in his neck. This rapidly expanding infection perforated into his esophagus, producing a draining infected tract through the side of his neck into his throat and esophagus connecting directly to his stomach contents. It required fourteen months of intense treatment, including molar endodontic therapy with a compound apicoectomy requiring perforation of his masseter musculature. This muscle raises the mandible to close the jaw during chewing. Eventually, the focused decontamination/bio-stimulation effect of the YSGG and diode lasers facilitated a complete resolution of the problem. Seen in April of 2008 left, Addra-290 is now going about the business of charming his ladies.

DENTIST GOES ANIMAL 66

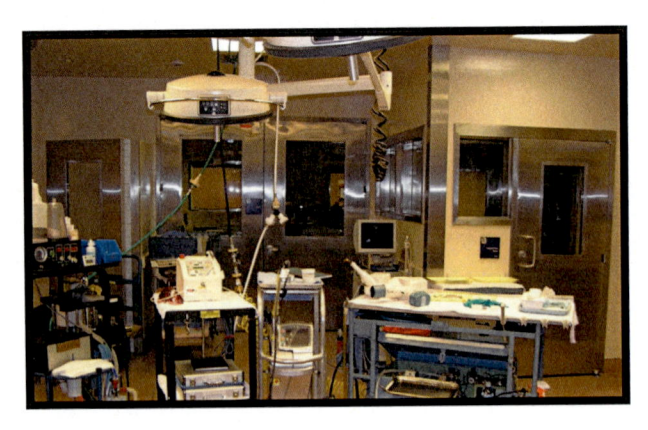

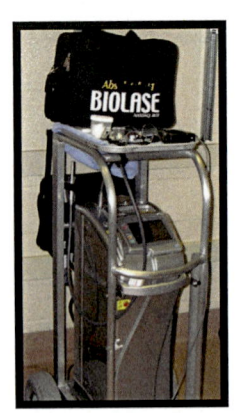

From the files of David A. Faan

My two dental laser units are seen above, with the 810nm diode on the left, the 2780nm YSGG-WaterLaser on the right. Both stand ready for clinical application in the large animal treatment room at the San Diego Wild Animal Park's ultra-modern, 66,000-square-foot Harter Veterinary Medical Center. My original mobile veterinary dental unit, built in 1977, is positioned to the right of the two laser units in the middle image above. Thirty years later it is still fully functional, and gets used with regularity. Several years ago it was happy to be painted a soft, refreshing, hospital blue in order to qualify for acceptance into this high-standard clinical and research complex with room to grow as future applications dictate.

---

neck with connecting infection to the fracture site in his hyoid bone. He was immobilized weekly for months, while we attempted to keep the infection contained and out of his chest.

Following extensive molar root canal therapy including a compound apicoectomy (see items 30 and 32 in Appendix B) the infection perforated his esophagus to drain down his throat, and then simply would not heal. Finally, with the help of our two new laser units, we managed to get the situation resolved. Surprisingly, one of the first clinical signs of successful laser-mediated tissue bio-stimulation and healing was a sudden increase in the rate of growth of his facial hair. After fourteen months in the hospital, Addra-290 was finally healthy, active, back out in the field where he belongs, and a success with the ladies as their alphamale.

We've incorporated our laser instruments into the treatment of a diverse assortment of animals including: the eye of a black milk snake; the hyper-extended knee injury of an Indian sarus crane; the removal of scar tissue in the nose of an Australian heeler domestic dog; the sterilization of the root canal of a very badly infected lower right canine in a California sea lion; disinfection of a facial abscess associated with a right tusk infection in an Alaskan walrus; treatment of a left canine root canal in a Chinese dhole; sterilization of a pulp canal in the broken tusks of a young male African elephant; and the dental treatment of a number of rhesus macaques. These lasers provide just another expanded new dimension to my continuously growing comprehensive clinical practice.

And, interestingly enough, it was my old friend, Trib the gorilla, who motivated the introduction, growth, and development of my interest in dental lasers nearly 20 years ago in 1990.

Chapter Seven
Lions and Tigers
and Teeth

Stroking its trunk with his small groping hands,
this student thinks, while the elephant stands,
exuding an odor of yams and hay,
and coating his fingers with smells of clay.

The student perceives at this critical junction,
he must learn to grapple with form and function.
With his eyes clogged, and his mind all but empty,
he perceives this machine as a most complex entity.

His haze of ignorance is slowly shifted
to the light of knowledge granted the gifted.
"I'll specialize in oto/rhino/laryngology,
with a side interest in anesthesiology."

My first out-of-town road trip as an expert from afar occurred in 1981, while I was working with Dr. Marty Dinnes, an experienced, internationally recognized zoo animal veterinarian. I met him at the annual American Association of Zoo Veterinarians meeting in Washington D.C. in 1980. Marty provided contract veterinary medical care to the Hollywood movie people, traveling circus animals, and a variety of animal-oriented amusement parks, as well as many large Texas-style game-ranch collectors. At that time, his home base was in Encino in the San Fernando Valley just north of Los Angeles, an area famous for spawning the "Valley Girl" sub-culture.

Marty had seen a lot of oral disease in a variety of circumstances all over the world, and provided valuable suggestions regarding the design of my mobile dental equipment package. For instance, he reminded me that it must meet the inflexible cargo access requirements of both commercial air transport and highway freight haulers—if I expected to get it economically relocated with any dependability. Marty was anxious to be one of the first zoo vets to have the ability to provide quality dental care to his clients. So as soon as I was ready to travel, we shipped my equipment north to the San Francisco area, booked into a motel near the park, and prepared to provide comprehensive veterinary dental care to Ron Whitfield's very unique, bachelor pride of African lions.

Marty was the park's consulting veterinarian. Ron and Roxanne Whitfield were animal trainers at Marine World Africa U.S.A. in Redwood City, south of San Francisco. The Whitfields assumed responsibility for the park's large cat and elephant shows, when Dave McMillan moved to the Great Adventure Park in New Jersey. The entire Marine World Park subsequently relocated across San Francisco Bay to Vallejo in 1986, where it is now located on the northeast corner of the bay near the mouth of the Sacramento River. They moved all of their animals in a modern day Noah's Ark-like flotilla, and got great media coverage during the event. The park is now called Six Flags Discovery Park, and is no longer much of an animal attraction.

Ron's wife Roxanne worked with him in the show. She had previously worked for a time as a clinical dental assistant, so she was one of the driving forces in our joint effort to insure proper dental care for their cats—but Ron's bachelor pride of eleven males did not like Roxanne.

Ron worked with the cats. He was a very conscientious and very pleasant individual; however, he had a fully functional split personality. When he left the world of bipeds and entered the caged world of his felids, he dropped the cloak of human civility entirely, and immediately became the alpha male of his pride. He had about a dozen male cats at that time, and he was one of the world's most successful big cat trainers. In fact, he put together the world's only all-male lion act.

The interesting thing about lion society is that generally only one male dominates in any given group or pride. And only the dominant male has access to any of the females. Occasionally, an alpha male may allow an uncle or brother to hang out with his pride, and then only they do the breeding. The females do the hunting. The dominant, male, breeding lion(s) routinely spend twenty hours a day sleeping, rolling over, watching the world go by, playing with his kids, or napping. During the other four hours, he is up, on full alert, looking for trouble, eating, fighting, or breeding one of the females. Lions usually give birth to an equal number of male and female cubs. All of the young females stay with their mother's pride, and have only minor social hierarchy difficulties. All of the females are expected to do the hunting, and have more babies. The young males, however, get thrown out of the family pride as soon as they reach sexual maturity. They form what's called a "bachelor pride," and Ron was the leader of such a pride.

A bachelor pride is composed of young male lions that hang out together, and fight with each other to practice their fighting skills in order to determine which one is capable of becoming the best, strongest, smartest fighter of the group. When one finally does become the undisputed local champ, and gets to feeling good about himself, he'll search out and challenges a dominant male with a harem of females. This is the way Mother Nature has arranged for the survival of the fittest. Once someone beats out the existing alpha male, the new male kills all his young offspring, the cubs, especially the male cubs, but quite often all of the cubs. He now takes over control of the pride; the females soon come back into estrus and are bred by the new male, and the cycle begins again. The old dominant male wanders off by himself, and generally becomes a solitary or roan animal, who eventually succumbs to old age or one of the ever-present predatory packs of cape hunting dogs or hyenas. Hyenas seem to harbor a strong hatred for lions, and do their best to kill every one they can.

Consequently, it is easy to understand that the process of assembling and maintaining an all-male group of lions is quite an accomplishment, as well as an inordinately risky business. Most of the other exotic cat trainers in the world thought that Ron Whitfield was just plain crazy. The rest admired his work, and figured he was a walking dead man, and that one of these days his cats were going to kill him.

In fact, one day in the mid-1990s they almost did. Ron's midday program began just as calmly and precisely as it had a hundred times before. Then about a third of the way into it, one of the cats got upset about something and a fight broke out. In a matter of two or three seconds all of the cats in the ring were fighting with each other and Ron was right in the middle of it all. One of the audience members had his video camera running and got the whole thing on tape. To this day, no one understands how Ron managed to live through it, let alone not sustain serious injury. That was the last show for that bunch of males. He retired the lions, and proceeded to assemble a new group with a more traditional mix of female lions with tigers.

I'd watched his work for years, and knew him to be a very talented and most interesting individual. In 1983, he collaborated with me on an article on the clinical importance of veterinary dentistry for the American Dental Association's *DENTISTRY 83* publication (see item 14 in Appendix B). The ADA then mailed the magazine to every dentist and dental student in the United States. Our article had a profound and immeasurable impact upon the increase of interest in, and the growth of the clinical practice of dentistry by veterinarians, which was our intent. It also contributed to the eventual recognition of veterinary dentistry as one of the accepted specialty practices of veterinary medicine.

It should be obvious by now that lions fight—a lot—naturally. This is their normal mode of behavior, and in the course of these events they break their teeth. As a consequence, over the years, I've repaired hundreds of broken canine teeth on a variety of big cats in all sorts of places. In October of 1982, my daughter Janet traveled to San Francisco with us to assist, while we cared for two more of Ron's male lions. Of all five of my kids, Janet was the only one who shared my interest in the animals. She had been one of my best clinical helpers, instrument cleaners, equipment packers, and surgical assistants since she was nine or ten years old. This was her first out-of-town trip. One of Ron's circus friends, a fellow by the name of Wayne Reagan, had a female lion-and-tiger act at the time with Circus Vargas. Wayne was staying over and working with Whitfield for a week or two waiting between bookings for his first trip to Hawaii. One of his tigers had a broken tooth, so we took care of Wayne's cat as well. Subsequently, Wayne and his wife traveled to Japan, the Pacific and then around the country with Circus Vargas, eventually to settle in the desert east of San Diego. Janet had a great time. We flew north on PSA airlines, and came back south on the Amtrak railroad along the coastline through Santa Barbara. It was a great adventure for her.

Whitfield was one of the first animal handlers outside of the more academic zoo settings to actively encourage and strongly promote regular dental check-ups and care for exotic animals. In the beginning, he did more than most of the other animal keepers and handlers in the zoo and amusement park business. Ron spread the gospel of the need for quality dentistry, and its value. To say that all circus and amusement park people fail to care properly for animals, is no more correct than to declare that all dentists or carpenters or teachers do not care about what they are doing. Ron Whitfield was a very gentle, gracious personality, and he did an excellent job with his lions and elephants.

Working with Ron's cats was also the first time I had a true test of the composite restorative material I used instead of the traditional human dental amalgam filling material. The product was called "Adaptec," and I had used a great deal of it in a variety of cats, as well as for the beak repair on the black eagle. It always seemed to hold up quite well. Ron had one old male in particular that tended to bite concrete when he got worked up for any reason. It was just like the way some humans punch the nearest wall when they get irritated. The lion had broken his lower left canine tooth instead of his knuckles. We fixed his tooth, and several years later he fractured it again, breaking off the other one as well. However, our Adaptic filling material on the first tooth held up quite well, in spite of the fact that much of the surrounding tooth had broken away from it. We called it the "concrete test," and I repaired his broken tooth a second time with a newer version of the same material.

Among the many trips I took with Dr. Marty Dinnes was one to Las Vegas to work on Siegfried & Roy's animals. The "Boys," as the locals referred to them, were indeed absolutely spectacular entertainers. Their cats lived the very best cat lives possible on planet earth.

We stayed at the Jockey Club because Marty had arranged for us to use the operating suite in one of the small animal hospitals located nearby. My daughter Janet and my regular dental assistant Gail King were there to help me. Ron Swallow, a certified animal health technician from Marine World, was there helping Marty. All of our equipment traveled well, and without damage. But the clinic facility was quite small, and became very crowded by the time we got everything in place and operational. The plan was to have Marty, Ron and Roy bring the cats over from their luxurious compound at Roy's home, one at a time. We would do the necessary dental work with the security of a fully equipped operating suite, and then when finished, the cats would travel back to their home in Roy's specially outfitted transport truck with Marty and Roy to recover in their own "bedroom," while the rest of us cleaned up and prepared for the next cat.

Roy was very tense for almost the entire week, and on several occasions really could have used a sedative himself each time one of his "babies" was immobilized. We worked on four of his prized animals that week.

The first cat was Rajah, a large male tiger that did a disappearing act into thin air over the middle of the stage. He was on the table from mid-morning to about 5:30 p.m., and needed a lot of work. Marty wanted to do another cat that day, but I was absolutely beat by the time we were finished. Of course, nothing went easily. Although the tiger was very stable during the long anesthesia, it was a day full of worry, because it was the first of Roy's cats to be immobilized. Roy watched the entire procedure peppering us with nervous questions. At dinner, Ron Swallow claimed that it was the most anxiety-ridden day he'd ever had monitoring an anesthesia. We cleaned up the operating room, took the cat back to Roy's house, and I had a chance to see their place, which was quite phenomenal. We met his mother and business manager, visited for a while as the cat recovered, and then Roy invited us all out to dinner.

We went to a small Italian restaurant in northern Las Vegas, and had a very nice, long, slow, delicious Italian dinner. It turned out to be Roy's birthday, so we all sang a little happy birthday number to him. Although the evening was wonderful, by the time dinner was finished, we were all completely wrung out. Shortly before midnight, I found it very difficult to maintain a bright-eyed, alert involvement in the conversation. Of course, Roy was just waking up. He is, after all, a night person. We, however, were completely wasted, and needed to go to bed.

At 7:30 a.m. the next morning we drove over to the hospital, and Roy was already there waiting for us with Leo, his prized African lion. Leo was another one of the major stars in their act. At the time, he was the cat standing behind the door on stage as Siegfried casually permitted his cage door to "accidentally" swing open. Needless to say, Leo scared the hell out of everybody in the first several rows, when he was cued to let go with his loudest roaring thing. He was very impressive. Roy had been very concerned about Leo, and thought that he had a lot of oral problems. We get him situated, checked out his mouth, and it turned out that his problems weren't nearly as bad as everybody had thought. I fixed him up, cleaned his teeth, and we were ready to take him back to the house.

Whenever animals are under anesthesia, time is at a premium, because of the necessity for someone to stay nearby to constantly monitor their vital signs during the recovery process. If one of our procedures ran late, someone's got to work the overtime shift watching the cat recover. Janet and Gail were both very good at their jobs, and very fast with the clean-up. They had the room and table ready and prepared for our next patient by the time Leo was securely loaded into the truck. They were always ready for the next cat long before they got to the clinic. The hold-up was we only had one secure transport truck—and it was busy at this time, moving Leo.

So, what do we do? Do we all stand around for a couple of hours, or what? At the pace we had been working, Marty was afraid that if we stopped for an hour or so, we'd all be asleep on the deck by the time the next cat arrived, which definitely wouldn't look good. The question was, how are we going to get the next cat over in a timely manner? Roy solved the problem.

Next in line was Sarah, a tiger, who was actually another of their stars. Roy only had one truck, so he didn't have any other normal way to get Sarah to the hospital in a timely fashion. Fortunately, Marty had rented a large station wagon at the airport for us to get around in. However, this time, after delivering Leo back to their compound, Roy's truck had to go to the airport to pick up a delivery needed for that evening's show. So to keep things rolling, Roy put a leash on Sarah, walked her over to the back of Marty's station wagon, and told her to jump in. She quickly jumped in and just sat there with him in the rear storage bed. The rest of us piled into the other two seats, and drove back over to the hospital. And so there we were, five fragile little bipeds in the car with this huge tiger in what suddenly seemed like a very small station wagon. It certainly seemed to have been more than big enough for all of us when we got in to it the first time at the airport. It can be very disconcerting to see a full-grown tiger loose in the back of a standard-sized station wagon, but it happened without incident.

Marty sedated Sarah while she was still in the back of the vehicle. Then we moved her onto the clinic's operating table with the soft cushion from the sofa in Roy's living room under her head. We were ready to proceed, and nobody had any trouble staying awake. I completed another giant root-canal job on her canine teeth, but had a variety of difficulties. I couldn't find the canal at first, broke off the end of one of my elongated instruments deep into the tooth, and had trouble retrieving it, but finally got it out before we finished. Eventually, Sarah went home in the big truck without incident. It had been another long, full, tiring day.

At dinner that evening, we discovered that Ron Swallow was a talented musician. It turned out he'd been a drummer with the Beach Boys for a while. The Diana Ross Show was in town at the time, and during dinner Ron announced that he would like to see her show. So after dinner we went back to the hotel, showered, changed, and all of us headed out to attend the midnight show. Tickets magically appeared, and we didn't get out of the club until 2:30 in the morning. As we entered our hotel lobby, we found Marty's wife Valerie sitting in deep conversation with Lynette, one of Siegfried & Roy's staff, whom we had met at their home the day before. Well, we all began to talk, and the next thing we knew it was approaching 4 a.m.

Eventually, everyone made it to bed, but the morning came to us with no mercy and great difficulty. We finally made it to the hospital after 9 o'clock. And there was Roy out in front of the hospital waiting for us with Magic, their male tiger. He was pacing about, waving his arms around, and was madder than hell that we missed our 7:30 a.m. curtain call . Marty dealt with Roy, and the rest of us worker bees quickly pushed our fatigue and hangovers aside, and got back to work. Once more, it turned into another long, killer day at the office.

All of Roy's cats travelled back and forth from their compound in his home, to the nightclub at the hotel, twice a day in the back of a special truck. For some reason, Magic had developed the habit of clamping his teeth around, and holding onto, the metal framework of this enclosure inside the transport truck. As a result of the normal side-to-side swaying action during the ride, he had abraded a notch into the backside of both of his upper canine teeth. It took a while to fix the damage, and Marty wanted to take some photographs of the repair process to show others how to fix similar problems, which we did. We showed Roy what had been happening, and Roy immediately had the truck's holding cages modified before the day was over in order to eliminate the cause of the problem. Roy didn't want it to happen again. The health and well-being of his cats was the most important issue on Roy's agenda.

There was actually an awful lot of tension through the whole day. Even though it didn't make our job any easier, I thought it was quite understandable, considering their animals were their livelihood. And in fact, they could not be replaced without a great deal of time, effort, and difficulty. That is why they raised their own replacement animals. Siegfried & Roy received the Entertainment of the Year Award in Las Vegas that year, and we heard a rumor on the grapevine that it had something to do with the fact that all of their cats had such bright and shiny teeth.

As almost everyone knows by now, Las Vegas is one of the top entertainment capitals of the world, and Siegfried & Roy were clearly one of the biggest entertainment acts in the world. To risk losing one of their animals because of some unforeseen medical complication was enough to drive anybody nuts. In the end, however, it all worked out well for all concerned, and by dinner that evening all was forgotten, and life was all good once more. In fact, we had another long, memorable evening, and I'll never forget the story that Roy told us at dinner. It concerned his lion, Leo, who "escaped" one day.

Roy had a special United States Department of Agriculture fish and game permit to keep his animals within the city limits. Strictly speaking, the living quarters for his cats were nicer than those found in 99.99% of the zoos in the world, and 99% of most homes for humans. Siegfried & Roy's main house at the time was "L" shaped, and they had built a mirror image L-shaped identical structure behind it in the back yard for the cats. The back wall of the cats' house faces south, and gets all of the heat from the blistering desert sunshine. A big swimming pool sits behind this wall, and the water from the pool is pumped up to the top of the wall, and falls over the entire surface of the wall, adding another cooling factor to the building's air conditioning system, which treats the air inside the open-faced building. The enclosures are partitioned, and everybody has a great space with lots of expensive engineering upgrades. They had every environmental protection, modification, mechanical and safety device on the market, from fly control to special sewage system to their own swimming pool. It was an extremely nice and very well built facility.

Roy decided one day that since they didn't have a zoo in Las Vegas, he would arrange to have little walk-through shows of his cats' home for some of the kids living in the neighborhood. So periodically, the local school kids would come over by the busload, and walk through Roy's air-conditioned cathouse to see, visit with, and in the process get to know and provide a little entertainment for his cats. He also put up a new rail about three feet away from the old chain-link fence in order to protect the kids.

Well, one morning for reasons that remain poorly defined, Leo got out. Somebody obviously left one of the gates open after the last show at 3:00 or 4:00 in the morning. So, a little later, and still early in the morning, Leo just walked out of his fancy home, down the driveway past the truck, and out to the sidewalk in the front of Siegfried & Roy's house. He saw some of the neighborhood kids he knows walking past his front yard on their way to school. So, instead of going on a lion rampage, he just walked along to school with them checking out the neighborhood.

All the kids were thrilled, and talked to him, saying, "Hi Leo, over here!," and they all walked toward the school together. After the kids got closer to the school building, Leo lost interest, and didn't have anything to do. Besides, he had had a hard days work last night. So the big cat walked over to a nice nearby shady spot, lay down, and went to sleep under a tree, on the freshly sprinkled, designer front lawn in the cool shade in front of a large fancy house.

It is important to remember that most of the adults living in Roy's corner of Las Vegas are night people, so usually there are not a lot of stray adults wandering around in these suburbs early in the mornings. The beautifully manicured front lawn Leo selected was also home to a little dog, who was wide awake, saw this big ugly interloper in its front yard, and began to bark.

The maid of the house came to the front room, opened the door to see what was going on, and the little dog charged out of the door into the front yard. The doggie in question turned out to be a pampered little Pekinese accustomed to having his own way, and routinely pushing giant human bodies around, and out of his territory. So, without a pause to think about it, he proceeded to hassle this huge strange creature in his front yard. Leo ignored him—for a while. The dog kept barking and yapping, running around, and growling at him, and finally ran up to Leo and bit him in the leg.

So what's a self-respecting, 500-pound, hard-working lion to do when he gets attacked?

Leo smacked the noisy little mutt with his paw, which is about the size of a heavy dinner platter, killed the dog on the spot, and then promptly went back to sleep. Needless to say, the women of the house went crazy.

I'm not sure how they finally settled the case legally, but at dinner that night Roy told us that they talked with the woman, and with the testimony from all of the neighborhood kids, they had proof positive that "the dog attacked the lion." It was a clear case of an unprovoked, viscious dog attack. And any little dog that was dumb enough to attack a 500-pound lion was bound to get into trouble sooner or later.

So, with some sweet talk, and no doubt a little bit of grease, everybody slowly settled back down, and life in the sunny Las Vegas suburbs slowly drifted back to normal—whatever that means.

Leo remained a huge star with all the neighborhood kids. The tours continued, however Roy beefed up their security protocol, added a second fence and security gate to double the protection, and one or the other has been locked ever since.

I did a lot of work with Dr. Marty Dinnes for a number of years, and always enjoyed every minute of it. We treated a lot of interesting four-legged Hollywood stars, and a bunch of circus animals—including several elephants. But that's another story.

Chapter Eight
The Hyena's Story

*Little bi-ped, take the time to appreciate
that Mother Nature's art does not depreciate.
Don't surrender to your visual defect.
Accept the growth of your budding intellect!!*

I've had a dog in my life from the time I was a little boy living in Germany. My first dog, seen on the left below, was a small, reddish brown, longhaired dachshund by the name of Moritz, who would sit up as straight and tall as an arrow to salute "Heil Hitler," when the occasion presented.

From the files of David A. Fagan

Number 5—"Schätze"—on the right, was a very dark black doberman/weimaraner/greyhound mix, whose name means "my dear little friend" in German. She had the deep-chested bark and the ultra-sensitive nose of a true hound-dog, could flash a huge mouth full of pearly white teeth like an alligator, loved to run with the wind, was nearly as agile as a cheetah, understood with equal ease both sign language and soft verbal instructions, was a very responsible and well-trained guard dog, and was as gentle and friendly as a baby lamb—with those she knew and trusted. She guarded our home, and protected all of our stuff exceptionally well—with diligence, grace, and a keen sense of perception for many years. She lived a fine, full life, and was my friend. Dr. O helped me put her down several years ago, when her kidneys finally gave out at the ripe old age of 17.

At the time I wrote this, my wife and I lived with Number 6, whose name was "Gemini". She was a mini-Pomeranian, who really did have a split personality. All the womenfolk said she was really cute. I've been told her ilk were bred down from the Norwegian elk hound. Gemini had exactly that sort of large-dog concept of self, in spite of her small size. She wouldn't hesitate a second to attack Roy's lion. There would be no second thoughts about it. She lived for several years with Schätze, and in spite of her minimal size, she always thought of herself as the alpha dog, and didn't seem to comprehend why the rest of us didn't understand the situation. Schätze politely tolerated her, thank God. Relatively quickly, Gemini taught herself all of the big dog's hand-signal communication behaviors, and quickly became one of the few non-circus doggies of her ilk who responds to sign language. As a result, shortly thereafter I taught her to salute, when she wanted to greet me on the stairway. When she started putting on age, and her hearing failed, the ability to communicate with hand signals was a big help for all of us.

Over the years, I have known and worked on many different domestic dogs, as well as a large variety of rare, exotic and celebrity movie dogs. But, by far, one of the most interesting canines I've ever encountered is the hyena.

Hyenas' behavior is very similar to that of their major rivals and worst enemies, the lion. In 1970, Hugo and Jane van Lawick-Goodall published a fascinating little book titled *Innocent Killers*, which is loaded with interesting facts like this spotted hyena item:

"It is not possible to distinguish, visually, between a male and a female hyena cub since the female is endowed with reproductive organs, which appear, externally, amazingly similar to those of a male. The curious phenomenon has led to a fallacy that the hyena is a hermaphrodite. One trapper, for instance, was asked to catch six hyenas, three of each sex. He rapidly trapped three 'males,' but had difficulty in finding even one female. Whilst he was still searching, one of his 'males' produced triplets." (pg. 158)

The female spotted hyena's urogenital system is unique among mammals. The female's clitoris is elongated to form a fully erectile phallus, and the vaginal opening is at the tip of this phallus. Only the shape of the glans at the tip of the phallus makes it possible to differentiate the sexes. The female urinates, mates and gives birth through this pseudo-penis. Since it is impossible to penetrate without the female's cooperation, these female hyenas also have full control over whom they choose to mate with. Of course, other mammalian females have this control as well, but not with this unique stratagy. The spotted male hyena's penis even lacks a baculum, the bone found in the genitals of many other male mammals. There is now clinical evidence that documents that during pregnancy, female spotted hyenas produce an abundance of intrauterine testosterone, and that this is the source of their genital peculiarity. For centuries, African legend had it that hyenas would give birth to all males one year and all females the next, which may have originated for the same reasons stated above. Hyenas live and hunt in groups, properly referred to as "clans."

The San Diego Zoo has had all three species of hyena in its extensive collection of breeding animals: the spotted, the striped, and the very rare longhaired brown. I have examined and worked on all three. Sissy, one of the spotted hyenas, held the geriatric age record for hyenas in captivity at the time we met early one morning in the zoo hospital's new surgery prep room. She was my first hyena encounter. She was so obese she looked as if she might burst. She smelled like a slab of rotting flesh, and was drooling copious quantities of sticky pink saliva from a foul and repulsive oral cavity. Upon completing my routine head, neck and oral exam, I couldn't tell if the mess in her mouth was causing the problem, or was the result of some massive systemic disease process. Stretched out on the stainless steel surgical table in front of us, this nineteen-year-old, arthritic spotted hyena was about to test my surgical skills to the limit, as well as launch me into the world of international television personality.

The lead keeper of the zoo's hyena string had arranged for Dr. Phil Ensley, one of the associate veterinarians at the San Diego Zoo hospital, to examine the animal and take a look at her mouth. Her keeper had noticed her usual drool puddles were now tinged reddish pink, and contained noticeable strands of clotted blood. Sissy's oral health problems were not so unique or uncommon for carnivores in captivity at that time, and most anywhere other than at the San Diego Zoo, they were still routinely overlooked. This carnivore would have been just another incapacitated old dog on her way to the boneyard without any particular attention paid to her oral problems or disorders.

The prevailing wisdom at the time was: "Animals don't get cavities and the like—some just have dirty mouths"—i.e., no need for a dentist.

Dentistry as a functional discipline of veterinary medicine was virtually nonexistent prior to 1975, and attributing any associations between an animal's oral health and its systemic physical well-being was fairly uncommon. Dr. Ensley knew better, and asked me to get involved. Thus began the first very public test of my freshly painted hospital green mobile veterinary dental unit.

One of the aspects I enjoy the most about the practice of dentistry with animals is the unlimited opportunity to design and fabricate new equipment. Although it always involves a lot of time and hard work, it provides great satisfaction. Sandy Walton, Dr. Oosterhuis' medical secretary at the San Diego Wild Animal Park's hospital joked with us about our non-stop collecting, fabricating and storing. At first, she called our storage shed the "hall of memories." But after she actually saw it all one day, she renamed our equipment stash the "Mile-o-Memorabili." A lot of the gear may only get used once every year or two, but like all good and essential stuff, it's there when it's needed, and it always makes the difference between clinical success, or failure.

My equipment was tested to the limit with Sissy, whose celebrity was enhanced by being one of the first dental patients in the zoo's new hospital following its dedication on September 10, 1977. Public relations representative Georgeanne Irvine cornered me early one morning when we ran into each other at the zoo's photo lab located in the Otto Center building near the Children's Zoo.

"We're planning to do a piece for Channel 39 News on the new hospital," she said, "but the hospital's surgical suite contamination protocol prevents us from getting cameras and a sound crew up close to the action in the OR during most of the interesting sterile surgery procedures. Can we do something with a dental procedure?"

"Sure," I replied. "Routine oral surgery is considered 'dirty surgery' as opposed to most other 'sterile surgical' procedures. I don't worry as much about contaminating the patient's mouth, as I have to worry about getting infected from it. Your whole crew can be in the room with us, and with a few minor exceptions can get as close as over my shoulder."

"Perfect," she responded. "I'll talk with Amalia Baretta at the station today and start the ball rolling."

"That'll be fine," I said. "I'm happy to help any way I can. As soon as you give me a time frame, I'll talk to Dr. Robinson about our caseload, and see if we can schedule something interesting."

Everybody was excited —the first big public relations story in the new hospital. "Veterinary dentistry, New Insights in the Field of Exotic Animal Veterinary Medicine," was not only to be covered in ZOONOOZ magazine, the zoo's monthly publication, but was going to be covered on local television, and perhaps go national—which it did.

"What do you think, Dave?" zoo veterinarian Dr. Phil Ensley asked as we returned to the treatment room after watching Sissy drool her way around her hospital "ward room" enclosure during our initial close-quarters visual examination.

"She's obviously distressed; and the problem certainly has a chronic smell to it. I think we should get a profile of her blood chemistry—a CBC with a kidney panel—before we get started to give us an indication if her kidneys can handle the anesthetic. And, it couldn't hurt to get some broad-spectrum antibiotics on board before we start to work in her mouth!"

"No trouble at all," Phil replied. "Ten days ought to be enough time to get the CBC back, and start getting some of the infection under control? Then we'll immobilize her for you to get some intra-oral x-rays, and figure out what it'll take to clean her up."

"Sounds like a good start," I responded.

The blood work confirmed that Sissy's kidneys could handle the anesthetic, and during the next ten days the antibiotics began to work their magic.

Georgeanne arranged with Amelia Baretta of Channel 39 News to do a feature news clip on "the completely mobile dental facilities at the new state-of-the-art San Diego Zoo hospital." For the television filming, Dr. Robinson had decided to use Sissy as the star of the show. I met with Amelia a couple of times to go over the surgical game plan, and help finalize her script. She was eager, professional, keenly perceptive, and asked a variety of pointed questions about the procedure as well as all of the equipment to be used.

"I believe most of our viewers will be surprised to learn that animals suffer from the same sort of dental problems humans are afflicted with. Do all animals have dental disease, or is it just those in zoos?"

"Both groups present with all twenty-six categories of head and neck problems described in humans," I answered. "They have a tough life, and generally their oral problems originate with traumatic injuries of one sort or another, and then proceed with subsequent local and/or systemic infections."

"Do animals get toothaches?"

"Absolutely, yes; but they go to great lengths to hide the fact, so they don't look weak or vulnerable, and make an easy target for other predators."

"What do they do in the wild?"

"They suffer quietly, and generally die the slow, hard way."

"How does Sissy's oral surgery procedure compare to what is done with humans?"

"Very similar about a third of the time, but much more complicated, and difficult. Hyenas' teeth are designed to be able to split open the leg bones of the larger herbivores like a zebra. Their teeth are big, strong and well anchored in their jaw bones."

The question-and-answer session was easy, but I found myself nervous with stage fright just thinking about facing my first all-seeing TV camera. When the lights finally came on, and the cameras started rolling, it felt like a surrealistic blanket of unreality had been wrapped around us all. Fortunately, Dr. Ensley's immobilization went very well, and we soon fell into autopilot, focusing only upon the task before us. In due course, we got our patient weighed, onto the surgery table, intubated, and hooked up to the monitors without difficulty with Phil's experienced direction leading the way. Finally, all of my attention was directed toward the mess in Sissy's mouth.

My experienced surgical assistant for the procedure was my daughter Janet, at that time a teenager, who was generally very quiet and conspicuously non-talkative. But finally, she blurted out,

"That's what I call a real nasty odor. Have you ever smelled anything like that before?"

"Pretty bad," I affirmed, ignoring the fumes.

Reality had just asserted itself, and it was time to forget the cameras and address the problem at hand. I began poking around in earnest to determine the exact extent of the tissue damage, and trying to determine what if anything, could be salvaged of Sissy's severely compromised masticatory apparatus.

"The pulp canal on the upper left first molar is exposed, infected and badly abscessed," I said as I began the auditory tract of our medical record for the camera crew.

Soon I was quietly enumerating a seemingly endless list for Janet to enter on our oral exam record form, which would ultimately determine the magnitude of Sissy's repair job.

"The upper left first premolar is abscessed; the second premolar is involved periodontally with severe bone loss."

Almost every tooth in her mouth was involved. With the visual exam and appraisal completed, we took a complete set of intra-oral X-rays to document the extent of the infection and bone loss. Phil had been maintaining her at a safe plane of anesthesia.

"How is she doing?" I asked.

"She's stable," he responded. "Respiration steady, and regular; blood pressure strong, and stable; EKG holding constant with no irregularity. Surprisingly, she's in very good shape."

"Good," I said. "I'd like to clean up the worst of the infection, while she's down. I'll need another hour or so. What do you think?"

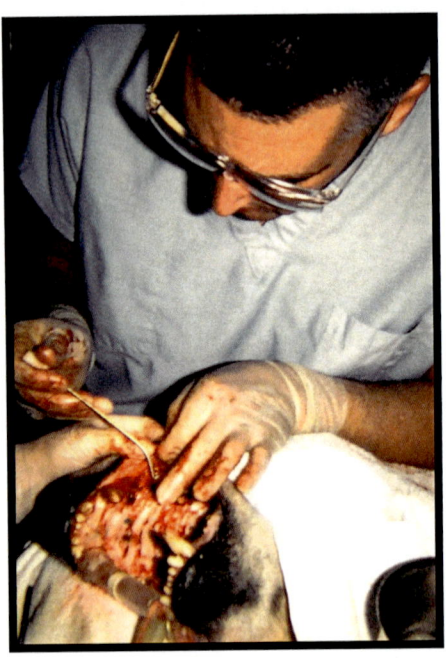

"I think she'll hold all right," he answered confidently. "If there's a problem, I'll let you know."

"It'll hurt and she's going to be losing a fair amount of blood." I said, "Try to give me a little notice if you see any problems developing. I'll need some time to close her up before we can stop."

I had great confidence that Phil could keep her blood pressure steady in spite of my unavoidable bloodletting, but I also knew I needed to let him know what I was about to do to our patient so he'd be prepared.

I ended up removing all of the teeth in her upper arch, except the two canine teeth and her upper right first premolar. The extensive apical infection associated with an unusually large upper right first molar had destroyed a portion of the bony orbit of her right eye socket, and an incredibly sticky, clear discharge came out of the hole where the tooth had been.

"What a mess," I mumbled to myself as Janet and I flushed, debrided and sutured it closed.

When I depressed the soft tissue in the back of her mouth to test the stability of my repositioned surgical flap, her eye bulged out. I was concerned she might lose the sight in that eye from the infection with the loss of bony structure between the eye and the mouth. Fortunately she didn't, but I wouldn't have bet on it that day.

The upper left second premolar had fistulated into her nose, infecting the nasal turbinates, and making a hole the size of a dime into her nasal passage. I packed her nose with gauze to stop the bleeding after removing the molar, while I closed the hole into her mouth. The soft tissue all around the tooth had been destroyed by the infection. It was a tough one to close, but I finally managed to get primary closure with a sliding graft of soft tissue from the inside of

From the files of Dr. David A. Fagan

My first surgery in the mouth of a hyena was a real eye-opener for me. I enjoyed oral surgery from the time of my first surgery case in dental school, where we were taught to treat everything and everybody that walked into the clinic off the streets of San Francisco's low-rent Mission District. Because the Vietnam War was generating numerous head and neck casualties, the need for trauma surgeons with oral surgery experience was great. I was provided ample opportunity to learn while in school, and my clinical practice during the 1960s hippie period added to my experience. So by the time I met my first hyena, I thought I had enough oral surgery experience to accept the challenge without hesitation. However, the size of their teeth, the hardness of the surrounding alveolar bone, and the overall magnitude of their problems made for a major trial by fire. With my able assistant (and daughter) Janet's help, I learned a lot of new tricks in a big hurry during those first few years of animal dentistry.

her cheek. The infection hadn't gotten into her left eye like it had on the right side.

"That's as good as it's going to get," I mumbled to Janet as we finished with the upper arch, and asked Phil to take a look.

"Let's not press our luck today," I said. "We've been at it for three and a half hours now, and she's had a lot of tough surgery for one day."

We were going to have to see her again anyway, and her X-rays indicated that her lower jaw was not as badly infected as her upper. We discussed the matter and decided that the lowers would hold for a while, and that a course of additional antibiotics would help stabilize matters—making it safer when we got back to her.

"The soft tissue oughtta heal alright, I suspect, but we'd better modify her diet to the soft side until we can confirm that her right eye is going to be OK."

Phil lightened her up slowly while she finished the IV fluids and antibiotics. Janet worked her magic again, cleaning up another surrounding mess of blood-stained instruments, materials and equipment we had created. I then began detaching and clearing everything away from our recovering patient. While rolling her out toward the heated holding pen for recovery, Janet was the first to sense there was something wrong with her, and said, "I don't see her breathing!"

"Stop the gurney!" Phil ordered.

We stopped in the middle of the doorway. Phil checked her heart and respiration rate. She was in fact having trouble.

"Let's get her back into the OR," he said.

She wasn't breathing through her nose. I pried open her mouth, Janet secured it open with a mouth prop. I quickly suctioned her throat, but there was nothing there. It was already clear. We gave her oxygen with a facemask, but she was gagging, heaving, trying to vomit with her tongue curling back into her throat. Closing her mouth suddenly, she easily crushed my rubber encased, heavy metal, mouth prop, and once again she couldn't breathe. We tried to open her mouth again, but this time it was impossible. Exhaling suddenly and forcefully through the nose, she discharged a large chunk of clotted blood, and then opening her mouth she inhaled a huge breath of fresh air. She looked me directly in the eye about eighteen inches away from my face, clearly madder than hell, and began breathing deeply and normally. She was very close to being wide awake.

"I think its time to get her back to her bedroom before she decides to take a bite outta your face," Phil said jokingly.

We quickly wheeled her back into the recovery area again.

Thrashing around during the recovery period, she banged her face on the floor a bit more than I would have liked, before the post-operative analgesic Phil had given her kicked in, and then she quickly settled down.

Amelia had enough raw footage to get her piece together for the next day's news. She was pleased, and so were we. After getting everything cleaned up, I went back and checked Sissy before I left. She was walking around "lookin' fer da bum that mugged her." I was just glad to see her up and breathing normally. During the years between 1976 and 1980, I restored the mouths of most of the hyenas in the zoo's large carnivore string. However, their successful long term recovery required a change of diet, so we took advantage of the situation to modify all of the hyenas' diets. A bit later in 1980, I presented a paper at both the annual meeting of the American Association of Zoo Veterinarians in Washington D.C., and the first annual Dr. Scholl Conference on the Nutrition of Captive Wild Animals at Lincoln Park Zoo in Chicago—

concerning the relationship between "Diet Consistency and Periodontal Disease in Carnivores." (See item 8 in Appendix B.) Then in 2001, I presented a similar paper at the Sixth International Small Felid Workshop at the zoo in San Juan, Costa Rica (see item 25 in Appendix B).

One of the primary objectives of all zoos is to encourage the reproduction of their rare and endangered residents. Maintaining healthy, well-nourished animals is the first step toward that goal. Zoo animals are fed a diet based upon a variety of factors including food preferences in the wild, local availability, perishability, economy, nutritional requirements of similar domestic species, and finally the "occupational therapy value" of the food items. Nutrition and dental health have a correlation coefficient well accepted by animal caregivers today without argument.

But, in 1977 it was still a new and debatable concept.

After eating a prescribed diet for several months, Sissy was sedated one day as part of her ongoing reproductive study. I had an opportunity to have a look at her dentition, while she was immobilized. The red eosin dye stain on the teeth showed between 60% and 80% less dental plaque, and almost no calculus.

However, the major surgery case of this morning was the rare male brown hyena named Scar—so-named for good reason. His body was beat up and scarred with complete abandon. This individual had come from the wild, and obviously ran with a very rough mob. His rank breath, multiple scars and distinctive body odor were all testimony to the fact that he was one tough cookie, who'd been through hell and back—probably numerous times.

Scar's dentition was not in instant need of emergency care, so on our first encounter, after establishing a complete diagnosis and treatment plan, I just cleaned up the right side of his mouth. We decided to do this, in order to be able to evaluate to what extent the industry standard—the commercial zoo carnivore diet, known as "ZooPreem"—had on the formation of plaque, calculus, and stain on his teeth. On the next occasion, his six weeks re-evaluation, his dentition was again badly stained, and covered with a mushy, bacterial-laden dental plaque. We were on our way to confirming that his diet was indeed a major part of the problem. He needed much more "hassle factor" per mouthful of nutrients.

Scar also shouldered the curator's hopes and expectations to become a major breeding sire. Although nowhere near as badly infected and debilitated as Sissy's, his mouth clearly required a fair amount of attention nonetheless, and during the following nine-month period, we slowly shaped up his general and oral health to nearly optimal physical condition. He had been in a separate enclosure all this time, not yet healthy enough for breeding.

"There are only twelve of this species in North America," Dr. Jane Meier, another of the hospita's associate veterinarians, commented as we watched Scar sniffing around his enclosure early one morning. "There's a lot of pressure to try to get some puppies out of this guy."

"Well, I imagine if he'll ever be up to it, now's as a good a time as any," I responded. "I'm basically finished with him except for the routine annual exam and follow-up. He's eating well now, and is looking good. As far as I'm concerned he's dischargeable." And so he was.

Two days later I stopped by Jane's office. "How did it go with Scar?" I asked as I entered the open door.

"Not well," she responded, swinging her chair around to face me. "The female attacked him immediately, as soon as she set eyes on him. She beat him up pretty badly—this morning we confirmed she broke his jaw among other things. If you have the time to take a look, he's in the intensive care unit. I don't know if he's gonna make it though."

In fact he didn't make it. After a few weeks it was clear the most humane thing to do was to euthanize Scar, and so ended his brief attempt at posterity. Scar was humanely euthanized on the morning of the 10th of April, 1978. Because there were only twelve of this species in the western hemisphere at the time, the decision was made to collect various tissues, blood and sperm samples for scientific study. All of these tissues were placed in the CRES research department's cryogenic freezers for long term frozen tissue storage. This was Dr. Benirschke's back-up frozen tissue bank project, known as the "the frozen zoo".

At the moment of his last breath, I felt a swirl of cool air envelop me as though Scar's departing spirit bid me "adieu." It felt like a brief, peaceful moment of what I imagined might sound like…

"Thanks for your help, Doc. But, I'm gettin' outta here! "

I spoke with Dr. Benirschke about the feelings that flood the mind after the loss of a patient following so much intense effort.

"Failure is a constant companion in the exotic animal business," he said. "Clearly, you're going to lose some from time to time. The practice of medicine, to a great extent, is a never-ending war."

I have slowly, and on occasion painfully, learned that this is true. If every member of our team pays close attention to all of the details, we'll win our share of the encounters. Our job is to direct our focus to the task at hand—the process. Over the years, I've learned that we are sure not going to win this war in my lifetime. There is no such thing as winning the war in medicine. We regularly win our share of many interesting battles, however. And, I've learned to appreciate the process, and accept the losses when they occur.

Twenty-plus years later, the hyenas at the zoo are weighed every month, and given meticulously well-calculated diets to maintain their overall systemic health. Now, the zoo has three full-time animal nutritionists on staff supervising the diets of all of the 6000-plus animals in their collection. The first was Dr. Mark Edwards. A few years back, I had the opportunity to examine another hyena with a fractured pre-molar found during his annual examination. It was a minor affair and easily repaired. And I marveled at how well their collective efforts had improved the oral health of these unusual predators.

In the front lines of the war to save the endangered animals, it is not at all uncommon to discover that the men and women who occupy these trenches find and implement very creative solutions to many very unusual individual problems. In fact, we all do this—through trial and error and learning—on a daily basis.

The death of Scar taught me something else about that in-between ground where everything is neither all right nor all wrong. This is what the Sufi Poet Rumi was talking about when he said:

"Out beyond ideas of right-doing and wrong-doing, there is a field of gray. I'll meet you there."

My experience with Scar and Sissy helped teach me to accept my share of the responsibility, maintain objectivity, and keep on performing my part of the job to the best of my ability.

Knowing that the war will continue, I remain alert to the fact that another healthy slice of humble pie may be waiting for me just around the very next corner. Dr. Benirschke's observations, and my encounter with Scar had a great deal to do with the development of my perspective on this issue.

Chapter Nine
Arusha Launches a Search

Colliding with the elephant's chest,
the fourth student uses his senses to guess
the probable function inside this space
located over its legs, and behind its face.

Hearing the rumblings of the various contents
He questions the cause of these gastric events.
Curiosity pumped beyond containment,
he says to himself in certain amazement

"This information is most clandestine—
I think I'll choose zoo animal medicine."

ARUSHA LAUNCHES A SEARCH

The first cheetah I ever touched was a young male named Arusha, and it occurred while he was in training to become a goodwill ambassador for the San Diego Zoo. His home was behind the stage of the zoo's Wegeforth Bowl Stadium, completed in 1936, and named to commemorate Dr. Harry Wegeforth, a local physician, who founded the zoo in September of 1916. Arusha lived with his older sister—and civility instructor—a playful, reddish-colored golden retriever named Anna. Anna taught Arusha how to associate successfully with humans.

Arusha was born at the Winston Wildlife Safari Park in Oregon, was orphaned at an early age, and needed to be hand reared. The zoo in San Diego was looking for a manageable animal PR personality, so animal trainer Kathy Marmack met Arusha, and a life-long relationship was born.

When Arusha was about eleven months old, and in the middle of a typical adolescent teething period, he had some difficulty shedding one of his baby teeth. Kathy (who has since become the animal trainer supervisor at the San Diego Zoo) immediately recognized the problem, and asked Dr. Ensley to arrange a trip to the dentist to have his dentition evaluated. My introduction to Arusha occurred at the Jennings Center for Zoological Medicine with associate veterinarian Dr. Jane Meier. The problem was a retained primary tooth, which was promptly removed without difficulty. However, by the time we completed my usual comprehensive oral examination, it was clear that Arusha also had mal-positioned lower first molars, which were noticeably tipped forward toward the front of his mouth and axially rotated. His problem is almost exactly the identical clinical presentation seen thousands of times a day by human dentists as human teenagers have their initial oral examination with an orthodontic evaluation.

The prospect of placing orthodontic bands, brackets and

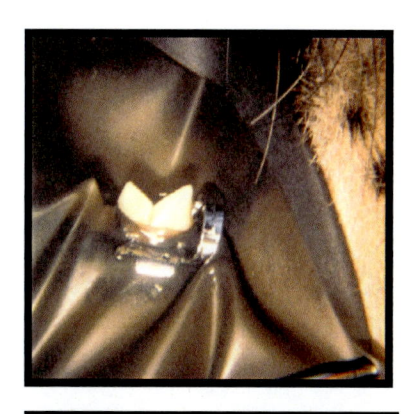

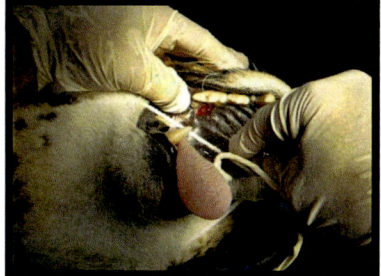

From the files of David A. Fagan

Arusha was my first cheetah encounter. Their primary teeth naturally exfoliate similar to normal human "teething" patterns, but his mandibular molars—seen at top—were over-sized, tipped forward, and slightly rotated axially. The sharp, pointy distal cusp on the molar created a localized puncture wound in the roof of Arusha's mouth. This was the tooth that launched our thirty-year, multi-institutional investigation. The small red area near my left thumb in the view on the right is the bloody hole in the roof of his mouth, which we named focal palatine rrosion or "FPE". At top, the entire molar tooth has been isolated under a "rubber dam" to insure that the exposed pulp tissue is not contaminated by oral bacteria during the dental treatment procedure to shorten it.

wires in a cheetah's mouth was a most impractical solution, so I needed a more appropriate alternative. The distal cusps of the two mal-positioned first molars were "topped," or slightly rounded off and blunted to eliminate the problem. I then treated the exposed pulp tissue with what's called a partial pulpotomy—a common dental treatment to re-seal the interior of the tooth, and restore the hole I'd made into the tooth's pulp chamber utilizing a tooth-colored composite restorative material. I used a rubber dam on this case to insure the protection of the remaining vital pulp tissue, while it was being worked on. Arusha, and his now famous molar, recovered without incident, and he went back to work in the goodwill ambassador business.

He was, by the way, a very popular and effective public relations ambassador. Joan Embery took him on local TV. He was a regular on the Johnny Carson show. He had a busy schedule at the zoo, in many local classrooms and numerous convention and entertainment venues. Arusha had countless human friends of all ages, all of whom came to know him on a first-name basis.

The lingering question for me, however, was: Why did this cheetah have such a typical humanoid-like orthodontic malocclusion? ? What was going on in his mouth? And did this dental deformity occur in other cheetahs?

Thus began another lengthy scientific investigation to discover the exact cause of the problem, and in the process, determine how to prevent it. Arusha single-handedly launched this, as yet unfinished, international research project.

Thirty years later, much has been learned about cheetahs and their dentition. However, the exact nature of all their various health problems seen in captivity still remains a subject of much debate, and is still under intensive investigation. It is quite conceivable, that in the final analysis, we will learn that close association with humans is a major part of their problem.

Cheetahs have been admired and revered for ages because of their unique beauty, incredible running ability, and pleasant personalities. For centuries noblemen and the wealthy of many cultures have captured and kept cheetahs for various reasons. In India, up until the late 1940s, the cheetah was use by humans as a hunting aid much like the falcon. In fact, hunters say they

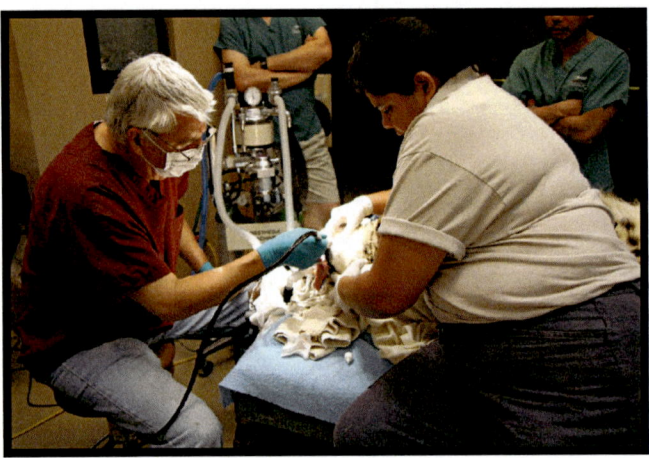

From the files of David A. Fagan

The FPE lesions come in a wide variety of sizes and shapes, like the one at left, and can inflict an enormous amount of damage on the surrounding bony structures and soft tissues in their oral cavities. On the right, the author is surgically correcting one of these erosive lesions on a cheetah at the Living Desert Reserve and Park near Palm Springs in the desert east of San Diego.

My good friend Ron Garrison, who was director of the ZSSD Photo Lab for many years, took these two images and the one on the next page. The Colyer Institute purchased the right to use a number of these images before he retired. I spent many enjoyable hours with Ron in his lab; at the zoo and WAP hospitals while he documented many of our clinical cases; wandering around the many exhibits with him; and at the WAP's off-exhibit cheetah-breeding facility trying to learn how he does it. He taught me to expect one good image out of every roll of thirty-six. Thank God for the digital camera. Ron started out as a military photographer, and has subsequently traveled all over the world leading his photo safari, and sharing his know-how with thousands.

"fly their cheetahs" when they turn them loose to hunt. And even today, a pet cheetah is a major status symbol with a small segment of the wannabe Hollywood set, in spite of all of the sanctimonious environmental-friendly talk.

Although they were exhibited in London as early as 1829, it was nearly 130 years later before one was born in captivity in 1960. In spite of a great deal of effort by many dedicated and knowledgeable individuals, cheetahs have not been able to maintain a predictable reproductive history in well managed captive environments. At the present time, the cheetah is in severe danger of becoming extinct for the third time for several rather poorly understood medical reasons.

Cheetahs are unique among all of the felids. Lions are the only true social members of the big cat family. The rest of the big cats are generally a solitary lot. The cheetah has a varied social structure, which readily adapts to the prevailing circumstances of their habitat. Males will sometimes form bachelor groups, and sometimes remain solitary. Females will usually be solitary except when they have young, and littermates will sometimes remain together after leaving their mother, if they live that long. Sometimes they will not. One of the reasons for this variation is that the cheetah is easily and regularly pushed away from its kills by lions, hyenas and jackals. Sometimes, a small group of two or three cheetahs defending a kill can more effectively deter a solitary, stronger predator from stealing their food.

Because of their dependence upon running ability and speed to obtain their food, cheetahs are very hesitant to engage in full-contact hostilities with any other predator, which may result in injury to one of their limbs. A cheetah's life depends upon having a good set of wheels. They cannot ever afford to risk getting a flat tire. However, injury is a relatively common companion of their lifestyle.

Territoriality also varies widely among individual cheetahs. Females will generally follow around the edge of a group of Thomson's gazelle, while the herd calmly wanders about in search of good grass. Some males will follow this same practice, while other males will claim small territories of good grassland or water supply, which are prime areas where many females will gather at certain times of year. These prime territories are often controlled by male coalitions, which gang up on other solitary males in order to control the reproductive benefits available in these favored locations.

When a female cheetah leaves her cubs to hunt, her offspring are extremely vulnerable to discovery by lions and other predators. Lions always proceed to kill cheetah cubs without hesitation. As a result of this sort of predation, only about 10% of the cheetah cubs born in the

"The cheetah is a strikingly handsome, unique animal. It is this uniqueness, which has, unfortunately, made it so difficult to maintain in customary captive situations. If there is to be any hope for a future for this animal, the cheetah must be managed differently, in a new, unique and bold manner."

—Elliot Handrus, MS

Photo by Ron Garrison

---

wild survive to adulthood. It appears to some investigators that cheetah population numbers vary inversely with lion population numbers. Consequently, cheetahs produce large litters to offset these risks and their related high infant mortality rate.

The genetic composition of cheetahs has been the subject of extensive scientific study for the past thirty-plus years. It has been determined that the genetic make-up of the cheetah is similar to that of "one hundred generations of an inbred strain of laboratory mice." The reason for this lack of genetic diversity could be explained by what is called a "population bottleneck." This is the scientific name for an event that results in the die-off of the majority of the animals of a particular species during a relatively short period of time. Detailed studies by scientific authorities lead to the assumption that there were in fact two such population die-offs in the cheetah's history. One was perhaps in the late Pleistocene epoch, followed by a recent bottleneck subsequent to the geographic isolation of the two sub-species groups in northeast and southern Africa, perhaps within the last 100 years.

Another problem for the cheetah, in both wild and captive environments, is that the number of motile spermatozoa found in the reproductive tract of a typical male is approximately one-sixth the amount found in your average domestic house cat. This is comparable to what would be considered clinical infertility in other mammalian species. Many scientists conclude that these genetic problems place the cheetah in severe danger of disappearing. However, there is also some argument to the contrary. If this lack of genetic diversity is the result of deleterious recessive genes having been selectively removed from the population, then it is possible that there are none of the usual negative inbreeding effects customarily seen in most other breeding groups, and this would be a good thing.

Based on biochemical analysis, the closest relative of the cheetah is the North American mountain lion. An extinct common ancestor of both species is known as *Acinonyx trunzani*, and has been found in the fossil record in the United States. Many suggest this may explain the relationship. An interesting article concerning this topic can be found on the Internet at www.colyerinstitute.org

There are also several rare color mutation patterns found in some cheetahs. The most common of these is referred to as the "king cheetah." This individual has a mixture of black stripes, as well as black spots. African legends proclaimed this animal centuries ago with the statement that "there are four big cats living in this wild land." At one time, this animal had been thought to be a distinct subspecies, but it has subsequently been found to be merely a color phase variation, much like the melanistic, or black, color phases found among the leopards.

A review of the scientific literature suggests the cheetah was originally brought into captivity in 1871 (Marker 1984). From 1956-1986, there were 385 animals imported, but only 193 were

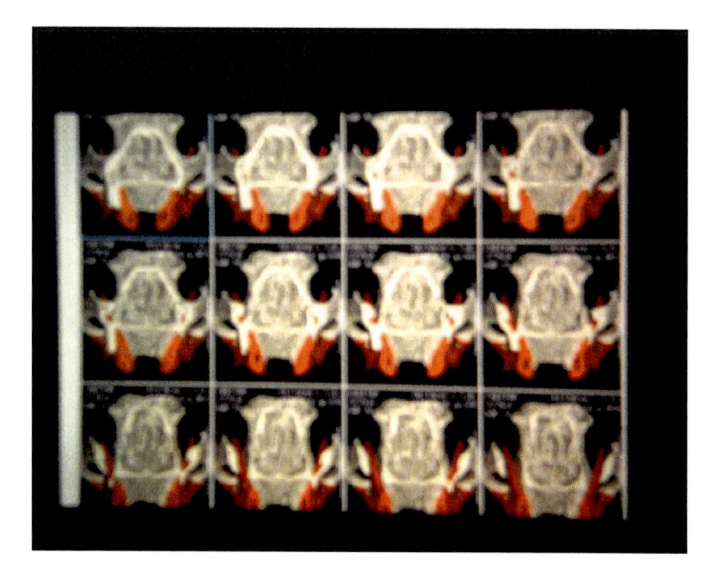

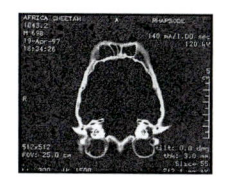

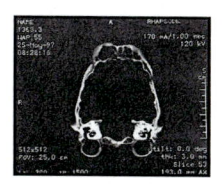

From the files of David A. Fagan

A CT-scan is properly known as a computerized axial tomography or CAT scan. It is a diagnostic imaging procedure that uses a combination of X-rays and computer technology to produce multiple cross-sectional, detailed images of any part of the body. The view at left shows a small portion of such a set of CT images of the skull of a cheetah with the mandible colored reddish. The two at above right are a typical individual's single raw X-ray images. On the left is the thicker, stronger, more symmetrical skull of a wild cheetah from Africa. On the right is a similar image from a cheetah born and raised in a captive environment showing much thinner skeletal bone. These three images and those on the next page are photographic reproductions taken from an X-ray viewing box.

alive at the end of this period (Marker 1989). In spite of some comments to the contrary, reproductive success numbers in captive groups seem to indicate that breeding cheetahs in captivity has on the whole not been very successful. This is despite all of the advances in captive propagation and management techniques. And, it has yet to be proven that captive propagation is a viable alternative for the survival of the species.

The king cheetah mentioned above also provides an interesting ethical question for captive management programs in zoos. Given that it is such a unique and beautiful animal, would it be better to breed animals for a specific flashy color pattern, thus decreasing the genetic variability of the breeding population even more, but perhaps increasing the number of visitors to an institution keeping these individuals? Or, would it be better to encourage the king cheetah to breed with normal-colored animals, perhaps injecting some degree of variability into the general population? This is the sort of ethical question that must be addressed by institutions engaged in captive breeding programs involving any endangered species.

As one small part of a very large, multi-faceted international scientific investigation of the cheetah, Dr. O at the Wild Animal Park and I were able to assemble and examine eighty-five cheetahs, fifty-nine live individuals and twenty-six museum specimens. Our clinical data profiled a developmental, self-inflicted, localized, disabling wound through the roof of their mouths, which we labeled "focal palatine erosion" (FPE), about which we published an article in 1982 (see item 13 in Appendix B). This disorder seemed to be associated with the diets fed in captivity, and was often associated with renal disease, and chronic suppurative infections of the nose.

Initially, we were unable to identify either a primary causative agent, or what's called the "pathogenesis" of the disorder. The pathogenesis of a disease is the mechanism by which an etiological factor actually causes the disease. The term is also used to describe the developmental steps of the disease, or the distinct steps by which the disease progresses clinically. The word comes from the Greek pathos, "disease," and genesis, "creation."

Nonetheless, our first impression was that FPE is the result of an atrophy of disuse of the animal's muscles of mastication. I refer to this issue when I say "their diet has insufficient hassle factor per mouthful of nutrients." Some studies suggest that cheetahs get to eat only one out of eleven trips to the kitchen. This means of course, that they must expend an enormous amount of energy or "fuel" to finally get a meal. Not only that, but they are very fast running machines that burn up a lot of fuel, and risk serious injury, on each of those failed ten attempts to get a meal.

Think of them as the animal equivalent to a top fuel dragster. No one would suggest or consider driving a top fuel dragster around town to work, or to the mall for a shopping spree. However, in captivity, cheetahs get their food delivered daily like a Domino's pizza. In captive circumstances, they do not have to do any work for their meals, and consequently, their muscles do not get exercised to the extent to which they were designed. As a direct result, their muscles and bones do not grow to their full genetic potential. Any good mechanic can tell you that the fastest way to ruin the engine of your dragster is to repeatedly start it, stop it, and do not drive it.

Think of the mammal's mouth as a picket fence. Then, if the bones of the cheetah's jaws and face don't get enough exercise, the picket fence doesn't grow to its fullest potential —because of the missing exercise. And consequently, the animal's teeth or "pickets" are too large to fit properly on the smaller fence. Or in other words, the muscles of mastication did not get enough exercise during their growth and development phase, and now the animal's head is too small for the size of its genetically predetermined dentition. Clearly, cheetahs need more hassle factor per mouthful of nutrients. But this requires lots of changes that are not forthcoming for a variety of very real-world practical reasons.

So, in due course, we decided to develop a series of surgical management protocols to deal with the most severe clinical signs and symptoms, while we continued to gather additional bits and pieces of information to add to our research study as circumstances permitted. Essentially,

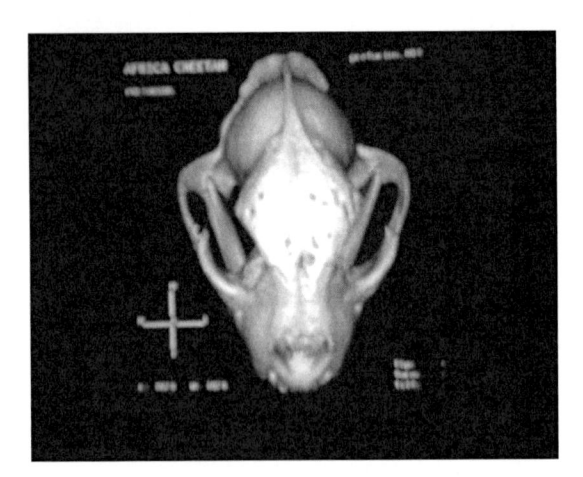

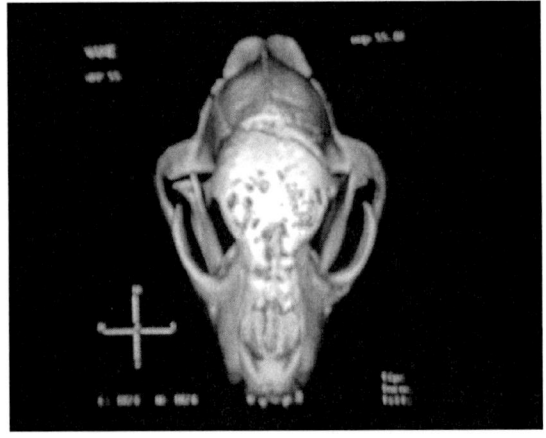

From the files of David A. Fagan

These two images are computer-reconstructed images of the skull bones of two animals compiled by a special computer program from the collection of single-frame images. On the left is the free-ranging wild cheetah, and on the right is the animal born and raised in a restricted, captive environment. This unique ability to create new perspective views from a single series of sequential X-ray images is what makes the CAT scan such a valuable instrument. Compare these images with those seen on the preceding page to better appreciate their diagnostic value.

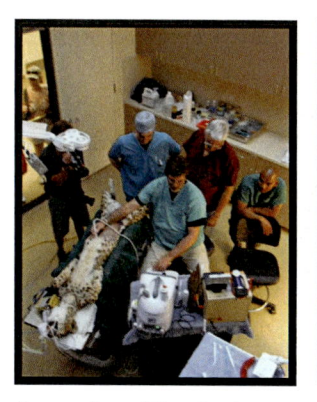

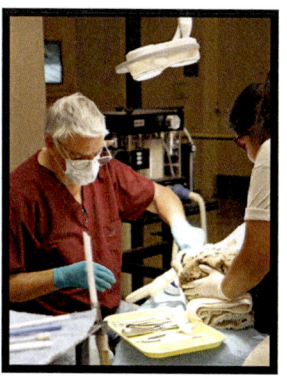

At right, the author examines "Jake," one of the cheetah ambassadors at the Living Desert Reserve and Park in Palm Desert. Jake and his companions have for the past six years participated in an annual gastric biopsy study conducted in conjunction with Veterinary Internal Medicine Specialist Dr. Peter Slusser in association with the Clinical Pathology Department at the University of California at Davis (UC-Davis). The left image shows Tom Baker, principle ultrasonagrapher and supervisor of small animal radiology at the VMTH UC-Davis conducting a complete ultrasound examination on the young female Sabe's reproductive system to better understand the reproductive physiology of the cheetah. From the left behind the cat the public views the activities through the glass viewing wall; the park's staff photographer Bert Buxbaum records the events; in blue is Pierre Comizzoli, DVM PhD., the surgeon and chief investigator working on the cheetah project sponsored by the Smithsonian Institute and the CCF - Cheetah Conservation Fund located in Namibia along the west coast of south Africa. Dr. Fagan is in the maroon scrub top; and Saldy Portacio, RVT, in green, is the park's registered vet tech. We are watching and discussing the procedure as Tom locates, identifies, measures, and records the cat's internal anatomical structures.

---

we were in the process of developing another new experimental surgical protocol specifically to fix this hole-in-the-roof-of-the-mouth problem. But we were once again working way out on the thin ice, and needless to say when the ice is thin everything doesn't always go according to plan. However in the process, we've managed to examine and work on a very large number of cheetahs.

I remember one occasion when Dr. O and I traveled out of town to another facility to work on a cheetah with a particularly bad FPE lesion. Everything went very well, until the actual moment of truth, when with scalpel blade in hand, it was necessary to decide just exactly where I was going to harvest the extra tissue necessary to close the hole between this cat's mouth and nose utilizing the double reposition flap procedure I had developed a number of years earlier on a little wiener dog named Red with the veterinary surgeons at Main Street Animal Hospital in southeast San Diego (see item 15 Appendix B).

Jim and I discussed the available options; I finally made the incision with a rock-solid pencil grip, and laser-focused determination as my dental school oral surgery professor had instructed. And in an instant, I completely severed a large hidden branch off the animal's carotid artery. In just one or two seconds at the most, we had a mouth full of arterial blood flowing everywhere, and just as quickly, we were all launched into full emergency mode. Seven hours later—following a tremendous amount of intense effort, including two cat-to-cat blood transfusions, an emergency telephone consultation with another trauma surgeon, some very fancy needle work, and a whole lot of good luck—we had the bleeding controlled, the severed vessels tied-off, the oral-nasal fistula repaired and closed, and the cat completely recovered from the protracted anesthetic ordeal to live a full life.

However, three surgeons, and a half-a-dozen techs were all exhausted, used up, and wrung out like a bunch of dirty dish towels. It was a long ride home. Clearly, we dropped that surgical approach from our short list of alternative FPE repair procedures. It was another hard lesson

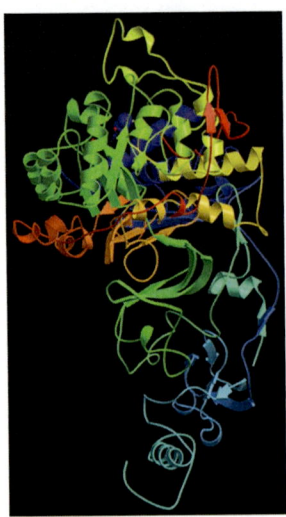

The image above is a molecular model of the H. pylori urease enzyme. Helicobacter pylori is a gram-negative, microaerophilic bacterium that infects various areas of the stomach and duodenum. Many cases of peptic ulcers, gastritis, duodenitis, and cancers are caused by H. pylori infections. However, many others who are infected do not show any symptoms of disease. H. pylori's helical shape (from which the genus name is derived) is thought to have evolved to penetrate and favor its motility in the mucus gel layer.

learned the hard way. But, this sort of "educated guesstimate risk taking" is a necessary and essential ingredient on the exotic animal experimental surgery dance floor we frequent.

By 1990, we had managed to obtain detailed sequential oral examination data on several developing litters of cheetah cubs, including full mouth intra-oral radiographs, impressions and plaster casts of their developing dentition. By coordinating efforts with another multi-species comparative muscle function research study under the direction of UC Davis, we also managed to obtain detailed CT scans of the skulls of eleven more adults, some living and some museum specimens. Preliminary analysis of this information suggested that FPE was a systemic problem. However, the digitized computer tapes of these scans from a mobile CT unit mounted inside the back of an older semi-trailer were not convertible into useable information by the powerful computers at General Electric research facility. This occurred because the constant road vibration had knocked this mobile unit out of calibration, and the data could only be recognized by the computer on board the now dismantled trailer.

Unfortunately, all of this information was lost to us. So, the direction of our search now shifted to locate a comparable set of cheetah skulls in order to determine by CT scan, if there was a bone-density difference to be found between captive and wild cheetahs. With the strict C.I.T.E.S. import prohibitions in place concerning all endangered species body parts, it was another four years before we were able to obtain three relatively fresh cheetah skulls from South Africa.

While we waited, we managed to secure accurate CT scans of the skulls of two equivalent animals, a male/female cheetah pair. One descended from South African bloodlines, yet was raised in captivity; and the other a male/female pair reared in the wilds of North Africa from a Smithsonian Museum collection circa 1910. But, in order to truly compare apples to apples, we needed to scan a third pair of contemporary cheetah skulls from South Africa. By the time we managed to do so, the CT scan and three-dimensional color re-construction computer software we had been using had been once again been upgraded, and now the prior work had to all be re-done, in order to comply with acceptable research protocol. The identically compiled comparative data was finally completed, and was presented to the scientific community in 1997 (see item 17 Appendix B). Preliminary interpretation suggests that there is a major difference between wild and captive skeletal anatomy, and that the FPE lesions may be just the first clinical signs of a much more complicated and significant systemic situation.

The summer of 1999 found me again back at the veterinary medical teaching hospital at the University of California at Davis, examining and attending to the oral needs of two additional fifteen-month-old cheetah cubs, under the experienced supervision of Drs. Karen Terio and Lynsey Phillips. Two more deserving animals were added to our growing list of regulars, while the search for the prevention and/or cure continues.

The importance of all this is that research is an essential, necessary, and expensive fact of life in the care and maintenance of any endangered species. The ultimate costs of not providing the funding or doing the research, are far greater than the costs of just doing it, and the research is usually a long-drawn-out, difficult, and expensive undertaking. Dr. Benirschke explains this situation in great detail in his white paper "The Mandate for Research in Zoos" written in 1976, and available on the Colyer Institute website. When we began thirty-some years ago, there was no previous work concerning oral problems in cheetahs available to help guide our investigation. We were starting from scratch. During our search, we found similar oral lesions in the skeletal remains of the clouded leopard, *Felis nebulosa*, and have subsequently seen similar lesions in the mouths of captive-raised tigers. Dr. Laura Marker, director of the Cheetah Conservation Fund, has identified similar oral lesions in the mouths of some wild cheetahs in Namibia.

Clearly, scientific investigation is a life-long process, and the investigators do not know where the path will lead them.

To further complicate the problems of the cheetahs in captivity, the poor genetic variability of this species makes it uniquely susceptible to disease. This in itself is an all-important issue in the captive management of any species. But it is perhaps not the most significant hurdle for the cheetah. That could be a captivity-induced digestive system disorder or gastritis, which slowly converts the cheetah's entire digestive system into non-functional scar tissue. The affected animal is then unable to absorb nutrients from the food it eats. Interestingly, the cause of this problem involves a microorganism known as *Helicobacter pylori*, which is very similar to the organism related to bacterial stomach ulcers in humans. However, for the cheetah, the result is that the animal slowly starves to death, because of an inability to absorb nutrients through the wall of its scarified digestive tract membrane. These three problems, combined with the other stresses generally found in captivity, suggest a dismal future for the cheetah. A novel new approach needs to be implemented for these unique animals.

Thirty years ago, Arusha may have been one of the first cheetah public relations ambassadors to effectively introduce and represent the plight of the wild cheetah. However, for the past 10 years or so, Dr. Laurie Marker in Namibia has provided a strong international voice for the cheetah, embodied in the Cheetah Conservation Fund (CCF), which she directs. The following is from their website, www.cheetah.org:

> *"CCF is currently the only in-situ based cheetah research organization in the world. And since the cheetah cannot speak for itself, researchers, volunteers, farmers and youth are now raising voices of support that will carry the cheetah with us through this millennium. The long-term goal of the Cheetah Conservation Fund is to secure the survival of cheetahs and their ecosystem... Fieldwork produces data that allows all parties to understand not only the role of the cheetah and other predators, but also the sensitive balance of nature... Zoos contribute to the conservation of wild cheetahs through education, research and support of in-situ work. To know how to save the cheetah and its habitat—now we need to understand the animal, and its role in the ecosystem."*

So the work goes on. And, like any good ambassador, Arusha helped launch this grand search for answers, which may, if we have a little luck, just help avoid the unpleasant consequences of another bottleneck.

Chapter Ten
Binky's Legacy

Impressed with the little fellow's persistence,
His heart's in the right place, this elephant senses
He can only hope that this one's head
is not yet too full of societal lead,
or overloaded with cultural rubbish.
Or too much heavy learning, which renders them sluggish.

Binky made headlines in newspapers all over the world in October of 1994, the day he mauled a twenty-nine-year-old female tourist from Sydney, Australia. For those enquiring minds who need to know all the facts of the case, the *National Enquirer* had a special sequence of "action photos" taken by an eyewitness whose "mouth turned to cotton" as he witnessed Binky's "blood-curdling attack." There was much debate in the press concerning who was to blame for this chilling encounter as a "crazed polar bear tries to eat woman alive."

Was this "enraged" bear a potential "danger to society," and if so, who must be made to pay for his appalling crime? Or, was the "victim" just another self-absorbed stupid human?

Surprisingly, in the end, Binky won the vote. Of course, most agreed that the "attack" with his "razor sharp teeth" was a tragedy—except for me.

I saw it all as an unsolicited testimonial for some mighty fine, high-quality veterinary dental care, which he had recently received from our team arranged by Alaska Zoo director, Sammye Seawell.

Bears tend to select small, dark, inaccessible holes as their preferred sleeping quarters. Consequently, I met Binky early one frosty morning looking into his confining, shadowy underground bedroom den behind his enclosure at the Alaska Zoo in Anchorage. I was about eighteen to twenty inches away from the front of his face, doing my professional best to determine if his canine tooth was really fractured, and if so, was it causing him any noticeable discomfort. What I saw, calmly looking back at me, was a surprisingly huge carnivore with a coal-black nose, and a pair of intently focused, bottomless eyes surrounded by 880 pounds of long, translucent, white fur, and absolutely no clue whatsoever about the health of his dentition.

Polar bears are unique among carnivores in that they do not display facial expressions, like snarling or growling, as a notification of intent to act. They always look cute, cuddly, relaxed, and loveable, right up to the moment they lean forward, bite your face off, and calmly start eating you for lunch. And that is one of the main reasons they are rarely seen in circus acts. They are very difficult, if not impossible to read, until it's much too late to do anything about it.

Binky was a large, mature, male polar bear. He was also very popular with the public. The slightly smaller female, who lived with him, was known as Nuka. Both had been rescued from certain death by Alaska's fish and wildlife authorities as yearling cubs. They were sent to the zoo to be cared for, and raised as public relations ambassadors, like the cheetah Arusha, only this time for Arctic wildlife. They were visited by thousands, loved by all, and posed for thousands of photographs each year.

Polar bears are by far the largest, strongest and most cunning predators in the Arctic, and they range all along the northern polar ice floe. They are also very agile, very fast, and very powerful, excellent swimmers. Their skin is naturally black, and their white fur is actually composed of hollow, translucent strands of hair in order to provide maximum protection from the sub-zero cold. Moreover, all of these hollow hairs also help keep them afloat in the water.

Technically speaking, the term fur is generally confined to mammals with very thick body hair. Therefore, all fur is composed of individual hairs. But not all hairs can be called fur.

The average full-grown male will often exceed 1000 pounds, and when standing upright on its hind legs to look around, it can look a large bull elephant directly in the eye. On all four legs, polar bears will measure eight to nine feet from the front of their black nose, to the tip of their short little tail. All of this bulk can, in a single bound, easily leap across a twelve-foot fissure in the ice.

They are indeed a fascinatingly accomplished "Super Bear." And, they all seem to know it.

When swimming they stroke the water with only their front legs, using their fourteen-inch-wide front paws like a wide hinged paddle or oar. They use their back legs as a rudder. Although they are not as agile in the water as a sea lion, they can give everything else an honest run for its money. Polar bears prefer to live on the pack ice. They are true marine mammals, and usually spend a large portion of their lives miles out in the ocean far away from solid land.

My old fisherman friend Dick Lynch told me the story of his only encounter with a polar bear one winter, while out in the sea aboard his commercial fishing boat over a hundred miles off the southern shoreline in the Gulf of Alaska northwest of Icy Straits. It was a couple of hours past midnight on a clear, cold, calm, early morning. Dick was sipping his ever-present cup of hot black coffee in the wheelhouse of his fishing boat pondering the uncertainties of spending so much of his life so far out in the ocean dodging large chunks of drifting sea ice.

Suddenly, the Molly lurched and rolled to starboard, like she'd hit a submerged mass of ice or tangled with some of the flotsam and jetsam that prowls the ocean's surface. Bolting out of the cabin's starboard door, he headed aft, only to come face-to-face with a huge polar bear trying to climb aboard his vessel. He quickly grabbed an oar off of the nearby skiff, and smacked the bear's right paw as it grasped the slippery transom rail. A brief but ferocious battle ensued. By the time his only shipmate, Red, reached the commotion, the bear had dropped back into the rolling sea, and was slowly drifting out of sight in the vessel's wake heading back towards the wandering ice floe.

Polar bears are basically solitary hunters with the stalking prowess of a jungle cat. But they are also exceptionally strong swimmers and fast runners when motivated. They have been observed overtaking a galloping reindeer on land. Various Arctic explorers and whalers have recorded countless stories of their incredible hunting skills. Bearded and ringed seals make up the mainstay of their diet, when they're on the pack ice. In summer, when they come ashore to molt, they are completely omnivorous, adapting their diet to that of their close relatives the brown bear, eating grass, lichens, blueberries, lemmings and spawning salmon, which they scoop from the narrow channels and pools with a quick flick of their huge paws. There have even been stories of polar/grizzly hybrid crosses.

The females will generally mate in April. Implantation can be delayed until September, and birth occurs in the dead of winter inside a dark, warm, snow cavern, which she prepares in the snow pack on the side of a hill for her three- to five-month winter hibernation. In the spring, her two to four cubs will each weigh about twenty to twenty-five pounds, but their mother will have lost as much as 500 to 700 pounds during her winter fast. Mother polar bears protect and feed their cubs for the next two years, while they grow and mature. She teaches them how to hunt, by passing along her favorite family tips, sites and skills, which she learned from her mother. Females generally mate every three years or so.

Polar bear population estimates are very difficult to determine with any real accuracy, because of their solitary, wandering ways. It's safe to say that humans and climate fluctuations are no doubt the bear's greatest challenges. However, it is also important to note that these bears have lived and evolved over the millennia in a very hostile, unforgiving, and extremely variable environment. Adrift on the ice floe, polar bears have been known to survive drifting 500-plus miles across the sea from Greenland to Labrador. Consequently, the education of humans concerning the true lifestyle and habitat requirements of these animals is one of the principal and important objectives of modern zoos. Media sensationalism is no longer a trusted or dependable authority concerning the truth about these animals.

The two bears at the Alaska Zoo normally consumed a dependable source of fresh Pacific herring supplemented with a fishmeal additive, providing all of their essential metabolites and nutrients. They were a pair of fine, healthy, and well-cared-for animals. However, they did not get to eat their regular allotment of fresh sealskin, which naturally flossed their teeth, and kept their mouths squeaky clean. As a result, like so many humans, over time, they developed the typical range of mammalian periodontal-related oral problems. Binky also fractured one of his canine teeth, as many other carnivores tend to do, in the wild as well as in captivity.

Dr. Riley Wilson, staff veterinarian for the Alaska Zoo, correctly diagnosed the situation as soon as it became clinically evident, but did not have all of the special equipment and instrumentation on hand to properly resolve the problem. So, looking for some help, he contacted one of his professional zoo vet colleagues, Dr. Oosterhuis at the San Diego Wild Animal Park. In due course, Dr. O assembled his team, with Dr. Stan Perkins—an M.D. anesthesiologist at Sharp Hospital in San Diego—assisting with the anesthesia, and me with my dentist friend, and occasional assistant, Dr. Lynn Shepard—another dentist—to evaluate and help resolve their dental problems. Within a matter of a week or so, we were all on our way to Alaska, to attend to the needs of these two locally famous bears.

Several periodontally involved molars were removed; all four of Binky's canine teeth were treated with root canal therapy, and restored with one of the new light-cured, dental composite resin materials. The prescribed antibiotics once again worked their magic, and in short order both bears were back in top shape. For Binky, this meant a renewed interest in stalking and hunting stuff.

Predictably, on October 18th, 1994, another self-absorbed, inattentive human provided the opportunity he had been looking for. This tourist ignored multiple warning signs, and "climbed over two chain-link fences with her camera to get close-up pictures of a 1600 pound polar bear, who appeared to be sleeping." With predictable success, Binky got his tourist. The press got its story, and we got an unsolicited testimonial for our quality dental care.

What was generally overlooked in the process was the fact that animals are maintained in captive environments for several specific reasons. Among the most obvious is the education of humans concerning issues like habitat usurpation, and destruction, as well as to teach the facts that wild animals are not pets, but they are indeed wild animals; and most importantly, that humans are obligated to follow a few of the basic rules of life on this planet—just like all of the other animal life-forms. Even though errant human misbehavior does not always result in the loss of life, as it so often does with other free-ranging animals, it does directly contribute to a gradual reduction in the overall quality of all of our lives over time. Regardless of how it eventually manifests, disregard for the basic rules of life—or a general lack of civility—is sooner or later noticed by someone; and gets punished one way or another.

Several years ago, one of my employees gave me a poster that states, "All I ever needed to know, I learned in kindergarten." The need to respect our planet and its wildlife, as well as each other, is one of those essential kindergarten lessons. Unfortunately, I have the nagging feeling that more than a few of our brethren have flunked this essential kindergarten lesson.

Several years passed, and another one of life's inexplicable challenges resulted in the interruption of the normal herring food source for Binky and Nuka.

The Exxon Valdez oil tanker ran aground contaminating a portion of Alaska's coastline and fishing grounds, and for a short while, negatively impacted the local supply of fresh herring. As a result, Binky and Nuka's diet was altered to the only other comparable commercially diet available.

This replacement herring was shipped frozen from a distant source on the Eastern Canadian coastline. This eastern supplier did not have a good history of dependability, but there was no other readily available source during the early days of the emergency. Soon, another series of human errors resulted in a decrease in the cleanliness at the replacement product's processing facility; and this was quickly capitalized upon by the ever-present local cockroach population. In short order, frozen cockroach bodies became incorporated in the replacement frozen herring feed product, purchased for the Alaska bears.

The cockroach has survived on our planet for over 100 million years, and according to some authorities, they are among the most likely inheritors of the planet, if and when the sum of our collective ineptitude finally overpowers Mother Nature, and can no longer be ignored.

Cockroaches are also a common intermediate host for a microorganism known as *Sarcosporidia*. This means that these little bugs carry the disease organism, like mumps, typhoid, AIDS, or hepatitis, but they are not personally infected by the disease process. These little microbes survive by encapsulating their offspring inside a tough little time-capsule-like cyst, known as a "spore." Spores are capable of withstanding all sorts of environmental adversity, including the digestive juices of a cockroach stomach. Spores can also survive the processing mechanisms and freezers of many commercial feed manufacturers. As a result, both Binky and Nuka became infected, in exactly the same way that many human tourists discover Montezuma's Revenge on a vacation trip into Mexico. And, within two weeks of their contamination, both bears died of a painful, antibiotic-resistant, intestinal disease known as *sarcosporidia enteritis*.

In spite of the untimely and unfortunate deaths of these two bears, theirs was not just another pathetic end to an unproductive animal life in captivity as some observers would proclaim. The clinical challenge to find preventive options, early identification, and develop an effective treatment protocol for tooth-related jaw infections resulted in a concerted effort to focus our clinical research on these objectives.

Motivated by Binky's untimely death, during the next 10 years, we treated and documented dozens of related cases in multiple species, including an elephant, a domestic horse, a very small Zulu suni antelope, an Artic walrus, and an assortment of other exotic antelopes like the rare black faced impala (see appendix C for a partial list of species treated). Our objective was to develop a more effective clinical protocol for the treatment of jaw infections of dental origin often referred to as "lumpy jaw" infections. After considerable time and effort, we finally worked out a reasonable solution, which we identified as the "beta–infusion technique with compound apicoectomy." This work was published in 2002 and 2005 as "Lumpy Jaw in Exotic Hoofstock – a Histopathalogical Analysis," along with Drs. Oosterhuis and Benirschke (see Appendix B - 30 and 31).

Our periodic trips to Alaska and elsewhere not only enabled us to provide much-needed veterinary care to deserving animals, but they have also confirmed the effectiveness of our multi-disciplinary, team approach to treating oral disease.

As a further bonus for me, these trips have also provided Dr. O with the opportunity to infect me with the fly-fishing virus. To date, I have managed to catch all of the major Alaskan sport fish, except the Dolly Varden trout, on my lightweight, Walton Powell hexa-graph fly rod. We've also managed to dip into some of the best fly-fishing waters around the world, as we go about our business.

On one occasion, after we had completed our assigned clinical responsibilities at the Alaska Zoo, Jim and I went fly fishing for king salmon far off the beaten path along the Susitna River drainage basin, northwest of Anchorage. As I was sitting quietly over a deep hole along the eastern bank of a narrow channel, a good-sized salmon suddenly took my line. Jim quietly released our mooring near the hole, and worked our boat over to the gravel bed along the western bank. While I was busy trying to land my prize king in the bright daylight at 12:45 a.m. in the morning, a patrolling Fish and Wildlife Officer stopped by to check out the activity. Needless to say, he asked to see our fishing licenses. In my haste to get onto the river that morning, I had left mine in our room at the lodge. With great skill, Dr. O began chatting with the approaching officer. As soon as he got close enough to see our faces, he said,

"Hey, I saw you guys on the news the other day. Aren't you two part of the group that operated on the polar bear at the zoo?"

Jim acknowledged that we were, and with the aid of a joke or two about dentists in general, the officer said he would "cut me some slack this time," because he couldn't believe that anyone who was "smart enough to operate on complicated zoo animals like the polar bear, would be dumb enough to go fishing without a current license in his pocket."

Education of all concerned is also an essential and necessary element to the understanding of our interactive and interdependent roles with the other wildlife with which we share this little blue planet we called Earth. Over the years, all of us have participated in dozens of televised segments of varying lengths, all of which have contributed something to this educational process. I have always been impressed with the power of television to influence behavior. Repeatedly, I have seen firsthand how it works. When our work with polar bears in Alaska, and at the Detroit Zoo, made it onto *CNN Headline News*, we received reaction from all over the country. On one occasion, I participated in four segments of *Animal Express*, hosted by Joan Embery for the San Diego Zoo, highlighting the role of dentistry in the veterinary medical care of animals. One afternoon a few weeks after completing one of these segments, I was hosting some out-of-town friends on a road trip south of the border. As we were walking through the bar at the Rosarito Beach Hotel south of San Diego along the west coast of Baja California, and we were suddenly greeted by my face on the television screen over the bar proclaiming the value of prompt, comprehensive dental care for animals. While eating dinner later that evening, I overheard a discussion at one of the adjacent dinner tables initiated by the earlier TV presentation.

We have created, over the years, segments for numerous television programs, which have aired all over the world, including a half-hour program for Japanese National Television called *We Are # One*. In 1983, we prepared an article for one of the publications of the American Dental Association called *Dentistry 83*. I was told this article on veterinary dentistry was sent to every dentist and dental student in the United States, and it helped precipitate a great deal of awareness, discussion and a keen interest in the subject of veterinary dental care.

When my first child was about to enter kindergarten school, I found and read a small book titled *Teaching as a Subversive Activity*, which addresses these issues of learning. This little book taught me that education is a process. It is not just a series of isolated events.

Biologist William Beebe expressed it this way:

> *"For in the end, we will conserve only what we love,*
> *we will love only what we understand, and*
> *we will understand only what we are taught."*

All of us are taught by what we see on television, in newsprint, in the movies, and by our particular sequence of educators. I believe one of the inherent obligations of serious professionals in the field of caring for animals, is to contribute something positive toward this body of educational material. The professionals I work with do this. And, I have tried to do the same by providing easy access to our clinical work via the ever-present eye of both the still and video media, and by encouraging easy access to our work along all avenues of the media and the Internet.

Practical, usable knowledge comes to us in small bite-sized chunks of information. All advancement in understanding is slowly marked by a series of small steps as these chunks of information come together to establish another pathway of further comprehension, and hopefully more understanding. I perceive it as something akin to working on an ever-expanding paint by number painting.

Binky, the Alaska Zoo's polar bear, established his legacy with his bite-sized contribution to the advancement of veterinary dental technology, care and understanding. In the process —and in his own unique way—he focused a small international beam of bright light on the issue of personal responsibility.

Binky and Nuka lost their lives to an avoidable, miserable, cockroach-vectored disease, because someone failed to learn and remember their lessons of personal responsibility.

Fortunately, many others have learned it, and practice it with great devotion and integrity.

Chapter Eleven
An Elephantine Challenge

This student feels, "there are flies in my face!"
And waving the swarm away with some grace;
She encounters abruptly the elephant's tail.
She stops, and examines it, in utmost detail.

This, she declares, is a useless appendage.
It obviously has no essential advantage.
In fact, it could cause a great deal of trouble.
Better remove it!! Right now!! On the double!!

Soon this student becomes even bolder,
and, as time passes, she grows even colder,
her desire to amputate grows more determined.
Among all the others, she's soon known as the "sturgeon."

When I was just a little lad in Seattle, our family frequently went for an all-day picnic outing at nearby park at Green Lake or to the zoo on the weekends. Each trip to the zoo would focus on a specific group of animals. My brother and I would select the animal(s) of interest for the occasion, and then we would all spend some time looking and learning about these particular creatures. The aviary, the monkey house, feeding time at the big cat house, or Prince Albert's beaver pond were all visited and enjoyed with some regularity. And then there were the elephants.

My earliest perception of elephants was that they were the smartest animals at the zoo. I knew this because they could give me "The Look." My mother also knew how to give us The Look. She usually did it whenever my brother or I were about to get into trouble. So, we knew a lot about The Look, regardless of where it originated. However, with the elephants, it always seemed to happen whenever I was near them. A slow, deliberate, movement of their heads often accompanied their Look, as one or two of them solemnly turned to watch me as I approached or walked nearby. At the time I had no idea what it all meant, if anything, nor if I was the only one who recognized or even got their Look. In any event, as I remember it, the whole encounter always seemed rather serious, and a little spooky. Not scary enough to want to avoid altogether, however, yet somehow mildly intriguing.

For me, the combination of The Look and their tracking eye-contact movement was a bit hypnotizing. I knew immediately, they knew something I didn't know. Just as my mother always knew things about my brother or me, like when we did or were about to do something she didn't approve of. That intense, direct look from the eye of those huge animals made me think that they were trying to pry some deep secret from my mind. Even later in life, The Look from an elephant feels to me much like the pinning stare from a leopard or tiger as it focuses to leap upon its prey. As a consequence, when as an adult I began to get involved with exotic animals, I tended to avoid the subject of elephants, and hoped that perhaps my path and theirs might not cross with any regularity.

Obviously, the tooth fairy had other plans, because it didn't work out that way at all.

Photo by Ron GRrison

My good friend Ron Garrison, for many years the director of the photo lab at the San Diego Zoo, took this photograph of two elephants in Africa. Each had lost a tusk, one the right, and the other the left. Ron told me they constantly traveled together in order to make a more efficient "two tusked" pair.

This is very similar to what Lucky and Maya did in their San Diego Zoo elephant enclosure, thus making my oral exam of Lucky's mouth much more nerve-racking and difficult for me.

AN ELEPHANTINE CHALLENGE 103

In the early 1970s, I was standing in the back of a crowd of students in the parking lot on the west end of the vet school building in Davis, the day Dr. Murray Fowler first used a new narcotic immobilizing drug, M-99, on one of Howard Johnson's elephants. As the elephant literally collapsed in a heap of avalanche debris on the ground, nearly crushing his keeper in the process, I watched in awe.

The elephant mystique I had harbored from my youth was suddenly replaced by intellectual curiosity. Immediately, I suspect, the elephant spirits began preparing my first elephant encounter of the close kind at the Sacramento Zoo.

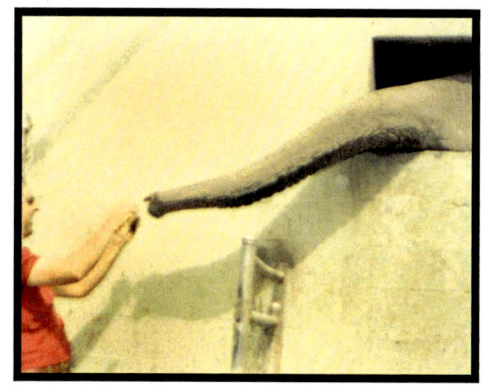

My next significant elephant encounter began to unfold in 1973 on the day I was introduced to Buster the camel at the Sacramento Zoo, described in Chapter Three. Just a few moments earlier, his veterinarian had administered the M-99 immobilization drug. At the first solid clinical sign, Dr. Hendrickson asked me to hold onto and help him guide one of the ropes he'd fastened around both of Buster's rear legs. We were in the process of trying to influence where Buster's immobilized body would finally come to rest in his hot dusty enclosure. It turned into a bit of a rodeo act before Buster finally landed in the middle of the paddock. I had become very focused on my role of helping to locate this 1200-pound animal in a mutually acceptable, safe position.

Intently focused on Roy's instructions, I was determined to deliver my portion of the task of keeping Buster's front end directed toward a cinderblock wall at the back of his paddock yard, and away from the fence along the front of his enclosure. I was leaning backward, gripping the rope, while the heels of my boots dug into the dusty soil. In due course, my back swung toward what I knew to be a large, solid barrier wall made of cinder blocks defining the back border of Buster's enclosure. I readjusted my footing again, and tugged both of us further away from the front fence, as hard as I could. Our tug-of-war quickly reached a stalemate, and I was soon standing quietly holding a steady tension on the rope with all of my strength as Buster continued to fade into unconsciousness.

From the files of David A. Fagan

At top, the author, at extreme right, is helping Buster find a mutually convenient location to come to rest for his dental procedure. On the bottom, the author is introducing himself to an inquisitive elephant trunk extending through an air vent in the wall at the back of Buster's paddock.

Just as I started to think we were winning the war, I heard a menacing, hissing sound coming from behind me, and felt a musky rush of warm air on the back of my neck. In my mind, it sounded and felt exactly like the hissing sound of a huge snake about a foot away from the back of my head. Once again, I instantly froze in my tracks. I am not very fond of large snakes.

The author Carl Sagan in his book *Speculations on the Evolution of Human Intelligence* suggests the hissing sound of a reptile is one of the "primordial danger sounds common to all mammals." As far as I'm concerned, he's correct. I quickly checked the ground around my feet, saw nothing, felt another warm puff of moist air on the back of my neck, and jerked my head to the right to see what was about to attack me. In front of my face was what at first did look exactly like the open mouth of a huge snake. I jerked away, holding the line tight, to discover that the "snake" was, in reality, the tip of an elephant's trunk. It took a moment for my mind to grasp the reality of this absurd situation. How in the hell could there suddenly be an elephant in the paddock with us?

Following this now slowly writhing object away from my face, I recognized that the body of the creature that belonged to this snake-like mouth next to my face was on the other side of the twelve-foot-tall cinder-block wall just behind me.

An elephant on the other side of the wall had stuck its trunk through a small ventilation hole near the top of the wall, and was trying to determine what was causing all of the commotion in the normally quiet yard outside the wall of its bedroom. The whole episode seemed to pass very quickly. I regained my composure; moved out of range; refocused my attention on our camel rodeo; and soon, I was busy dealing with Buster's filthy mouth. The elephant was forgotten.

Well, not completely. Repeatedly during the following months I found myself reflecting on that afternoon, including my sudden introduction to this strange elephant body part.

At one point, I actually became a little disappointed that I hadn't been able to remember more about this strange event. I began visualizing how this nasal extension of the elephant had been quietly searching up and down my torso sensing... what?

What could this animal "see" with its trunk? How had it perceived my presence? Conversely, without seeing the rest of the elephant's huge form, and not being subjected to the riveting gaze I dreaded from my youth, I was now able to consider the elephant intellectually, from a different point of view.

This experience personalized for me the Sufi tale of the blind men examining an elephant. The many versions of this often told traditional tale relate the story of a group of blind humans, who are trying to identify the true essence of a passing elephant using only their senses of touch, smell and hearing. In my version of this tale found at the beginning of each chapter of this book, I identify them as blind medical students, and the elephant gets to express his thoughts as well. Each blind human obtains a completely different perception of the animal, because of the elephant's great diversity of body parts. In my strange elephant encounter that afternoon in Buster's paddock, the elephant was the blind explorer trying to identify me with only its sense of smell. Thankfully, it didn't evolve into a touching episode before I realized what was happening.

I have often wondered what that elephant learned about the sweaty, noisy little biped she discovered on the other side of her enclosure that hot August morning. Somehow, for me the experience seemed to overshadow some of the uneasiness I had previously harbored toward elephants. It had leveled our playing field, so to speak, and I realized I had become very interested in learning more about these unusual and inquisitive animals.

My next significant mental encounter with elephants occurred nearly ten years later at the Marine World Africa/USA Park, when it was located in Redwood City south of San Francisco. I was working again with Drs. Marty Dinnes and Ron Gutter on Ron Whitfield's large group of all-male African lions. Our operating team of four or five always stayed at one of the nearby hotels, while working on two or three lions each day. This work with Ron's lions was the subject of an article in the *Journal of the American Dental Students Association* titled "Veterinary Dentistry: Preserving Exotic Animals through Clinical Care, Research, Education and Teamwork" (see Chapter Two and Item 14 – Appendix B).

Ron also had five elephants. One of them was a huge African bull known as Samson, who, it turned out, was the tallest elephant in the United States at the time, at around fifteen feet. All five of Ron's elephants, including Jenny and Samson, occupied a very nice sheltered bedroom area across from the rolling runway chute Ron used to move his lions back and forth from their bedroom area to their working area in the park's nearby show arena.

In order for us to get back and forth from our vehicle to our makeshift dental office operating room, all of us had to walk along the chute holding the lions, and as we did so, pass in front of the shed holding the five elephants. Regardless of what they were doing at the time we passed, the elephants always stopped, and gave us The Look as we approached. Generally, one if not all of them would extend their trunks, and sniff at us as we passed along in front of them.

It was an opportunity to observe them as they tried to figure out what was going on, but for me it quickly became a rather disconcerting distraction. For some unexplained reason, my childhood memories resurfaced, and each passing became another primordial elephant gauntlet. We routinely passed back and forth in front of these elephants at least half a dozen times each day for close to a week, and every time, the elephants would reach out, and get a whiff of us, or blow a puff of hot moist air and/or straw our way.

Samson made me the most nervous. He would stick his trunk out like the others, pretending that it was at maximum extension. As soon as I passed into his strike zone, he would suddenly stretch it out an extra three feet or so, and gently tag me with a sniff.

In order to avoid or minimize his gentle tagging, I tended to crowd toward the lion's chute as I passed, but this always produced a snarling commotion from the lion's enclosures as I was then invading their space—just to let me know that they also knew I was passing by, and that I was still an unwelcomed interloper as far as they were concerned as well. They too could play this game, and tag us whenever they really wanted to. Very quickly, I was threading the needle between irritating the lions, or getting tagged by the elephants. Both groups of animals were very clearly playing with us. During the week we were there, Samson had managed to train most of us to behave according to his liking. He ensured that we all behaved respectfully, each and every time we passed him.

I didn't particularly like the feeling of being played with, but I damn well did my best to not to let it show. I began paying more attention to each passing by making silent, mental notes of my observations. I'm sure Samson knew he was making me nervous—and I'm also quite certain he understood I realized he enjoyed doing so.

During the intervening years, I have come to understand them much better. At this point in my life, I have actually evolved a very strong personal commitment to their care and conservation. I now have enormous respect for elephants, and on occasion, suspect they are much more intelligent than a large number of the humanoids I've encountered over the years.

My first elephant oral surgery, or more specifically first elephant molar extraction surgery, involved a female Asian elephant known as Lucky, and occurred at the San Diego Zoo in 1981. With the clarity of 20/20 hindsight, this procedure was absolutely, without any doubt,

DENTIST GOES ANIMAL 106

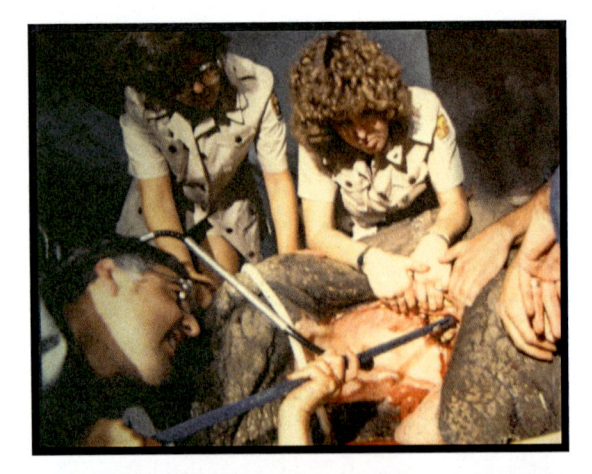

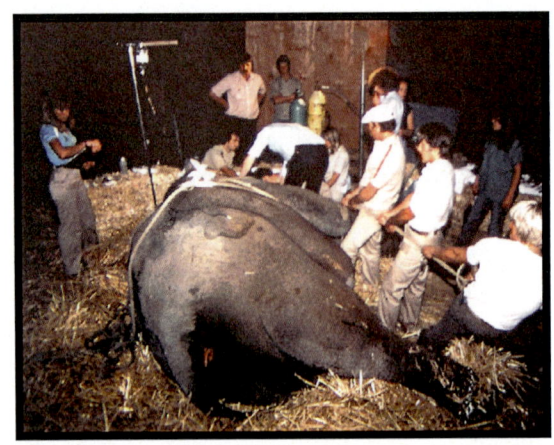

Above on the top left, in 1981, the author is utilizing the second of four progressively larger industrial-strength crowbars to dislodge a deformed fragment from elephant Lucky's molar. Lucky's bloody deformed tooth fragment is seen in the lower middle image, and the cleaned up deformed tooth is seen on the lower left. Approximately one year later, as seen at top right, I'm doing it again with another elephant, Jenny, in Northern California, and her equally deformed molar is seen in the bottom right image.

---

the most physically demanding and difficult surgical procedure I have ever undertaken. I suspect a more rational human dental surgeon would have declared it their last elephant, as well. It occurred with the help of a fellow by the name of Red Thomas at the west end of the old mesa elephant yard just outside the yard door to the elephant barn at the San Diego Zoo in May of 1981. Red, the lead elephant keeper, had noticed what appeared to be a retained segment of a used-up tooth in the process of exfoliating or being shed. I was asked by Dr. Phil Robinson, the zoo's veterinarian at the time, to go down to the elephant barn, talk with Red, take a look at Lucky, and determine what if anything needed to be done about her apparently insignificant teething problem.

I was eager to learn exactly what the task of elephant dentist entailed. As a consequence, before I met Red and our patient, I spent a good deal of time at the nearby UC-San Diego library familiarizing myself with elephant dentition in general. Lucky had been a circus elephant, I learned. About twenty years previously, she had been very well behaved around humans, but over the years, she had assembled a plan to take more control of her situation. She had worked out an arrangement with one of her companions, another female elephant by the name of Maya. The two of them were, essentially, inseparable. As a consequence, together, they could be double trouble in any situation. With this finely tuned approach, they tended to rule their living quarters with a rack of four tusks.

Lucky wouldn't hold her trunk up for more than a few seconds at a time. As a result, I couldn't see into her mouth very well. Red would ask her to put her trunk up; she would do it, and then immediately begin to slowly drop it down a bit. Red would immediately give her an apple, she'd eat it, and then we would do it again. Essentially, she had reversed the tables, and was now training Red how to feed her an apple every time she began to lower her trunk. So I really wasn't able to see exactly what was going on inside her mouth before the immobilization procedure.

So I just stood there looking into her mouth waiting for another fleeting partial view of her dentition whenever she was ready for another apple, and put her trunk in the air. What I remember the most from my first-ever elephant introduction is a vivid image of just how easy it would be to get squashed into the ground, or pile-driven into the dirt with a slap on the head by either Lucky, or her too-close-for-comfort companion, Maya. This never happened, of course, and slowly those thoughts slid back into secondary consideration. Finally after many apples, I saw the small, retained segment of what looked like a normally exfoliating tooth fragment. Immediately, my brain forgot the danger, and began dealing with the mechanics of how to get the job done.

Lucky's problem proved to be a case of concrescence, i.e. a dental abnormality characterized by an unusual overlaying of the roots of at least two teeth by excessive cementum, thus joining the two of them together. The cause can sometimes be attributed to trauma or crowding of teeth. Surgical separation of these two teeth may be necessary if one is to be extracted. The fusion or concrescence process is analogous to the formation of a large burl surrounding a defect on a redwood tree. In Lucky's case, a portion of a second partial or supernumeral tooth bud fused to a normal molar to form one enlarged deformed tooth.

Instead of finding a small worn-off cap weighing a few ounces at most, I found a secondary mass of tooth structure welded onto the main body of Lucky's functional molar tooth. I had expected, and was prepared to remove, a little fragment of tooth from the surrounding soft tissue, and maybe some bone. I was completely unprepared to deal with a fused burl of deformed tooth structure.

With considerable effort, I finally managed to fracture off the defect with the help of two strong, burly men holding a very heavy six-foot steel crowbar, wedged into a narrow "moat." I had finally managed to cut into the normal molar with the help of a half-inch electric drill holding a three-eighths inch carbide cutting tip. The magnitude of force required to remove this burl-like defect had grown from my anticipated few hundred pounds of force to tens of thousands of pounds. Miraculously, we succeeded without breaking Lucky's jaw, or fracturing her skull in the process.

Lucky had also become a very lazy animal, and she certainly didn't get anywhere near as much exercise as any free-ranging or circus elephant. Consequently, she was not wearing away the normal growth of skin on the soles of her feet, and they needed to be manicured or trimmed on a regular basis, just as humans and their pet dogs need to trim or manicure their toe nails and cuticles periodically. Also like many humans or pet dogs, Lucky had gotten to the point where she didn't like to have her feet trimmed, so she stopped cooperating, and wouldn't let anybody touch her feet.

Foot problems are a very common concern with elephants in captivity, and are generally resolved by teaching the elephant to hold its foot up on a stand, while one of the keepers trims its toenails and/or the soles of its feet. Elephants also get ingrown and cracked toenails, again just like humans. On occasion, these can lead to serious local infections and foot abscesses.

These problems must be aggressively treated and resolved early, in order to avoid the commonly fatal consequences of infection invading the bones of the feet, which results from timidity of care. As I discovered during my first elephant oral exam, Lucky would not go along with her planned routine foot-care program any longer. It had gotten to the point where they had to be immobilized in order to have their feet pedicured. Thus, I couldn't perform my first real hands-on oral exam of any elephant until the next time Red scheduled the soles of one of his elephants' feet to be trimmed.

When that opportunity arose, I was immediately awestruck by the magnitude of the problem I was facing. The logistics of trying to do something as simple as hold its massive mouth open, presented a formidable task. I wasn't quite sure how I was going to manage it. My education as an elephant dentist had to begin with the absolute most fundamental basics.

It wasn't too long before I had another opportunity to address the problem, under considerably more favorable circumstances. Treating a medical or dental problem in a properly trained elephant is always significantly safer, and often much easier on both the patient and the clinician, than trying the same treatment on a poorly trained, frightened, or medically debilitated animal. Later in 1981, I had an opportunity to test this hypothesis under actual clinical circumstances with another case: Hattie, one of the elephants at the Circus Vargas.

From the files of David A. Fagan

In the view on the left, Rex Williams and I stand in front of Hattie discussing the immobilization details concerning where it's best to locate our operating area, including details like exactly where to place Hattie's head/mouth, and which side of her body needs to be on the down side. Rex told me to "just drop that little blue towel on the ground where you want her mouth, and I'll put her there." So I dropped the blue towel, and, to our delight and amazement, Hattie's mouth was within eight to ten inches from the towel by the time she was completely immobilized.

Hattie, a thirty-five-year-old Asian female elephant, normally weighed about 7000 pounds. Rex Williams, the elephant trainer at Circus Vargas, and his crew monitored their elephants' physical condition extremely well on a daily basis. In the last eight months Hattie had dropped 1800 pounds in spite of their best efforts. Now, when she was having trouble masticating her food, they knew she needed help, and had arranged to have exotic-animal veterinarian Dr. Marty Dinnes diagnose the problem and recommend a solution when they got into town.

By this time Marty, Dr. Ron Gutter, another exotic animal veterinarian, and I had worked together on a variety of cases, and were all comfortable and compatible with each other's style and clinical skills. Both vets examined the elephant, and our consensus was to set a date to surgically remove Hattie's deformed tooth. Since the circus was wintering for a couple of months at the old Lion Country Safari Park in Irvine, California, it was a mutually convenient time for us to get together and take a look at her. In distinct contrast to Lucky, Hattie was precision trained and very sociable, like all of the twelve elephants who lived, ate, and slept together with Circus Vargas at the time. Hattie's trainer, Rex Williams, was one of the most experienced and well-respected elephant trainers in the world. He was also soft-spoken, friendly and honest. I found him very likeable, and extremely easy to work with.

When I first looked into Hattie's mouth, the upper left first molar extruded from the surrounding gingiva about an inch and a half to two inches, and was rounded like a polished softball. Ordinarily, a normal elephant molar tooth should only be visible about one half of an inch above the gum line, three quarters of an inch at the outside. Normally, its chewing surface is always reasonably flat, and very rough. Looking rounded and deformed, the unusual overgrowth of Hattie's tooth looked like an elongated, smashed softball, and suggested a polished, abnormal dental growth known as an "odontoma."

But an odontoma would have formed during the early developmental phase of the elephant's molars, when the enamel plates were still soft. However, since this problem had just recently materialized, it most likely was not an odontoma. Recent improper wearing of a malformed or improperly positioned tooth seemed to be a more likely cause of Hattie's problem.

"Since we are wintering over now, I can't afford to pay you guys for at least thirty to sixty days," Cliff Vargas informed us, "not until we get back on the road again."

Fingering through another handful of her partially digested dung, I addressed myself to Marty, and said, "Her fresh stool is very course, a sure sign of inadequate mastication. I don't think we should wait that long and risk an impaction colic, which could possibly kill her. She's lost an awful lot of weight."

"We can live with the delay in getting paid, Cliff, but let's schedule the surgery as soon as possible," Marty said. "How about next week?"

"Done," Cliff replied, and so we began our preparation.

This was going to be a rare opportunity to see Rex, a world-renowned professional, handle his elephants during a medical procedure without the distractions of a couple of daily performances.

On Wednesday, December 22, 1981, at 6:00 o'clock on a damp, overcast, foggy morning, we arrived as scheduled, and by 8:30 a.m. we were ready to begin.

Our well equipped, temporary "operating room" was located just a few yards away from our patient's eleven comrades. Rex had selected this familiar spot because he knew Hattie

The Circus Vargas

In the mid-1960s, Clifford Vargas began laying the foundation for rejuvenating the traditional big-top circus into an actual traveling circus tent, and out of the concrete sports arena auditoriums to which circuses had become relegated. He was undoubtedly influenced by his childhood fascination with the circus. He was a frequent spectator at circuses that every year visited his hometown of Livermore, California, where his Portuguese-descended family maintained a farm. It was always the Big Top itself that intrigued Vargas the most, capturing his heart and imagination. "To me, the big top was quite a sight, sitting splendidly on some vast flat field that only the day before was totally vacant and lifeless," he often said. With the sawdust, spangles and billowing canvas, Circus Vargas is a time machine that transports its audience back to the glamour and heart-pounding excitement of the authentic old-time circus. See the Vargas schedule at www.circusvargas.com.

This view clearly demonstrate the earthy arrangement of our dental operating arena in the field. Here, Rex, Marty and I are discussing Hattie's dental problem with some hands-on probing and groping.

From the files of David A. Fagan

would respond better to his instructions if she were closer to the other elephants.

By 10:30 a.m. the sun was up, and had warmed away the night's frosty chill enough in our "operating room" to enable Marty to begin the procedure. All my equipment cases, instruments and tools were positioned within easy reach on a crescent of hay bales around our operating site. On top of them were several vital-sign and EKG monitors, an operational IV drip attached to the handle end of a pitch fork, and a variety of medicaments, supplies, anesthetics and drugs Marty and Ron thought we would need for anything unexpected. We were ready to begin.

Bringing Hattie over to us, Rex swiftly and gently moved her into position and softly spoke the words, "Stretch out, Hattie." She immediately and calmly lowered herself to the ground within five feet of our temporary operating room full of expensive, specialized surgical equipment, next to the little blue towel I had laid on the ground to mark the spot where I wanted to have her mouth positioned.

Selecting an exact location for the animal to place herself required an abundance of trust and communication between Rex and Hattie. It reflected the animal's acceptance of Rex as her trusted herd leader, and many long hours of working together. During Hattie's initial training, every time she responded correctly Rex rewarded her with a carrot or an apple. Eventually she no longer needed these instant rewards, and her positive reinforcement became verbal encouragement, a pat on her shoulder or sometimes just the feeling between man and beast signifying common respect and trust.

This win/win relationship between Rex and his elephants offered multiple rewards for all involved. Hattie's understanding, cooperation and responsiveness to Rex's every thought and word were directly beneficial to her by providing a stress-free lifestyle with quick relief to any occasional problem. Spectators coming to the circus were entertained by the elephants' range of unique behaviors, while they learned about these magnificent animals. But most importantly, Rex could interact with a relaxed harmony in the middle of a group of trusted, old friends all working towards a common objective.

Bringing over an "anchor" elephant from Hattie's group of companions, Rex quickly hooked her shoulder harness to a chain. Placing a rope around Hattie's right front and rear legs, he pulled it under her belly, attached the rope to the chain and whispered, "Lie down, Hattie." These words completed the process.

Our massive patient slowly and carefully rolled over toward Rex, while he carefully coaxed the anchor elephant to move back a few feet. Hattie rolled slowly to the ground onto her right side, while we carefully constructed a straw pillow under her head and ear to prevent unnecessary pressure spots. Her eye was exactly over my little blue towel, and her mouth was within eight inches of where I had requested it.

While one of his helpers returned Hattie's companion to her position along the nearby picket line, Rex lifted and held her left ear into a vertical position, while speaking softly to her. Marty sedated Hattie with an injection of a powerful narcotic analgesic into the large vein on the back of her ear. Within several minutes she was relaxed and groggy. Calmly watching us as we hovered over her, a few minutes later she was quietly at the desired surgical plane of anesthesia.

It was the textbook-perfect induction to an ideal immobilization.

Finally in her mouth, I could closely examine the deformed-looking tooth, and took about ten minutes to probe around and get acquainted with the rest of her oral tissues. All of the soft tissue and the other molars were clinically healthy in spite of this one's unusual appearance. My initial diagnosis of odontoma would have rendered the surface of this upper left molar harder and smoother than it turned out to be. And it should have been considerably more worn down if it was being used at all. This was not an odontoma, and this molar was not being used. It was just a massive crusted cap of moist calculus on top of a normal, but currently non-functional or unused, molar.

From the files of David A. Fagan

In the view above, Dr. Ron Gutter is intently monitoring Hattie's vital signs with the help of a couple of battery-powered vital-sign monitoring instruments in his hand, and sitting on the wooden stool between her legs. Ron was an extremely intuitive and reliable veterinary anesthesiologist. He also took care of many of Hugh Hefner's animals at the Playboy mansion.

Since she was lying on her right side, her upper right molar was now on her down side buried under a couple hundred pounds of sagging cheek and tongue. The rest of the oral examination was much more difficult now because everything was under the extra weight of her flabby tongue and cheek. And I could still find nothing causing the problem. Thinking the problem might be caused by a possible tumor in her throat, I took another ten minutes to thoroughly check everything as far as I could extend my arm around the back of her mouth.

With my arm now up to my shoulder down her throat, I finally announced, "There's gotta be something else causing the problem, something other than this upper left molar. Guys, we need to talk some more."

Marty and Rex looked in her wide-open mouth again, and agreed. It was clear our original plan would not address the problem with Hattie's mouth. This calculus formation was the result of a problem, not the cause of her problem.

Grabbing a loaf of bread for positive reinforcement, Rex called for me and Marty to follow him over to the other elephants, while Ron continued to monitor our patient. We started down

The view above is our operating arena. My assistant Gail King is standing below the IV drip. Dr. Ron Gutter, to the left in the white shirt with stripe, is watching Hattie's respiration, ready to adjust her medication. Rex is kneeling with the cowboy hat, and I'm on the ground in front of Rex. Immediately above me is Tom Ables, one of the three original incorporating directors of The Colyer Institute, and a public relations professional/photographer, who photo-documented the entire procedure. The container in the background was the circus's used manure receptacle, and all of the other onlookers are circus people. Even the animals stood nearby, and watched the entire procedure with focused attention.

the picket line calmly checking all of their opened mouths for a clue to a correct diagnosis. Under Rex's guidance, Marty and I were roaming up and down this row of eleven elephants freely and safely looking them in the eye, and searching their wide-open mouths for any clue to help us figure out a solution to their unconscious companion's dental problem.

Deeply anesthetized, Hattie just lay there motionless. At that time, it was thought that each passing minute diminished our chances of helping her because the weight and size of her lungs tended to compress the down-side lung tissue as it does in other mammals, thus limiting the time an elephant can be down without increased risk of developing major anesthetic complications. Subsequently, we've learned that the elephant's lungs are actually attached to the inside of their chest wall. So they do not have a pleural space. And now we know that time is not such a concern as it is with other large mammalian general anesthetic procedures.

After looking at all of the other elephants' mouths, we determined that all of their upper teeth extruded out of the gingiva about a quarter inch to a half inch or so, in order to function normally with their lower teeth. Hattie's lower molars were properly positioned, but both of her upper molars were hyper-extruded two inches or more.

"Thanks for your help, girls," I whispered softly as I caught the eye of the large female at the end of the picket line.

Returning to Hattie, I said, "I'm sure this is not an odontoma."

Picking up a hammer and a small cold chisel, I gingerly whacked the surface of the crusty upper left molar. Off popped a huge chunk of calculus. It was just polished calculus, about the size of the outer shell of a regulation soft ball. This was now even more confusing, because now it proved this tooth was not being used at all—but why?

Pondering this dilemma, I remembered a leg problem with one of my racehorses we treated at the UC-Davis large-animal hospital. Kicked by another horse, he had a small, painful hairline fracture in his right knee. Compensating by carrying most of his weight on his left, he stressed the tendons on the left front. Of course when pushed, he limped on the left fetlock first, but it was really the right knee and leg with the major injury. This "using the other to favor the injured" concept set me to thinking about other possible causes. We discussed our options.

I decided to recheck the mostly hidden upper right molar now buried in a mass of soft tissue. Now with purpose, and more aggressive direct probing, I finally discovered the small and elusive draining fistulous tract buried deep under a pile of sagging cheek tissue, which led me to a large, deep and completely hidden apical periodontal abscess. This smelly mess on the other side of her mouth underneath the upper molar was the real source of Hattie's painful toothache.

Without further delay, we proceeded to remove the mostly hidden upper right molar, which was much more difficult to reach because it was on her down side. With a Black & Decker half-inch electric drill, I created a moat, or trough, around the tooth. My crow-bar nail-puller turned elephant periosteal-elevator could now be positioned in this moat to provide sufficient leverage. Combined with a half-inch ratchet, and six-inch socket-extender turned elevator attachment I had made after the difficulty of my first elephant procedure with Lucky, I now proceeded to quickly loosen Hattie's tooth.

On my back with my head almost in her mouth, I could precisely position the working tip of a bone chisel, while Marty operated the manual-impact hammer. Rex stabilized the chisel's position up or down for proper leverage, while Ron monitored and adjusted her anesthesia. A grueling hour later, we had successfully extracted an eight-pound, relatively normal-appearing upper right molar. It had a long, sharp, spiky-looking root apex, which had not resorbed properly.

"Damn," Rex sighed under his breath. "She will do anything you ask her, but she can't tell us what's bothering her. This thing musta hurt like hell."

The pressure of masticating her food was driving this sharp root tip spike up into the sensitive tissues underlying the tooth, causing symptoms similar to what we humans often experience with an abscessed wisdom tooth while trying to eat. This was the same problem Trib the gorilla had had. The bad tooth hurt too much to chew on. This was the real cause of Hattie's chewing difficulties.

"I just have to remove this flap of gum tissue on the lateral wall of the right molar, flush out the socket site again, clean up her mouth, and then we're outta here," I informed Ron to give him an idea of how much longer the procedure would last. Ron then began making the appropriate adjustments to her anesthesia cocktail to begin the process of bringing her back home to us.

I was thankful we had solved the problem, and a major part of my satisfaction was being able to discover the true source of the problem before we ran out of anesthesia time to get it resolved.

Under Ron's attentive supervision Hattie's vital signs were strong and very stable. We kept her quiet for another ten to fifteen minutes, while a secure blood clot formed in the deep socket site of the extracted tooth. This was because getting to her feet would drive her blood pressure up, and risk hemorrhaging from the extraction site. This was to be avoided.

In due course, Ron and I disconnected the monitors and IV line, and all of us relocated

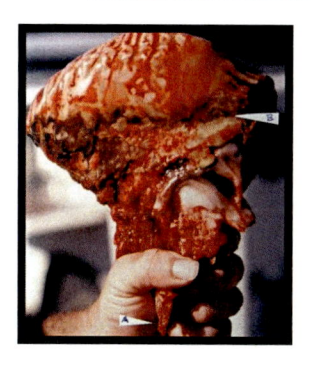

From the files of David A. Fagan

This is a view of the eight-pound molar tooth we removed from Hattie's mouth. More smooth, polished calculus can be seen along the top or upper third of the tooth. The top arrow marks the gum line transition. The arrow at the bottom identifies the sharp dentin spike that was causing Hattie's toothache every time she tried to chew on this tooth. The presence of this sharp non-resorbtion area at the base of the tooth confirms the difficulty she was having with the malposition of this molar.

our gear away from Hattie's legs. Marty continued monitoring the patient, while Rex brought forward two of Hattie's favorite companion elephants, stationing one on each side of her.

"The antagonist drug is in," Marty said, and we moved back a few feet from the patient, aware of the fast action of the potent reversal drug.

All of Hattie's companions on the picket line had been observing us quietly throughout the entire procedure, and the moment she stirred, one of them emitted a tremendous trumpet, helping to wake her from the final stages of sedation. Immediately all of the other animals on the picket line, including the nearby horses, llamas and camels joined in with an ovation of snorting, foot stomping, whinnying and trumpeting. They continued thunderously for about five minutes, while Hattie got her bearings.

From the files of David A. Fagan

Immediately upon standing up, Hattie and both of her companions began probing the socket site of the missing molar inside her mouth. All three animals were very intent during their examination, and seemed to be communicating about the event. Dr. Dinnes and Rex stood nearby watching the three elephants looking for signs confirming Hattie's full recovery. A few moments later, Rex instructed one of his stable hands to lead the three animals around the training ring for a while to walk off the remaining systemic effects of the drugs.

Within a few minutes, Hattie began to rock up onto her sternum. As she moved, her two companions would step closer so she could lean against their legs. One put an encouraging trunk down around Hattie's face, and within a moment or two our patient began to stand. Without any commands from her trainer, her two trusted companion elephants spontaneously snuggled up a bit closer, bringing Hattie up slowly and gently, just as she had gone down.

It was a rare and magnificent sight to behold.

Standing between the two helper elephants for about ten minutes, Hattie regained her balance and composure, and stabilized her blood pressure. All the while, her two companions followed the tip of her trunk until all three of them were probing the inside of her mouth, inspecting her extraction site. Soon she was well recovered, but still standing quietly with her companions. When Marty finally determined she had recovered enough to walk, he asked Rex to have them walk around a bit to shake out any stiffness in her legs. Rex then quietly instructed one of his stable hands to walk the three of them around in the nearby arena.

"Tail up, girls," Rex instructed them in his usual soft, calm voice.

Hattie grasped the tail of the lead elephant on her left with her trunk; her other companion took her tail in its trunk, and the three of them calmly followed Rex and one of his helpers out into the nearby training ring in military precision. All three elephants moved away together in unison, while I stood there stunned. Rex had them walk around the arena for half an hour or so, while we packed up our gear and headed home.

"It was so incredibly smooth and uncomplicated, the way they helped each other when Hattie was waking up at the end," Janet told her brother Pat that evening at the dinner table.

Jan was convinced our hypotheses had been proven without a doubt. I poured myself a glass of Krohn's Ruby Port wine, and wondered if I'd ever see anything like this again. We toasted to the value of maintaining manageable, well-behaved elephants.

It must have been a worthy port, because in the intervening years I've had a great deal more elephant business than I would ever have imagined when I began. Generally among the most interesting and challenging of animals, my elephant cases always seem to require new and innovative equipment developments, specifically intended to resolve another one of a perplexing host of elephant specific clinical issues. And we also slowly learned how to approximate the ease and success of Hattie's immobilization with predictability and grace in some other rather unlikely and difficult circumstances.

In the beginning, I thought that an animal the size of an elephant would have a proportionately large oral cavity or mouth. But, in reality, the elephant's mouth is not very large at all, and there is no extra room for many man-made objects.

The very first elephant dental issue encountered by any attending dentist involves the question of how to hold the animal's mouth open, while looking or working on the teeth. This is actually much more difficult than imagined. The usual bite blocks are either too feeble, too large, or tend to fall out. Ropes work fairly well, but need to be positioned carefully, and often need to be adjusted or repositioned during the procedure. We finally settled on an older style "jaws of life" hydraulic device used for years by the fire departments to open damaged auto doors in highway accidents. We subsequently fabricated a special set of adapters, which attach to the "jaws" to increase the utilization options so I can apply controlled force to the dentition in any desired direction during oral surgery.

Over the years, with each new elephant encounter, we added another batch of tools, grinders, saws, etc. to our elephant stash until we now have a fairly complete rolling cabinet full of essentials, including a wet-dry shop vac from Home Depot, which functions very well as an elephant-sized surgical evacuator system. The quick-connect hose attachments make a very adaptable Water Pik. Inflatable truck tire inner tubes make highly functional pillows and a container full of soft ropes and pulleys round out this portion of our special equipment stash.

The view at top is our hydraulically operated "jaws of life," which is one of the best bite blocks for large animals like elephants, rhinos, etc. Below it is a typical Home Depot wet-dry shop vacuum with a protective face shield, and a set of quick-connect hose units to simplify field use.

In the late 1990s, I was looking for a professional medical illustrator to help with a writing project. This quest resulted in a random dinner meeting one evening at a Japanese dinner house in southern Orange County. One of the attendees owned a trucking business nearby, and we were invited to his warehouse after dinner to sample his favorite sake. In the process

DENTIST GOES ANIMAL 116

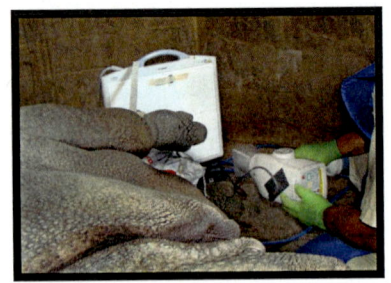

From the files of David A. Fagan

Above, the green-gloved hands of the clinician easily hold and aim a relatively small, portable, battery powered, direct-current, 75 kvp/2mas NOMAD X-ray generator at the digital sensor plate of an EKLIN radiology system. Within a matter of a few seconds, the image on the right appears on the Eklin unit's monitor screen located behind the clinician, and confirms the fractured bone in the rhino's left foot.

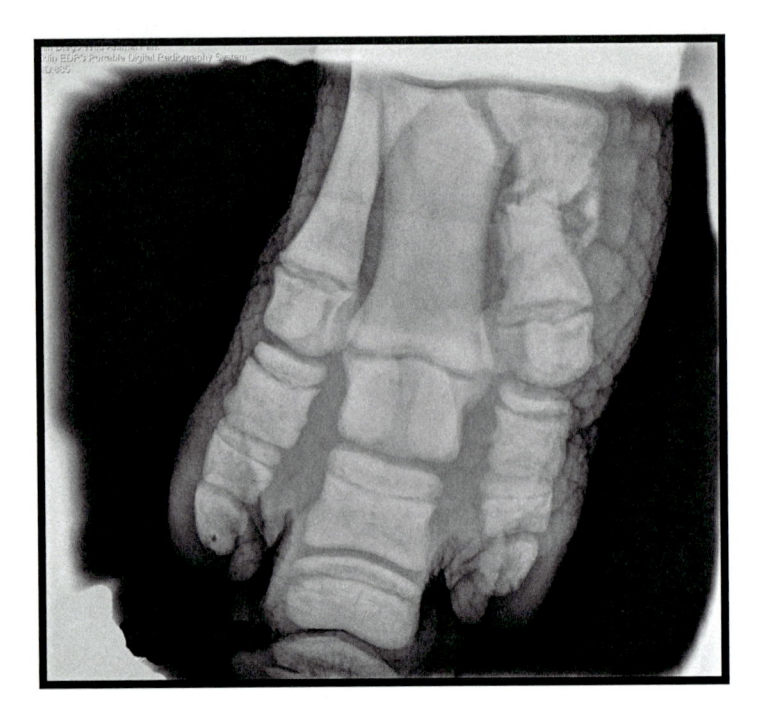

Previously, in order to get an X-ray image of this animal's foot, a five hundred pound traditional X-ray machine had to be positioned in the animal's stall, maintaining both 110 AC current, and proper positioning to expose the view. Then the team and animal had to wait for thirty or forty minutes while another member of the team returnsed to the hospital to develop the images in an automatic processor. Each new image required a repeat of this time-consuming procedure.

With the new NOMAD and EKLIN equipment, set-up and break-down time are just a matter of five to ten minutes, and multiple images can be obtained at the rate of one image per minute until the clinical team is satisfied. These new technologies are having a huge, profoundly positive impact on the quality of clinical care available to all sorts of animals in many new and unusual locations.

---

of entering the back of his place of business, I noticed a pile of thick-walled, clear, 60 mm diameter, soft plastic tubing coiled on a pallet near the back wall. It immediately set me to thinking about the next elephant immobilization we had pending. We sampled his sake, announced our pleasure with his fine taste in after-dinner drink, and I asked if he would like to donate a six-foot length of the plastic tubing to a noble cause. After a lengthy explanation over a good deal more sake, he agreed. And, so began our quest to design and fabricate the worlds first set of elephant endotracheal tubes.

Needless to say, it didn't happen overnight. But after ten years of methodically plowing along, and with the help of a rubber manufacturing facility in the Pacific Northwest, in November of 2006 at the first European elephant school in Hamburg, we were finally able to display the first package of the five sets we made. The Colyer Institute donated one set to Drs. Thomas Hildebrand and Frank Goritz for use in their elephant and rhino research at the IZW (Das Institut für Zoo-und Wildtierforschung/Institute for Zoo and Wildlife Research) in Berlin. One set went with Dr. Zuba to help with the immobilization of bull elephants for a joint sterilization-by-vasectomy study project with Disney's Animal Kingdom, San Diego Wild Animal Park, and CATCHCO in South Africa. And one set of tubes stayed at the Wild Animal

Park to be made available under the direction of Dr. Oosterhuis to any American Assocition of Zoo Veterinarians member with a need to immobilize elephants. The project has proven very helpful, and has enabled both the collection of good, new data concerning elephant anesthesia, as well as helped facilitate the development of Dr. Zuba's unique elephant ventilator system, completing clinical trials as of this writing.

Essentially, I function within a team of specialists in the arena of "technology transfer." That is, we help facilitate the exchange of information, techniques, materials, instruments, and protocols from the fields of human clinical medicine, dentistry, and biotechnology to the disciplines of veterinary medicine, with a special emphasis on exotic animal medicine and veterinary dentistry. Over the past thirty years there have been numerous examples of "stuff" transferred. Obviously, some have been more productive than others.

A recent example involves the clinical application of the new prototype NOMAD, handheld, portable dental X-ray machine developed for use in human dental offices, which we transferred to field applications in veterinary medicine, shown in the photos on the previous page. Anyone who has ever wrestled with a heavy, cumbersome medical X-ray machine, immediately understands why the heavy metal support framework is so difficult to move. The NOMAD machine is small, lightweight, easy to use, and provides a great solution to a longstanding, difficult problem. With the growing clinical acceptance of digital radiography, a compatible, portable, direct-current, X-ray generator is a very welcome addition. We have been working with this product for the past several years, and have clearly demonstrated a new market in veterinary medicine. The NOMAD unit also enables many routine radiographic views to be accomplished without the need for immobilization of the animal. And, when used in conjunction with a digital X-ray sensor system, it significantly reduces the difficulties traditionally associated with radiographic efforts in the field environment.

Needless to say, with the rapidly evolving developments on the human side of clinical medicine, there is absolutely no end in sight to our ability to locate and transfer a variety of practical solutions to many remaining clinical problems on the exotic animal side of the equation.

Chapter Twelve
Elephant Dental School

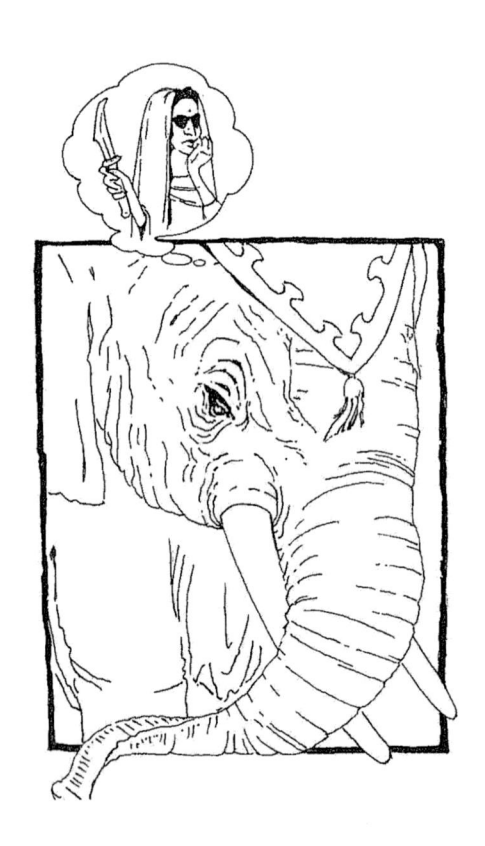

*As he watches this biped, who has much to learn.
This elephant instinctively grows more concerned.
Natural selection does not stand a chance
'gainst a ruthless surgeon with a probing lance.*

Since my introduction to elephant dentistry in 1981, I've participated, directly or indirectly, with the diagnosis and treatment of dozens of additional elephant dental problems, ranging through the entire spectrum of oral issues. These have included severe periodontal and/or peri-apical abscesses, the removal of impacted molars, the treatment or repair of numerous infected, damaged, and/or broken tusks, and three colossal necropsies. These cases have involved young elephants, old ones, and both males and females ranging in age from three to sixty years. Some were California cases, while others came to me from many other corners of the world including Perth in Western Australia, Kiev in the Ukraine, Vienna in southeastern Europe, Tyler in the piney woods of eastern Texas, the frozen earth of Anchorage in southern Alaska during the darkness of the winter solstice, and numerous other points in between.

It wasn't until some years had passed, however, that I slowly became consciously aware of what all this diversity of elephant dental dysfunction meant to both me, and my personal little cluster of enormous patients. I suspect it is rather like asking a woman to discuss the meaning of childbirth during the process. I'm certain a much more balanced perspective emerges with the passage of time. So it has evolved with me, and elephant oral surgery.

Although I have fathered five children, I have never actually had or delivered a child. I have however, helped to "deliver" a calf, several horses, some small dogs—and a number of elephant molar teeth and tusks. It is my experienced opinion that all of these elephant dental procedures have issues very much in common with what I understand about the birthing process.

Each and every time I'm asked to participate in the resolution of another elephant dental problem, a bit of a chill rattles around in the back of my brain.

Fortunately for our team, only one of these elephant surgical encounters proved fatal to the patient. And that animal expired as a result of very bad case of terminal tuberculosis—not because of her oral surgery or related anesthesia. However, even in spite of this one unfortunate incident, more often than not, each case turned out to be something of an accomplishment, adding another, valuable pearl of wisdom to my long string of lessons, all learned the hard way.

Consequently, when viewed before the fact, each new case always presents a daunting, fresh surprise twist or two, wrapped inside an enormous task, involving a minimum of a dozen individuals, and on occasion as many as three dozen.

All of this is so because the dentition of the elephant is exceptional in every respect.

Unlike humans and other mammals, which have only two sets of functional dentition, elephants are issued with the genetic material to grow six successive sets of four functional molar teeth, each with a different predetermined unique size and shape for a total of twenty-four molars, assembled from between 200 to 250 individual, primordial dental plates, which slowly and continuously develop throughout their fifty- to sixty-plus year life span.

Consequently, a thirty-five- or forty-year-old elephant can present with a molar eruption complication involving a brand new tooth, similar to the teething problems characteristic of a six-year-old human.

Furthermore, elephants have only one pair of front teeth, or tusks. These are continuously growing teeth, much larger than, but similar to, the incisors of rabbits, beavers, capybaras and the like. Some elephants, most commonly Asian females, do not have any tusks at all, while others have a pair of small vestigial tusk remnants known as "tushes."

In 1999, we published histopathologic evidence to support the notion that elephants do not have any sensory nerve fibers within their dental pulp tissues. This means that elephants never get the classic toothache. (See item 22 in Appendix B.) However, they can, and on occasion they do, get very nasty and painful jaw infections as the result of broken teeth and/or fractured jawbones.

The molar tooth of an adult African male is about the size of a Los Angeles telephone book. But it is much more densely packed, and can weigh as much as two or three of these phone books. However, it is when one of these huge, iceberg-like teeth has to be removed, that someone has—literally— a very big problem on their hands. The logistics of trying to do something as simple as hold its massive mouth open, presented a formidable task. I wasn't quite sure how I was going to manage it. My education as an elephant dentist began with the absolute most fundamental basics.

My first serious surprise involved the relatively small size of their oral cavity with respect to elephants' overall body size. Their head is huge; their cheeks are massive, wet, flabby and very heavy. Their tongue is equally large, very slimy and slippery, and tends to roll around like a giant, drunken slug. Moreover, everything is very difficult to retract out of the way under all circumstances. And although their teeth are just an enlarged assembly of normal mammalian tooth parts: i.e.: enamel, dentin, and cementum, there was no indication of just how hard an elephant molar was to cut. My first impression was that these teeth were harder than teak hardwood, and had more in common with kiln-fired ceramic material surrounding small slabs of granite rock. Genetically, all elephant teeth are composed of the same materials as all other mammalian tooth structure, including human. And since I'd drilled, cut and repaired thousands of human teeth, I knew that enamel and dentin cuts very well with a high speed, water cooled, carbide, or diamond bur. The problem is that an elephant's tooth was so large, it would require a thousand-fold increase in drilling capability over the puny little human dental drills I had used for so long.

I immediately set about assembling another species-specific set of operative instruments, which I thought would do the trick. But this time they were very large. One of the first essential steps was to make a set of elephant-specific bite blocks. Bite blocks are devices designed to hold the patient's teeth apart. These devices are essential when any dental patient is unconscious or uncooperative. All dentists have them, and most patients dislike them. My first elephant set began with a two-by-six-inch wooden plank, which I cut into a series of triangular-shaped blocks. I made a set of six various sizes all with a thirty-degree taper. I assumed I would be able to pull the elephant's mouth open with a rope, select an appropriate sized block, place it in between her teeth, and it would hold the mouth open. It didn't work that way—at all.

The bite block would stay in place as long as I didn't move anything in the animal's mouth. But the degree of force necessary to do anything with the animal's teeth required a fair amount of pushing and shoving. Consequently, the bite block tended to wiggle loose rather quickly. Although initially it seemed like a very good idea, in reality, they were all useless and nonfunc-

ELEPHANT DENTAL SCHOOL 121

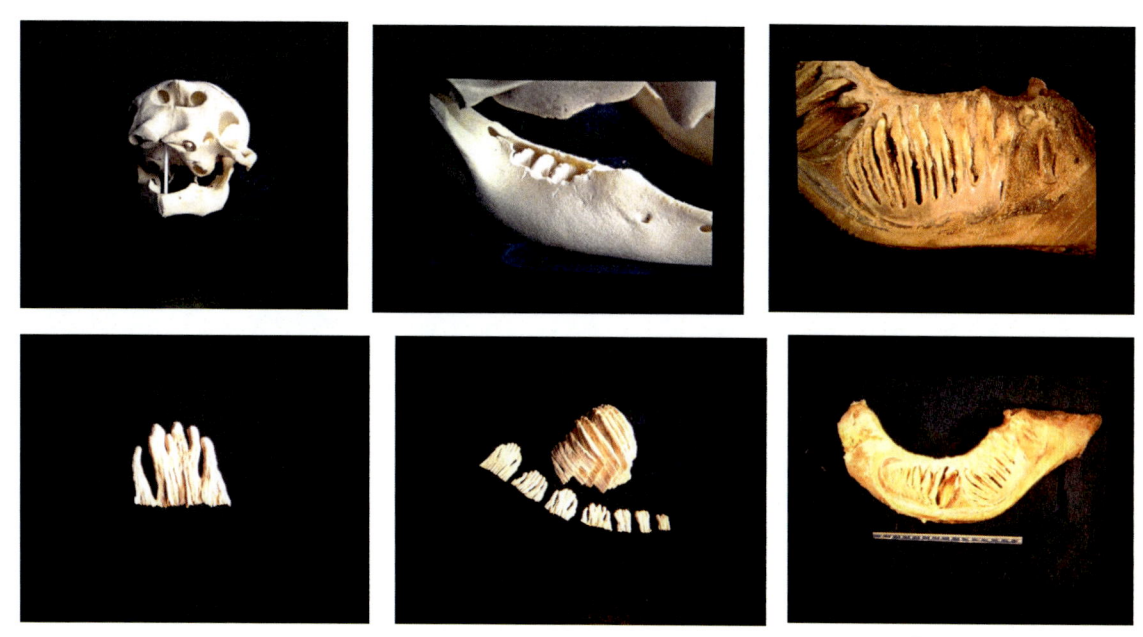

From the files of David A. Fagan

At the top left, a cleaned neonatal elephant skull shows the tip of the developing but not yet erupted left tusk tooth bud. The top middle image shows a row of unique mineralizing enamel plates within the body of the animal's left mandible. In the top right image, two elephant molars develop from the genetic reorganization and mineralization within a gelatinous protein mass in the interior of this sectioned neonatal mandible, similar to that seen in the top middle image. Slowly, a series of fifty to sixty small, thin, hand-shaped enamel structures take shape as seen in the lower left image. As seen in the lower middle image, seven to fifteen little individual plates slowly fuse together to form the first of six continuously growing elephant molars, as seen immediately above this row of seven individual developing enamel plates. In the lower right image, the developing first molar is seen in close up just as it begins to erupt into the oral cavity near the time of birth.

tional. I needed a better alternative. I eventually made another adjustable metal set, which worked a bit better. However, I learned, halfway through my first procedure, that the only sure way to hold an elephant's head still while I worked on it, was to securely tie both the mandible and the maxilla at the base of the trunk to separate steel tie-rings set into the concrete floor or a nearby wall. Subsequently, I now always tie my patients to something solid. Then, with the help of a jaws of life hydraulic device, I open their mouth and secure it with the rope tie-down lines.

My second heavy dose of elephant reality came with the discovery of just how much preparation, difficulty, and trouble is involved in the task of getting an elephant to lie down in a convenient, operative position and location. All animals seem to have a built-in tendency to resist force. If you push them, they push back. If you pull on them, they tug back. Horse handlers have known and used this fact for years to back a stubborn horse into a trailer. When it's time to position an elephant down on the ground for a specific procedure, it is unsafe for all concerned to just let 'em fall wherever they please. Before any immobilizing drug is administered, the animal must initially be secured to and/or within something indestructible in order to hold them in an acceptable position. Otherwise, once the immobilization medications start to work their magic, the animal begins to wander around like a drunk, and could easily position itself with its head crammed into a concrete corner, where you can't possibly reach the parts you need to work on, and they can't move itself once they are down. It may even manage to obstruct its airway in the process making matters impossible for all concerned. Safety demands that the clinicians properly position the elephant before it becomes uncooperative or unconscious. In order to accomplish this, the patient must be able and willing to obey instructions before the procedure begins. Otherwise, the anesthesia team is obligated to get creative and properly tie its patient securely in place in order to muscle the elephant into an acceptable position, before the immobilization drug(s) overwhelm the animal's sensibilities.

A poorly trained, apprehensive, or unmanageable elephant is much more trouble in all respects. As the immobilization drugs go to work the animal begins to get very groggy and unstable. At this time, the animal automatically resists everything, and instinctively struggles against the immobilization chemicals. Invariably, a tug-of-war begins. If all restraint measures are not fully secure, before you know it, the front legs may be heading north, while the back legs are heading south, and what should be a smooth, atraumatic induction turns into a commotion. A major exercise then follows as the immobilization team attempts to keep ten thousand pounds of confused elephant from injuring or killing someone or itself during the struggle to find a mutually acceptable, safe, reclined position.

As I participated in my first elephant immobilization, it immediately became abundantly clear to me that complete, proper control of the entire induction process is an issue of absolute, major importance with any large animal immobilization procedure. On our team, Alan Roocroft addresses these issues with great skill, apparent ease, and nearly always to clinical perfection.

My third major elephant dental surprise occurred when I finally discovered just exactly how hard the elephant's teeth are to cut. I had spent time at the museum. I had studied elephant skulls. I looked at their teeth, and I analyzed the surrounding bony anatomy. From everything I saw, it looked like my first elephant's tooth—Lucky's—was going to be a simple, straightforward removal of a small fragment of worn-down, used-up tooth structure in the process of being naturally eliminated from the mouth, and it would require minimal drilling and/or cutting. The exfoliating fragment appeared to be the final ten percent remaining chunk of the original phone-book-sized tooth structure. What I discovered was: elephants can, and often do, have deformed, damaged, and genetically abnormal teeth.

Developmental abnormalities are a common occurrence associated with the normal dental development process in all species, and regardless of why, how or when they occur, the result is the creation of a deformed tooth of one sort or another as seen in the summary chart on the next page. In Lucky's case described in the last chapter, her tooth was actually deformed by fusion or concrescence during its early developmental phase, resulting in two or more tooth parts joining into one larger deformed structure, which was having trouble moving forward in her mouth.

Early along this path of hard lessons learned the hard way, I was introduced to my fourth elephant dentition surprise. Following the removal of any elephant tooth, there is very little in the way of leftover soft tissue remaining to be utilized for post-operative suturing, or post-surgical socket site closure. Proper oral surgery protocol instructs the clinician to vigorously protect all of the soft tissue surrounding the designated tooth being removed. This is

A Classification of Common Dental Abnormalities

1. Environmental Causes

During tooth development: Enamel hypoplasia – Turner's hypoplasia – Dental fluorosis- Hutchinson's teeth
Destruction after tooth development: Attrition – Abrasion – Erosion – Abfraction- Internal resorption – External resorption
Discoloration caused by: Chlorophyll-rich foods – Tobacco – Tea – Coffee – Chlorhexidine – Congenital erythropoietic porphyria – Alkaptonuria – Erythroblastosis fetalis – Tetracycline – Minocycline
Alteration of eruption: Impaction - Ankylosis

2. Developmental Causes

Abnormality in number: Anodontia – Hyperdontia – Hypodontia
Abnormality in size: Microdontia – Macrodontia
Abnormality in shape: Gemination – Fusion – Concrescence – Talon cusp – Cusp of Carabelli – Dens evaginatus – Dens invaginatus (or Dens in Dente) – Ectopic enamel – Taurodontism – Hypercementosis – Dilaceration – Supernumerary roots
Abnormality in structure: Amelogenesis imperfecta – Dentinogenesis imperfecta – Dentin dysplasia – Regional odontodysplasia

because once a tooth is removed, there remains a very big hole in the jawbone, which must be addressed. Ordinarily, post-operative socket site management protocol dictates the detachment of a portion of the surrounding soft tissue to be re-positioned over the anticipated hole, which is then filled with blood, synthetic bone particles and perhaps other clot forming materials, all sutured securely into the socket site, and thus restricting bacterial access into the exposed alveolar bone (see Appendix B items 15 and 21). This process helps establish a stable blood clot within the bony wound in order to promote what is referred to as "healing by first intention."

With Lucky, we didn't have enough anesthesia time left, in the first place. I didn't have any available soft tissue to reposition, in the second place. And in the third place, the hole in the bone was so large that I didn't know if I could get it done, even if I could have found the materials and the time to do it.

As a result, oral surgery with elephants generally requires that the socket site is left open, and treated post-operatively as an open wound to heal by "saucerization." This leave-it-open approach dictates the pre-operative necessity to be prepared to deal with the legendary complications of a post-operative alveolar osteitis. "Osteitis" is the general term for infection and inflammation of bone. It is sometimes incorrectly referred to as a "dry-socket," and it is similar to the painful dental complication that so commonly occurs following the removal of wisdom teeth in humans. In doctor-speak, this prolonged healing process is referred to as "healing by secondary intention," which implies healing from the bottom up, rather than from the top down.

Consequently, in order to address this problem in subsequent elephant cases, I designed an elephant water-pic-type rinsing device for the keepers to use post-operatively to help keep the wound clean, while it slowly heals. Obviously, this device functions better with some animals than with others.

DENTIST GOES ANIMAL 124

The fifth surprise lesson for me was that the size of the dental instruments I had initially forecast was grossly insufficient to address the size of the problems that routinely materialize in an elephant's mouth. Although I was able to tug, pull and wiggle several thousand pounds of head around, the fact was, I didn't have sufficient leverage, or what is known as "focused mechanical advantage" to get the dental task completed smoothly, efficiently, and in a timely manner.

Fortunately, we did Lucky's procedure in a large, well established zoological facility with easy access to a very well-equipped workshop. I was able to rapidly improvise as we moved along, and somehow, we managed to get the job completed in a reasonable time frame in spite of my initial inadequacies. As a result, in the months that followed, I designed, and fabricated, a complete new set of dental instruments that could be used for just about any oral procedure on an elephant. They reside in my still growing elephant bag of tricks ready for use whenever the occasion presents.

By the time I got to Hattie, who was a superbly well-trained elephant, I was overjoyed to discover just how easy it can be to proceed though an elephant induction procedure—if the animal is well trained and cooperative. Although I had brought up the question of training Lucky at San Diego before we operated on her, the fact was then and still is now, there are substantial economic, political, safety and management-related reasons and concerns that prohibited what's referred to as "full contact" training of elephants. So re-training a behavior isn't really a very practical option with many untrained animals.

Somewhere along the way, my sixth surprise taught me that it could be a relatively easy matter to add a new behavior to a well-educated, cooperative, older elephant. It usually takes about two weeks. On occasion the animal's trainer will utilize another well trained "anchor elephant" to help focus attention to get the task completed in a timely manner. There is no debate involved, if the procedure is necessary for the one animal's health and safety, a

From the files of David A. Fagan

The molar image at extreme left is a typical maxillary elephant molar with its chewing or occlusal surface slightly distorted and facing downward. It is about the size of a Los Angeles telephone book, and is quite heavy for its size. The image in the middle is a normal occlusal surface of an Asian elephant molar for comparison. On the right above is an African elephant mandible showing a typical molar developmental sequence with a small "cap" remnant exfoliating at the front of the animal's right jaw, with a portion of a fully functional molar fused together just behind the cap, and five new molar enamel plates in the process of being fused together in the back of this right mandible.

The two images at bottom right show how the tooth is formed with enamel, dentin, and cementum, and the differences between the enamel patterns on the occlusal surface of the Asian (ovoid shaped) and African (diamond shaped) elephant molar. A number of the elephant dental images used in this book were provided by Alan Roocroft, who has one of the world's finest collections of elephant photos, images, books, coins, and stamps.

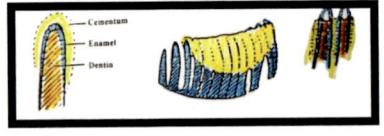

second well-trained helper elephant can and will provide the support, confidence and muscle necessary to get the sick elephant to do what needs to be done. In a matter of a few days to several weeks or so, the sick animal throws in the towel, decides to take the easy way out, stops resisting, and does what it's told to do. To train one elephant with the help of another is a historically well-tested and routine matter. It has a lot in common with teaching human children how to behave in public.

Over the years, because not very many elephants are as well trained as we'd like, Alan Roocroft has become my preferred position-the-elephant expert. Alan is an excellent, experienced elephant trainer with a solid international reputation. One way or another, with very little commotion, he always gets his elephant to assume the proper position prior to immobilization. I remain totally astonished at the ease with which this skilled elephant trainer positions his animal. The whole pharmacological exercise of having a skilled trainer get such a huge animal onto the operating table is less than one-hundredth of the complexity and danger of immobilizing an untrained animal with inexperienced, or less knowledgeable individuals.

Surprise number seven occurred the day I learned that "What you see is not necessarily what you're gonna get." The elephant's mouth is not designed to facilitate human visual access. It is also not possible to see their entire oral cavity at one time, even in the best of circumstances. Normally, as an elephant opens its mouth, the copious soft tissues of its cheek flex inward toward the mid-line in a manner designed to push food onto the biting surfaces of their teeth. Actually, all mammalian cheek muscles are designed to function as a pushing device, working in concert with the tongue to position food onto the biting surfaces of the animal's dentition. During mastication, the cheek muscles are normally stretched taut so that when the teeth close, they slide over its surface, and the cheek doesn't get bitten. The primary musculature of the mammalian cheek is known as the "buccinator muscle," so named from the Latin word for their horn blowers or buglers, who always had very large cheek muscles. The buccinator is normally a very thin, flexible muscle, but it is a very effective structure, designed to improve the function of the elephant's grist mill–like dentition.

Initially, I didn't think it was possible to remove an elephant's tooth if the tooth was on the wrong, or down side. Any look into the mouth of an immobilized elephant will confirm that the entire mass of their downside cheek, tongue and lips are smashed around, against, and nearly completely bury the entire downside dental arcade. There is always very poor access to these teeth and gums. But, over time, I learned it could be done—surprise number eight. In fact, it is fairly straightforward to do, once you learn how to position the head correctly.

I've operated on several elephants outside in the elements, but most often our immobilization procedures occur inside a barn or enclosure of some sort because of weather or security considerations. In reality, it is possible to operate on an elephant just about anywhere, if the team is properly prepared. Properly trained and experienced veterinarians can even begin the immobilization procedure from a helicopter many miles out into the African bush, and many major surgical procedures have been performed way out in the field.

When Dr. Dinnes scheduled the molar extraction involving Ron Whitfield's Asian elephant Jenny, the only area large enough to do the procedure was in an old hay storage barn. Marty had arranged to move Jenny away from her companions, and into this large—but to Jenny very unfamiliar—barn. Elephants are very intelligent animals. Although she was a well trained, cooperative individual, when she figured out she was about to be immobilized, she got very upset very quickly. She arrived calmly into the barn, didn't like what she saw, and became an enormous amount of trouble and a danger to immobilize. In addition, the structure was a relatively flimsy building, as hay barns go, just a covered hay storage shed actually. The elephant could have easily pushed a hole in the wall or caused the entire building to fall down, if she had hit one of the tall six-by-six upright posts. In fact, at one point during the induction, she started to fall toward one of the building's center-row support poles. All of us inside the barn knew that if she had hit the center up-right, the roof of the barn was on its way down to greet us. It was a difficult induction, and immobilization. But, it was a very easy, soft tissue molar extraction once we got to it.

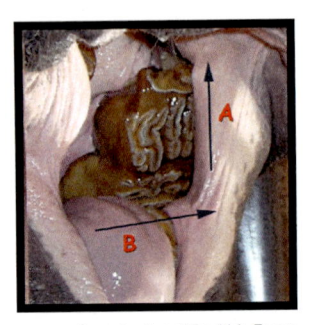

From the files of David A. Fagan

Like any logjam or pile of pack ice, the elephant's molar dentition displays an astonishing array of complex deformities. This image shows a most dramatic 90-degree rotation of just a portion of the enamel plates from the normal "B" axis to the "A" axis. How this happened is completely unknown, but it must have occurred before the plates mineralized. Although this image represents a rare "good look" as compared to the average partial peek, notice how the tongue and lips pull inward to hide the animal's dentition, providing a very limited view.

Although I didn't realize it until some months later, it was actually Jenny who taught me lesson number nine: that the dentition of an elephant has a lot of similarities with an ice- or logjam on a river. One of the contributing reasons why elephant malocclusions tend to occur in the first place is that diets fed in captivity tend not to match the abrasivity found in the diets eaten by generations of that individual animal's ancestors in the wild. Generally, when an offending tooth is removed, the remaining teeth have a tendency to straighten themselves out over time, just like a logjam. Slowly, the natural reparative processes associated with normal tooth eruption sequence takes over, and the rest of the elephant's teeth start moving again into their proper positions. The surgical event itself releases the pressure on individual logs in the logjam, and this release of pressure stimulates the eruption of the next successor teeth. This is exactly what occurred with Jenny. I took out the large right mandibular impacted tooth in March. Two or three months later, the corresponding well-used mandibular molar on the opposite side of her mouth came out, exfoliating naturally of its own accord. A couple of months after that, the new opposing right maxillary molar tooth came in, and by October the opposite left maxillary tooth was replaced and in operational position. Within a year of the initial extraction, Jenny had a complete new set of four fully functional molars.

On several occasions, we came across an astonishing degree of dental malocclusion with molars six to ten inches out of alignment, rotated and/or severely malpositioned. With that amount of malocclusion, our detailed pre-planned treatment plans immediately became another of our "best laid plans go down the drain in a hurry" stories. Unexpected phenomena require flexibility and improvisation at the time of surgery. What I've repeatedly learned over time is the absolute necessity to think fast, stay flexible, embrace creativity, and adjust our plan to respond to particular circumstances as they arise. This lesson has been driven home with each successive case.

On one occasion with another Circus Vargas elephant named Joyce, we were unable to find any contributing cause for her protracted slow weight loss except her malpositioned molars. Following correction of the dental problem, Joyce quickly recovered fully from her anesthetic medications, but then had a heart attack and died from the physical exertion while attempting to stand up afterwards. An extensive post mortem examination revealed a severe human strain of a tuberculosis (TB) infection invading her entire body with only five to ten percent of her pulmonary capacity remaining. Amazingly, this was enough to successfully carry her through the immobilization procedure, but not enough to get her back on her feet afterwards. This case launched an intensive investigation, and on-going study of TB in elephants, which has confirmed that elephants do indeed get TB from humans. Moreover, they do not seroconvert, or produce specific antibodies in their blood in response to the presence of the human TB antigen. Consequently, they do not display expected changes in their blood chemistry, nor do they show any clinical signs or symptoms until death. Nearly ten years later, the scientific community finally produced a reliable new clinical test, which now enables these infected animals to be identified.

Asian cow: Annabelle

Photo by John Seawell

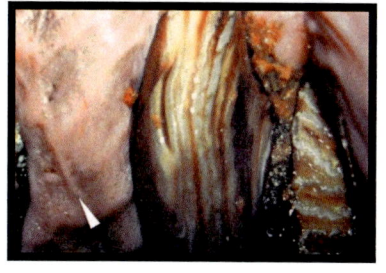

My first trip to Anchorage concerned the removal of a midline impaction in the roof of the mouth of Annabelle, the signature elephant star at the Alaska Zoo. Annie, as she was known to her public, came to Alaska as the prize in a bathroom tissue sweepstakes award contest forty-five-plus years ago, when our world was quite a different place. The winner of this typical award contest of the time lived in Anchorage, and he elected to take the baby elephant instead of the $3000 cash.

When the novelty of his pet elephant wore off, the rapidly growing "baby" was boarded at the local equestrian stables owned and operated by Ms. Sammye Seawell. Sammye and her husband John later built the Alaska Zoo in order to provide an adequate home for Annabelle. Annie lived a full and rich life in a strange and far-away place because of the loving care from an entire neighborhood of folks and their children supporting the Seawells and Annie. Our team not only removed Annie's impacted tooth, but on a cold, dark morning of the winter solstices one year, we also repaired a cracked tusk on her young African companion elephant, Maggie.

It was an early version of our team of emergency elephant-care specialists, with Susanne Schofield occupying the veterinary assistant slot that responded in 1981 to the call from the Alaska Zoo. Over the years, Jim, Alan, Stan and I have returned to the Alaska Zoo repeatedly to assist its veterinarian Dr. Riley Wilson and staff with the resolution of a variety of other clinical health care issues involving both of their elephants, as well as several of their other animals.

Over and over again, the success of our team has depended upon our balance of surgical skills, experience, mechanical skills, and a working knowledge of how instruments and machine tools function. The entire process of how to identify and resolve unusual clinical problems, and get things done quickly and safely, represents the focus of our team working together as jacks of many trades.

We all enjoy traveling, and the challenges of thinking fast, staying flexible, and being creative. Our team approach helps us realize those expectations, and our periodic trips to Alaska and elsewhere not only provide needed medical care to deserving animals, but also over the years they have documented the efficiency and effectiveness of our team approach.

African bull: Chip

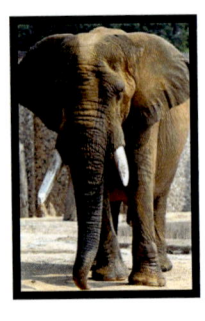

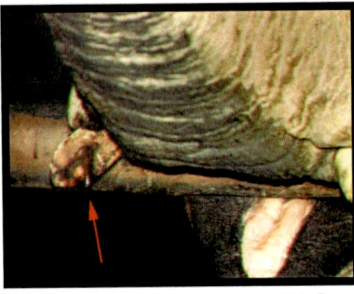

Chip is seen at left; at right, the dangling pulp tissue that convinced everyone—wrongly, as it turned out—that dental pain must have been causing his aggressive behavior. Good detective work by Alan Roocroft identified an "invading" trash-removal truck as the real culprit, and more research by Roocroft, myself, Jim Simon and Kurt Benirschke later determined that elephants to not have nerves in their dental tissue, and hence do not experience pain in that tissue.

Male elephants tend to have more trouble with their tusks than with their molars. This is no doubt because they generally have bigger, longer tusks than females, and they tend to be more aggressive, which is hard on their tusks, both in the wild and in captive environments. It was an example of male territorial aggression that prompted my introduction to Chip, a large African bull elephant at the Caldwell Zoo in the piney woods of eastern Texas in the town of Tyler.

Although I don't think he was named for this reason, Chip, who arrived at the Caldwell Zoo in 1982, repeatedly cracked, broke, or chipped off pieces of his tusks crashing into the heavy, hydraulically operated metal doors on his barn, as well as a sturdy welded iron fencing around the perimeter of his large, outdoor paddock enclosure. At the time, Dr. Doyle Starnes was the zoo's veterinarian. On this occasion, I traveled with Dr. Lynn Shepard, an associate dentist who worked with me from time to time, and Alan Roocroft in the capacity of elephant behaviorist and husbandry specialist.

The dangling three-inch fragment of bloody pulp tissue shown in the righthand photo above convinced everyone that Chip was experiencing excruciating dental pain, and that this constant "dental" pain was the cause of his aggressive behavior. The question of "How do elephants tolerate such obvious dental pain?" remained unanswered until 1999, when Alan Roocroft and the author in collaboration with Jim Simon, an endodontist, and Kurt Benirschke, a clinical pathologist, finally determined that elephants do not have sensory nerve fibers in their dental pulp tissue. This material was published in 1999 (see item 22 in Appendix B).

Although it took several trips, we managed to repair Chip's tusks, in spite of the fact that at one point everyone became so engrossed with the volume of blood pouring from his amputated tusks that no one noticed that the IV bag dripping the immobilization drug into the vein in his ear had run dry. Chip then woke up during the procedure. Over the years I've only had a few animals wake up on me while I was working on them. Chip was the largest, and a major surprise.

Concurrently, Alan Roocroft recommended several changes to Chip's environment, and modified his daily routine to eliminate the cause of his destructive behavior. The underlying root cause of Chip's problem was not the bloody pulp; it was the service road, which passed along the far side border of his outside paddock enclosure. Every week when a large trash-collection truck would show up, Chip would perceive the motion through the fog of an irritable musth/testosterone-induced frenzy, as a territorial invasion of some sort. He would immediately charge forward to confront the intruder to drive it away. The invading truck always left with the garbage, so it was clear in Chip's mind, his territorial defensive behavior was very effective and should continue.

Roocroft resolved the problem by taking the time to thoroughly analyze the facts, and then recommended the installation of a tall, visual barrier fencing to hide the truck, along with several root-ball swinging toys inside his enclosure, which "fought back" with him, and provided a non-destructive object upon which to focus his attention. In a matter of days, the destructive behavior was a thing of the past, because there were no more invaders encroaching upon his territory, and he was required to pay attention to an annoying new pine tree root ball hanging just outside his bedroom doorway.

Asian bull: Tusko

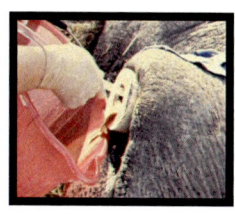

From the files of David A. Fagan

On the left, the entire team has assembled for a daily tusk-flushing and disinfection procedure, which continued for nearly two years. At right, the completely necrotic pulp chamber is drained and cleaned to within three centimeters of the elephant's left eye. The infection was eventually contained, the eye was not lost, but an effective root canal procedure could not be completed. Fifteen-plus years later the remnants of the now fractured tusk were surgically removed.

Tusko was an Asian bull living at Gary Johnson's privately owned elephant breeding facility in Riverside County just north of San Diego. Gary and Kari Johnson own and operate "Have Trunk, Will Travel," an elephant education and entertainment business, which provides a great many of the elephants seen in various Hollywood-produced movies, the Pasadena New Year's Rose Bowl Parade, and around the country at numerous county fairs. Their facility is among the finest in the world, and in 1999 produced two new baby Asian elephants. Their animals all get the best possible husbandry, health and medical care and attention.

Tusko's life however, had been another issue. He had been imported into Florida as a baby, lost his right eye and right tusk early in his youth when they became badly infected, and then killed a keeper who surprised him on his blind right side while living in Canada. In spite of this history, his new job in Riverside was to produce babies. However, he arrived at Gary's place with a very irregular musth cycle, which lasted for months at a time. Although this state of nervous irritability occurs periodically in all male elephants, Gary recognized Tusko's problem immediately as being associated with a badly infected left tusk. He contacted Alan Roocroft at the Wild Animal Park, and once again our little team was on the road.

What began as the planned amputation of the diseased portion of pulp tissue inside his left tusk, turned into two-and-a-half years of daily endodontic tusk treatments, after we uncovered a severe underlying tusk infection extending twenty-three inches up into his head, draining out under the skin of his face, and on the verge of destroying the vision in his only remaining left eye. A blind bull with a history of killing humans does not have a secure future. So, with Gary's undiminished determination, support, and incredible hard work, we managed to save Tusko's eye, as well as the tusk. This case also contributed to our understanding that elephants do not have nerve tissue in their tusks. Years later in 2007, Dr. Mitch Finnigan and his staff at the Portland Zoo in Oregon successfully removed the fragmented remnants of this broken tusk.

Asian cow: Megan

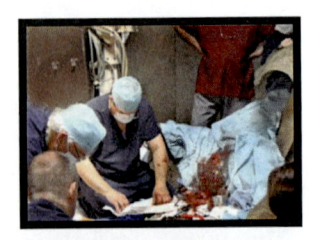

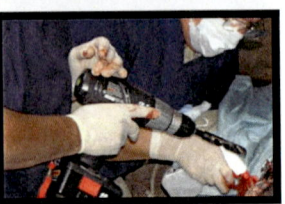

From the files of David A. Fagan

The upper left image shows Megan, a middle-aged African cow living at the Kansas City Zoo under the care of Dr. Kirk Suedmeyer, their zoo veterinarian. The center image shows Drs. Oosterhuis and Fagan working on the immobilized elephant. The top right image shows Dr. Suedmeyer conversing with Drs. Fagan and Oosterhuis as they perform an apicoectomy on the infected molar. The bottom right image clearly shows the author's elephant dental drill ready for action. The infected site was accessed through the lateral bony wall of the mandible, following debridement, and placement of medication in a special blend of particulate bone grafting materials, the lesion took nine months to completely heal (see Item 33, Appendix B.)

During the past thirty years, our team has collectively and individually been involved in numerous innovative procedures involving many elephants, as well as a fair amount of elephant research. In 2004, Dr. Oosterhuis and I joined Dr. Kirk Suedmeyer's extensive team of specialists to perform the world's first elephant molar apicoectomy on an African cow at the zoo in Kansas City, Missouri.

For what remains an unknown reason, this cow developed an unresponsive draining abscess along the lower border of her left mandible. Utilizing a state-of-the-art hydraulic elephant-restraint device, and at the time completely new Eklin digital radiographic X-ray sensing unit, we were able to localize the source of the infection to the distal root section of the animal's primary functioning lower left molar. Following extensive preparation, Dr. Suedmeyer assembled a large team of radiology, internal medicine, anesthesia, and dental experts. The elephant was immobilized for a second time, operated, recovered, and in nine months was declared healed. This case confirmed again the value of the broad-based team approach necessary to address these most difficult elephant dental problems.

African calf: Vus Musi & his tusk pearls

The year 2005 saw the addition of state-of-the-art laser equipment to facilitate the bacterial decontamination of infected pulp tissue in order to insure asepsis prior to the sealing and restoration of an exposed dental pulp canal. We have also developed a new set of surgical instruments to enable repeat access to contaminated canals following the principles developed during Tusko's endodontic treatment more than fifteen years earlier.

More recently, application of these techniques have included a laser-assisted partial pulpotomy on the tusks of a four-year-old African bull calf at the San Diego Wild Animal Park. Our one-year follow-up radiographs confirmed the successful formation of a substantial secondary dentin (ivory) bridge, and this data has enabled us to properly document the forma-

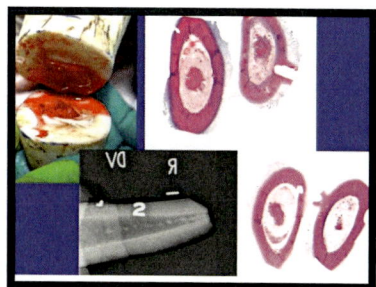

From the files of David A. Fagan

Above left, a three-year-old African male calf named Vus Musi displays his fractured right tusk. The right image shows a radiograph of the freshly exposed pulp chamber with a series of radio-opaque "nodules" extending back into the patient's circulatory system. 2.5 cm of the tip of the tusk was amputated to gain access to the now infected pulp chamber, and following demineralization, histopathalogic sections clearly display the microscopic nature of these osseous structures.

tion of what has historically been referred to as "ivory pearls" to facilitate the natural healing processes of elephant pulp tissue. Microscopic analysis of the tusk's pulp tissue confirms that the "pearls" are actually osseous or bony structures, not ivory or dentin structures.

The actual healing mechanism of the secondary dentin bridge formation consists of stimulated osteoblasts and odontoblasts working together to create an effective, natural re-sealing mechanism within the pulp chamber by the adjacent vital pulp tissue immediately following a traumatic exposure. The eventual success or failure of this natural self-repair mechanism to maintain a vital, aseptic pulp depends entirely upon both the health of the animal, and the virulence and quantity of the invading organisms. If the entry hole is small, invasion is slow, and the pulp tissue healthy and vital, self repair by natural bridge formation is likely. If anything swings the odds the other way, a necrotic pulpitis will most likely follow. This work seems to confirm the clinical validity of an early partial pulpotomy with composite restoration as a beneficial clinical treatment alternative, which promotes and insures the healthy repair of traumatically exposed tusks.

More than twenty-five years of experiences with elephants have provided a multitude of thought-provoking experiences and lessons. And through it all, I remain fascinated by humanity's response to the subject of dental disease in animals, and especially in elephants. People immediately tend to relate the animal's oral problem to their own dental experience. Whenever the subject arises, there begins an emotional dialogue concerning one of their personal dental issues, and then that of friends or relatives, who have had similar discomforting oral experiences. Most everyone it seems has a vivid memory of a bad trip to a dentist, but almost all have great empathy for the poor helpless animal forced to endure a similar negative encounter. All of this talk seems to generate a recurrent theme with an addictive fascination.

I first became aware of this when I worked on Lucky in 1981. There was a great deal of fanfare about the freshly removed, huge tooth. It was suggested at the time that we enter the bloody five-pound molar into the Guinness book of records as "the heaviest tooth ever extracted." To my knowledge, this was never done. Subsequently, I have removed elephant teeth that have weighed eight to nine pounds. The whole idea of the suggestion for a record struck me as an interesting expression of the depth of interest on the part of the public. I was actually approached by a fellow after one procedure, who wanted to make T-shirts with a photo of the elephant's bloody tooth on the front.

The *That's Incredible* TV series actually filmed and broadcasted a short sequence about the removal of Lucky's tooth. At the time, and because of the sensational reputation of the program, I was very concerned that we would be depicted in some sort of foolish format such as leaping off of the head of an elephant into a blood soaked sponge, while snatching the tooth out of her mouth. As it turned out, we appeared following a motorcycle-jumping stunt, and looked reasonably professional in their short, informative news clip. I heard, but never confirmed, that when we operated on the Annabelle elephant in Alaska, we were again nominated to the *Guinness Book of Records* for the "Northernmost Dental Procedure on an Elephant," but I also don't know if this occurred. We finally did make it onto *Ripley's Believe It or Not* TV series, but not for an elephant procedure. The Ripley people selected one of our cheetah procedures, as I remember. And *CNN Headline News* did a nice little clip concerning our polar bear work at the Alaska and Detroit zoos. There has always been a very serious degree of publicity and interest associated with animal dentistry.

However, I was totally unprepared for what occurred at Brookfield Zoo, when we operated on its elephant. There were thirty-seven separate media teams at the zoo covering the procedure. This included all three of the major television networks, local newspapers, *Time*, *Newsweek*, and *National Geographic*. The story covered one half of the front page of both the *Chicago Tribune*, and the *Chicago Sun Times* newspapers the next morning, and was read by an estimated four million people. All of us involved spent the entire next day participating in various print and radio interviews. I was astonished at the amount and extent of the coverage. It is a good thing that people seem to care so much about animals, and if this is the sort of subject matter that can capture their interest for a few moments, then I suspect it is also a good thing. Education concerning environmental issues is the objective, and the nature of the messenger it seems to me, is a matter of secondary importance.

In the 1970s, against an abundance of disinterest, we discussed the need to address oral disease in captive species. Throughout the 1980s we published an assortment of case materials, and participated in a variety of public relations venues to further this awareness. In the 1990s, we extended our field of involvement into the international community supported by significant new information strengthening Dr. Frank Colyer's groundbreaking work presented a century earlier. In 2003, we participated in the establishment of the first European Elephant Management School in Hamburg, Germany at Tierpark Hagenbeck, as discussed in Chapter 13. In 2006 we completed a prototype, developed, and manufactured the world's first set of specialized elephant endotracheal intubation tubes, now being utilized by an international team of clinicians in South Africa to help develop and perfect a vasectomy protocol for male elephants—which will have a profound impact upon their future in-situ conservation strategies.

And as of this writing in 2014, we continue to plod forward.

Based upon my experience, and from comments made by other elephant experts from all around the world, we know for sure that the destiny of the elephant is, to a great extent, subject to the political whims of the public, and their ultimate financial value to various wildlife administrators. This fact, and the urgent need for a dramatic, visionary effort to guarantee a future for these animals in both private and public venues was underscored by the 1997 report from the North American Asian Elephant Studbook group, which noted that, in spite of the best efforts of numerous individuals and organizations, the Asian elephant in North America has passed the point of statistically irrecoverable extinction. That is, by 2001, eighty-three percent of the Asian females in North America that year would be beyond prime breeding age, and most of the remainder of questionable fertility. The April 2006 issue of *AFRICA Geographic* presented a similar detailed special report titled "Elephants & Us."

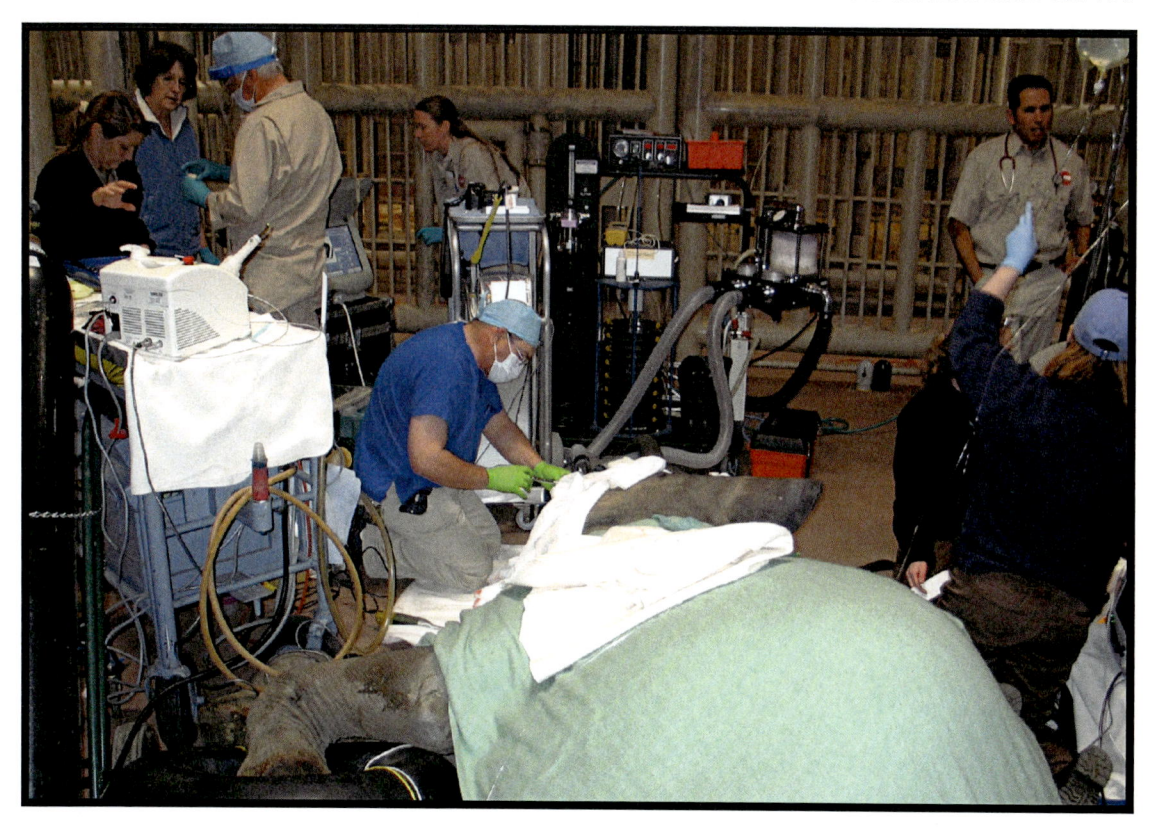

From the files of David A. Fagan

This photograph shows Dr. Oosterhuis in blue preparing the tusk of the Vus Musi elephant under the blue-green blanket. Dr. Fagan in the brown jump suit is standing to the left preparing instrumentation with his surgical assistant of many years Paula King in blue, and Kristin McCaffree, RVT to her right. Directly behind Dr. O is Rachel Peters, one of the RVTs at the San Diego Zoo's Wild Animal Park Harvter Veterinary Medical Center. To the right is UC-Davis third-year exotic animal medicine resident Dr. Julio Mercado, who moved on to become staff veterinarian at the Audubon Zoo in New Orleans. The small white instrument on the left is our diode laser, and directly behind Dr. O's head stands our YSGG-MD hard tissue laser unit.

The implications of all of this reminded me of the Sufi tale found in Robert E. Ornstein's version of the Sufi tale about the blind men and the elephant, in a little book titled *The Mind Field*, which also describes a small group of blind medical students as they examine an elephant. It is interesting to note that Ornstein, himself a leading psychology expert, has his version of this tale end with the observation that the students "fell to quarreling among themselves as to... the elephant's structure... and although they all differed flatly from one another on all these points, they all agreed that the psychiatrist was a fool."

Perhaps the Sufi wise men were on to something. Maybe, we need to be a little foolish to work on, and care about these giant, intelligent mountains of flesh and blood. But then again, maybe we're just foolish enough to be able to think outside of the box, and that's what it takes to try to do something about a few of these "statistically irrecoverable" issues.

In any event, for the past thirty years, we've done what we could both individually and collectively. We've cured some disease. We've participated in a fair number of educational programs. We've done a fair bit of significant research, and we've done some soul searching.

But, it may still require a few more of us—or perhaps some of you—to become aware of the still urgent need for a fresh, rational prospective to help cut through the media smokescreen, or what some call the "KulturSmog," in order to pursue the more rational and practical solutions for a few of these issues. We can choose to act constructively with a fresh awareness, and perhaps we'll find the willpower to back away from the confrontational, ineffective approaches of much of the current politically motivated environmental policies of many NGOs, much of which is built on the thin air of educated guesswork.

In his extensively referenced book *In a Dark Wood*, Alston Chase clearly identifies and defines this issue:

> *"An ancient political and philosophical notion, ecosystem ecology, masquerades as a modern scientific theory. Today, not only does it infuse all environmental law and policy, but its influence is also quietly changing the very character of government. Yet, as I shall show, it is false, and its implementation has been a calamity for nature and society.*
>
> *"Since the 1960s mainstream America had touted moderation but practiced extremism, preached conservation and practiced profligacy, extolled reason while engaging in the politics of emotional manipulation.*
>
> *"Each side has its share of saints and sinners. But the extreme polarization that characterizes preservation fights derives not from the virtue or turpitude of individuals, but from the polarity of the ideas they believe in. Environmental battles are not between good guys and bad guys, but between beliefs. And the real villain is ignorance."*

Chapter Thirteen
A Trip to Vienna

The last blind student remains detached.
His many perceptions can't find a good match.
He seeks for a focus in the conversations
of the mob of spectators who seek revelations.

This man has a sense of powerful pulsations,
and experiences multiple deep sensations.
The elephant's thoughts have showered his mind
with towering images of a simpler kind.

He continues to reflect on the sounds of this throng,
then the elephant moves—and is suddenly gone.

Knowing static impressions can hinder the mind,
As they color and cloud the dynamic in kind,
he refuses to form attitudes or connections,
thus remain undistorted his primal reflections.

And letting his mind float, the student now knows...

That all Earth's inhabitants will take their place,
with the laws of nature controlling the space.

In 1999, my years of fascination with elephant dentition garnered me an invitation to speak at the oldest continuously operating zoo in the world: Schoenbrunn Tiergarten, in Vienna, Austria.

Schoenbrunn is the name of the beautiful spring or fountain that flowed from the site several hundred years earlier. This zoo's animal collection began in 1552, when Crown Prince Maximilian of Austria, later to become Emperor Maximilian II of the Austro-Hungarian Empire, began to stock his deer park surrounding their castle at nearby Eberdorf with various exotic animals. In due course, it became a well stocked private menagerie. One of the first really strange new animals to arrive was an Indian elephant, which Maximilian brought overland by caravan all the way from Spain. After a hundred years or so of maintaining successful animal operations at numerous different game park locations around Austria, Maximilian made the decision to bring all of his royal animal collections to the grounds of the Imperial Schoenbrunn Palace in Vienna, now the home of Empress Maria Theresa.

In addition to running the Austro-Hungarian Empire for forty-three years beginning at the age of twenty-three, Maria Theresa was the mother of seventeen children, among them the future wife of the French General Napoleon Bonaparte. Napoleon took up residence at her Vienna palace during his occupation of Vienna in 1805 and 1809, and his son Napoleon II died in the palace in 1832 at the age of twenty-one.

Maria Theresa allowed only herbivores to reside in the Schoenbrunn Zoo during her reign. She knew the history of the old menageries, and used an eighty-year-old tragic story of "The Lion's Bride" to forbid any "ravenous" animals at Schoenbrunn.

In the old days, it was the gardener's daughter who was responsible for feeding the lions. It was told that on the day of her wedding, she went to feed the lions, while wearing her wedding dress. Her favorite lion, distressed by her pending betrayal and loss of his keeper, killed and ate her in a fit of jealousy. Schoenbrunn remained free of carnivores until 1781. Maria Theresa's husband, Franz Stephan, had a profound interest in zoology, and commissioned a private menagerie at Schoenbrunn for the royal family. A simple layout of thirteen wedge-shaped enclosures surrounding a beautiful elevated, octagonal pavilion became the foundation of their animal park, and their Frühstück Pavilion remains standing today in the heart the Tiergarten Schoenbrunn.

I can personally attest to the charm of both the gardens and the Tierpark. My wife Paula and I were married in the beautiful gothic chapel within the Schoenbrunn Palace, exactly where Napoleon was married. Our first meal as a married couple occurred in the Kaiser's Frühstück Pavilion in the center of the zoo. All of this occurred while we were in Vienna attending an international conference in May of 1999. Our hosts at the Tiergarten treated us as guests of the court, and provided us with enough memories to last more than one lifetime. The Tierpark's photographer, Ms. Jutta Kirchner, photographed our wedding and activities, and took many of the Vienna wedding photos you see here.

Photos by Jutta Kirchner

Three weeks of wedding, conference, exploration, travel, and relaxation at the palace, in the nearby Vienna Woods, and along the Danube River with wonderful new friends and a lovely new wife, was a magical adventure. At the top left, we were guests at a formal pre-wedding dinner party with a private Mozart concert inside the hexaganal Frühstück Pavilion. The following afternoon during our post-wedding luncheon, we received a magnum of palace wine from the chef, which we shared with our family and friends five years later in San Diego. At the top right is one of our favorite wedding party photos, with Paula's maid of honor, Ms. Charlotte Deutsch, to my left. In the middle right image, Paula and I are horseback riding through the famous Vienna Woods; then we toured the beautiful Benedictine Abby at Melk. And, finally we enjoyed a relaxing, memorable, summer picnic along the bank of the River Danube.

Today the zoo, known as Tiergarten Schoenbrunn, receives more than a million visitors each year. After the destruction and losses incurred during the two world wars, the buildings of the former imperial palace menagerie were renovated, the grounds enlarged, and under the expert guidance of director Professor Dr. Helmut Pechlaner, new projects were constantly being undertaken. As a result, the Schoenbrunn Tiergarten is once again being appreciated by a host of international visitors in all of its earlier imperial splendor. The new zoo facilities include a state-of-the-art home for six elephants. Several years ago, two of them had minor tusk problems, and because of some questions raised by local animal activists, I was contacted by Dr. Heinz Burger, who was their senior zoo veterinarian, and director of veterinary medical services. We carried on a long-distance consultation, as I assisted him with the resolution of the problem.

Dr. Pechlaner and Dr. Burger were also my two best men. They stood up for me before the Vienna magistrate, and helped get me through three weeks of wedding ceremony—and many late nights of extended activities.

In May of 1999, the newly refurbished Tiergarten Schoenbrunn joined with the University of Vienna's School of Veterinary Medicine and the Institute for Zoo Biology and Wildlife Research (IZW) in Berlin, to host the 39th International Symposium on Diseases of Zoo and Wild Animals. In attendance were over 350 individuals from 30 countries all around the world. Because of my work with elephants, I had been invited to present a scientific paper titled "Significant Dental Disease in Elephants" (see item 19, Appendix B).

What began so many years ago in Seattle's Woodland Park Zoo as a distrust of some huge elephantine creatures, had slowly evolved into a position of spokesperson on their behalf, addressing issues that contribute to the well-being of these largest of all land mammals. With the input and help from my good friends and co-authors Alan Roocroft, Jim Oosterhuis and Kurt Benirschke, I was able to present new data concerning the elephant's dentition, which now appears to be leading to a better understanding of their needs, behavior and overall care in both captive and free ranging environments.

After the conference, my new wife and I lingered in Vienna and the historically famous Vienna Woods and Danube River for several weeks. One beautiful sunny day after his morning rounds, we joined Dr. Burger at the Kaiser Pavilion to enjoy a traditional late-morning cup of coffee with a small breakfast cake. In short order, Burger and I lapsed into predictable man-talk, while Paula explored the beautiful surrounding spring gardens.

In the course of our conversation, Heinz mentioned that now that the conference was over, he was scheduled to accompany a tiger into Libya in North Africa to be delivered to Moammar Khadafy. Because of our various traveling experiences, it was natural that our conversation slowly drifted to the fact that earlier in the spring of 1999, my friend Alan Roocroft had been asked to go to Brazil to help save another "abused" elephant.

The story of what Alan encountered in Brazil is an indication of the extent to which emotionally motivated good intentions can often fall short of their stated objectives, and actually interfere with the proven, focused efforts of more qualified professionals.

In the jungle of Brazil between San Paulo and Rio de Janeiro, there are a multitude of small circus groups traveling between hundreds of small isolated towns and villages. Many have animals, a few have an elephant, and all provide welcome entertainment and a much anticipated distraction wherever they wander. On occasion, some have also experienced behavioral difficulties with one or more of their animals.

Elephants are notoriously difficult to maintain—anywhere. Males in particular, even in the wild, are capable of creating a great deal of trouble with very little notice of intent. This is why dominant free-ranging female elephants routinely drive all sexually maturing males out of their extended family group. Undisciplined individuals are too much trouble to be allowed to stay in the quiet, stable environment necessary for their mothers to raise their other youngsters to become normal adults. The big trouble with male elephants is they periodically go into musth.

Above left, the author and Dr. Devaka Weerakoon/Sri Lanka, one of the twenty-four instructors at the first European Elephant Management School in Hamburg, Germany, raise a toast. At right another of the instructors, Dr. E.K. Easwaran, is seen in Kerala, India. (See instructors' profile at www.elephant-management.com/home.html for complete list.)

This male hormonal, PMS-like state of nervous frenzy and dangerous irritability has been the subject of volumes of research, speculation and opinion. Suffice it to say that maintaining either sex of elephant is a difficult, complicated undertaking requiring specific knowledge and skills. Even the females get very upset from time to time, just like their human counterparts.

Well, the news of some difficulties with an elephant in a particular circus was announced in one of the local newspapers. So a small group of wealthy animal activists in the San Paulo area contacted one of the well-known International Animal Activists Groups, and decided this was a good time to "Save another elephant from a life of constant abuse by another evil, small-time circus owner." This was an obvious overstatement of the actual situation, but sufficient to create a major emotional uprising, with lots of good copy for the local newspapers.

In short order, a group of activists converged on the circus in a small coastal town not too far from San Paulo, and demanded that something be done immediately. After some time, and with no luck trying to resolve the difficulties with the activists, the circus owners decided to let them "save" the elephant, any way they saw fit. So, the elephant was securely chained to a nearby tree, and supplied with plenty of food and water. The circus troupe then went back on the road to their next appointed location, and abandoned their elephant to the care of the activists.

During the next several weeks, while debate raged in the press, the elephant was "maintained" by a local group of concerned activists. The process was complicated by the fact that the activists really didn't know very much about elephant husbandry. With several weeks of inadequate care, the elephant became more dissatisfied, increasingly irritable, and very difficult to deal with. Concern that their plan was not proceeding very well prompted the wealthy activists to contact Alan Roocroft in San Diego, and arrange for him to travel to Brazil, and move their now enraged and truly dangerous elephant to the safety of a nearby zoo. Alan agreed to evaluate the situation, and news of the new plan was also printed in the local newspapers. Immediately, a different group of activists saw the article, and threatened publicly to kill both Alan and the nearby Sorocaba Zoo's director, in order to save the elephant from "a life of abuse in the restrictive confines of another inadequate zoo."

However, no one was able to offer an acceptable alternative. Alan learned of the threats, and declined to show up for his scheduled killing.

More time passed, with more Mafia-like threats and declarations in the press, while the now really unhappy elephant remained tethered under the tree in the jungle. During the next six weeks, as the situation deteriorated much further, the activists finally decided that something needed to be done to conclude their saving process. Legal papers were filed, arguments were made by some of Brazil's best (read most expensive) legal minds, money was lavished on the lawyers, and the court decided that the circus people should be allowed to come back, and reclaim the elephant from the tree. They were further instructed to deliver the now very dangerous elephant to Alan, a "real elephant expert," who would help arrange a new home for this animal somewhere, perhaps in one of the larger zoos nearby. The circus owners must also pay a large fine to the court to cover all of the costs associated with saving the animal from the alleged, but unproven, abuse. And oh yes, Alan would not be killed for participating.

So finally, Alan flew to San Paulo to meet with the group of wealthy activists. This well-intentioned group quickly became very unhappy with him, because he would not agree to modify the court's directive, and magically whisk the elephant away to a new life of freedom in some unidentifiable, ideal location of safety. Consequently, Alan spent much of his time enjoying lavishly prepared meals with the wealthy activists' cook and chauffeur, while they pondered their next move.

Finally, in the company of the two instigating activists, who wore disguises, because of the death threats announced next to their photos in the local newspapers, Alan made several unannounced inspection tours of the small Sorocaba Zoo west of Rio de Janeiro, as well as a couple of the small traveling circus groups—all the while expecting bullets to fly, or a car bomb to go off. He discovered that the two peaceful-looking elephants at the Sorocaba Zoo were in fact themselves killers—one had killed two keepers, and the other had killed eleven humans. The Sorocaba Zoo was absolutely not a safe place to bring another irritable elephant. In due course, word arrived that the circus owner had been notified that they must bring their elephant to the zoo in Sorocaba, so Alan and the activists all relocated there to await their arrival.

Ten days passed with more lavish meals, and neither the circus nor the elephant showed up. It seems that the circus owner had paid a small bribe to one of the court's lesser officials, was released from all responsibility, and promptly disappeared back into the jungle—now with his famously rehabilitated elephant. The wealthy activists remained unhappy, and no doubt selected an easier animal to "save" for their next activity. Alan flew home after having an opportunity to inspect another of the worlds 830-plus zoos.

So why did this ridiculous sequence of events occur in the first place?

It is generally assumed by the public that activists are active because they have good intentions, and they "know stuff." But this poses the questions, why do so many of their do-gooder activities go so badly? And why isn't more said about it when they do?

The answer, I suspect, is related to a tremendous lack of big-picture understanding concerning the true current state of environmental affairs, in spite of all the rhetoric to the contrary. The simple truth is, complex, multi-faceted problems generally require complex, multi-faceted solutions, conceived and implemented by knowledgeable professionals with experience relative to the subject.

I submit it is time to get over the notion that all established, self-proclaimed political and environmental authority is somehow endowed with superior knowledge and understanding of these complicated scientific issues. Narrowly focused, emotionally motivated, political and/or activist interests are not generally the best source for an effective solution. As a general rule, over time they routinely become a large part of the problem. If the activists/media objective is nothing more than a thirty-second crisis for the day sound bite for the evening news in order to maintain votes and cash flow, then educated viewers must learn to recognize and accept that this is what's going on, and not support such self-centered foolishness.

Dr. Billy Karesh states it thus in his book *Appointments at the Ends of the World*: "As conservationists we face enormous challenges. Rather than thinking we have all the answers, we must acknowledge that one of the most important keys to success is working closely with local people and agencies to develop strategies and implement programs."

Over the years, I have been fortunate enough to have had the opportunity to visit a large number of zoological parks, stationary and mobile menageries, and private housing facilities for all sorts of wildlife. I have seen everything from the most squalid and depressing of enclosures to the Taj Mahal of animal living quarters. I am impressed by the insatiable desire of humans to associate with animals—often well beyond the limits of their financial capabilities to do so.

It seems to me, the animal mothering behavior of many humans is motivated by something subliminal, internal and very personal. I suspect it can be found in nearly all of us to one degree or another. Perhaps it's something primordial, associated with our biological role as just another one of the species sharing space on planet Earth. I suspect we need all these other animal and plant species in order to maintain ourselves as stable, functional beings. Consequently, I think its time to utilize our intellect and capacities to work together toward a common end. All the bickering over minor issues of organizational dominance is not only detrimental for all concerned, but is human political behavior at its most shallow level. It is definitely not productive conservation.

Although the activist-driven environmental movement has resulted in some notable achievements, there is a growing realization that many of these emotional crusades, which embody so much hype and hope, routinely have not lived up to their earlier promise, and are currently gripped by pessimism and distrust. Opinion seems badly polarized. There now exists a strengthening anti-environmental campaign, arguing that the environmental movement is not only not liberating nature, but is actually detrimental to developing society and damaging to the environment.

Alston Chase in his book *In a Dark Woods* states this very clearly: "When the search for truth is confused with political advocacy, the pursuit of knowledge is reduced to the quest for power." I encourage those who are interested in investigating this thesis further read this well-documented book, as well as *Blue Plant in Green Shackles*, by Vaclav Klaus, former president of the Czech Republic, addressing the negative consequences of "ideological environmentalism."

During the time when Europe was ruled by an assortment of monarchies, it was implicitly understood by all that the children of the ruling family must be properly educated before advancing into their future roles as rulers. The form of government in the United States is a representative republic, not a monarchy. Therefore, it is the people, all of us—not some smiley-faced mob of political clowns—who eventually must shoulder the responsibility for decision-making.

Certainly, it must be equally as important for us to insure our future leaders are properly educated; are taught to understand the concepts of personal responsibility; and are not just being slowly brainwashed into accepting the thin air of un-educated guesswork to be the truth simply because its easily and quickly downloaded onto an iPod.

Fortunately there's still hope. There remains a host of dedicated, experienced, hard working individuals out there quietly making a real difference dealing with the truth. I encourage you to get a substantial education; go find one of them; then strap on your tool belt; and join them.

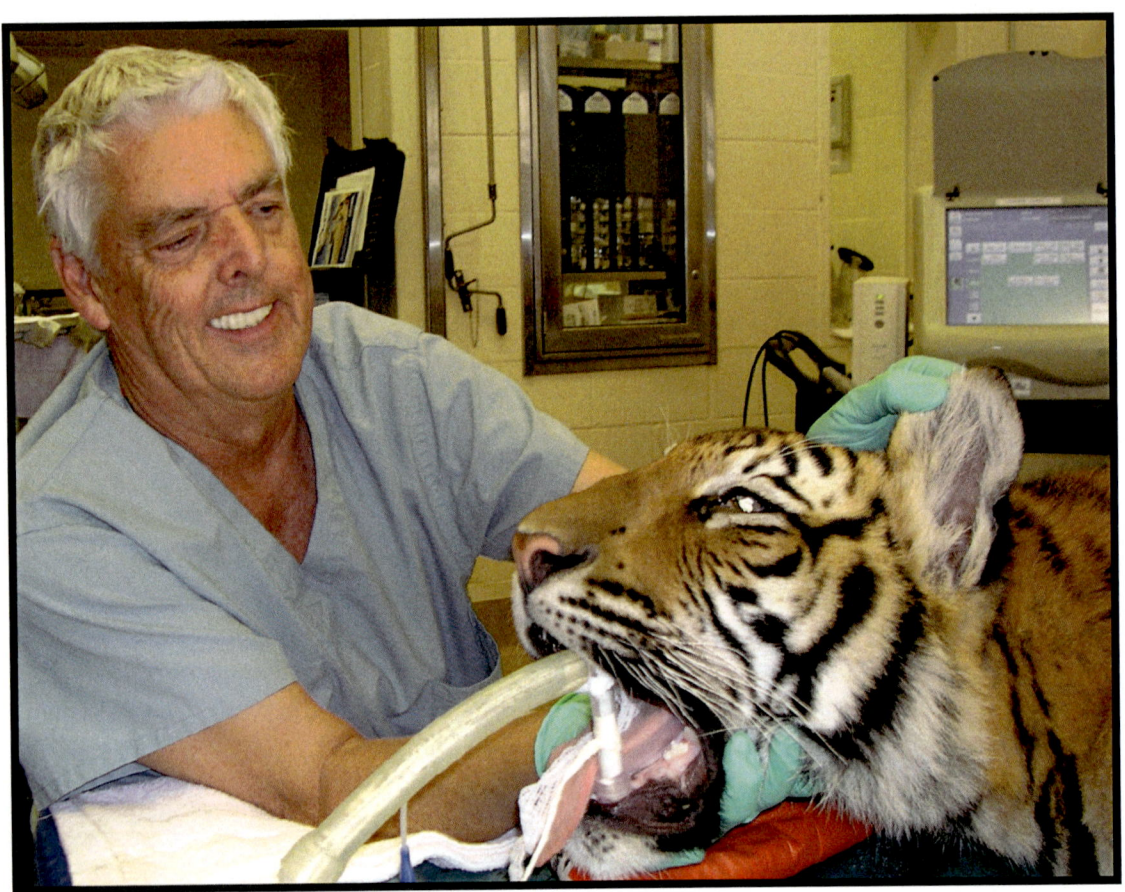

From the files of David A. Fagan

My wife Paula named this yearling Malaysian Tiger cub "Keemasan Mata." The name is Malaysian for "Golden Eye." His pappy was a young male tiger captured and removed from the wild. The locals named him "Awang Relak," and allegedly he was a man-killer. He was sent to San Diego to make more of these beautiful babies. During his quarantine exam, it was discovered that Awang's dentition was grossly malformed and severely infected. It took my assistant PK and me approximately twenty-six hours of oral surgery in four phased procedures to clean up all of the infection, remove his deformed dentition, and then support his jawbones with a massive amount of particulate bone grafting material. Awang also has the distinction of having had three CT scans (see Item 34 in Appendix B) during the process.

At one point, there was serious question whether Awang would live, let alone reproduce. Therefore, two years later when two healthy cubs arrived, there was great joy in Mudville. I was honored to be asked to name one of the cubs.

Chapter Fourteen
Who Was Sir Frank Colyer?

The elephant feels the biped's anguish,
Knowing it seeks simpler rules to distinguish
the natural laws it's begun to perceive.
With his animal wisdom, he too grieves.

He knows that morality is not just intention,
And "a life worth living" demands invention
As all contend with this most complex struggle,
That often gets stuck in a terrible muddle.

He senses a time of conflict and debate,
with tumultuous upheavals that all tend to relate.
A new, stable balance is the ultimate goal,
with ALL species playing demanding new roles.

And, this elephant knows . . .

that the winners will adapt to the changing new game,
with each player observing the rules on this range.

Sir Frank Colyer was a dentist born near London, England in the later half of the 1800s, and was a truly amazing individual.

Shortly before the turn of the last century, this English dental clinician was one of the first to clearly demonstrate the critical link between dental disease and overall systemic health in both humans and animals. What Dr. J. F. Colyer documented well over one hundred-plus years ago remains true today. Yet, sadly, only in the most recent few years has the general public begun to seriously support an unemotional, scientific effort to preserve the very existence of some species, let alone adequately address the nutrition, dentition and oral health of many animals.

Painting by Clarece White, by permission of the UK Royal College of Surgeons

This portrait of Sir Frank Colyer hangs in the museum room holding the Odontological Section of the museum of the U.K. Royal College of Surgeons. The section displays an astonishing assortment of rare and unusual dental artifacts from Colyer's years of research and collecting. It was commissioned by a group of subscribers in 1954, and a digital version of the image was provided to us courtesy of the Royal College of Surgeons.

Moreover, the early scientific endeavors of this very prolific English dental surgeon have, more than one hundred years later, directly contributed to the development of the modern practice of veterinary dentistry—now recognized as one of the specialty practices of veterinary medicine. His contributions were fundamental, substantial and without peer.

In early 1978, I was working with Dr. Jim Oosterhuis at the San Diego Wild Animal Park on the gorilla Trib. We felt that the medical circumstances unique to this particular case needed to be presented to the entire community of animal health-care specialists in the form of a peer-reviewed scientific article published in a respected journal. In order to substantiate our findings and present our conclusions in proper context, we conducted an extensive literature search—not such an easy task in 1978 as it is today—to support and guide our in-progress clinical research concerning the unique triad of oral problems presented in this gorilla's story, as told in Chapter Six.

During our library searches, references to a "J.F. Colyer" revealed an individual who had published two highly relevant books: *Dental Disease in Its Relation to General Medicine*, in 1911; and *Variation and Diseases of the Teeth of Animals*, in 1936. After reviewing these two books, it was obvious that Sir Frank Colyer had written the fundamental textbooks on the subject of dental disease in animals before the turn of the last century.

Colyer had, from the late 1800s into the early 1900s, traveled the world conducting research, analysis and gathering physical documentation to support his thesis that animals in the wild do indeed have the same variety of oral diseases and dental maladies he'd seen and treated in humans in his clinical practice in London—and that these diseases have the same profound systemic impact upon the animal's general health. He was a tireless clinician, researcher, teacher, and eventually Dean of the Royal Dental Hospital in London. He was a prolific writer, who compiled and published his views and findings in numerous articles and textbooks.

We found a brief note posted by one of his dental society peers on page 314 of the *British Medical Journal* dated August 31, 1946 by one C.F. Porter, who obviously knew Dr. Colyer personally, soliciting donations for the presentation to Colyer of the portrait seen on the previous page, on the occasion of his 80th birthday, as a gift "not from any learned society, but from the rank and file of the dental profession." He writes, "Sir – I would like to quote the old proverb, 'Whatsoever thy hand findeth to do—do it with all thy might,' for in suchwise Sir Frank Colyer has ordained his life should be lived, and the dental profession has reaped in full measure the harvest of his strenuous labours...."

In 1979, I was invited to make a presentation before the American Association of Zoo Veterinarians gathering in Washington, D.C. I presented two papers at that meeting. One was titled, "Diet Consistency and Periodontal Disease in Exotic Carnivores," and the other, "The Pathogenesis of Dental Disease of Carnivores" (see items 8 and 9 in Appendix B). We were particularly interested in expressing a concern regarding the systemic effects of untreated oral disease in American zoological collections. We wanted to emphasize the impact these disease processes were having upon both the general health and reproductive success of numerous carnivores in their captive environments. In order to add weight to our thesis, we elected to reference Colyer's work, which goes into great detail on both of these subjects. On page 690 of his book *Variation and Disease in the Teeth of Animals*, Dr. Colyer concludes with the following remarks. Although initially written well over one hundred years ago, they were our conclusions in 1980, and they essentially still ring true today:

> "*The conclusions I have arrived at after my investigations into the (oral) disease in animals are as follows:*
>
> *1. The disease starts as an injury to the gum margin caused by food. This injury may be of a traumatic or chemical nature; when traumatic, the food in the process of mastication penetrates the soft tissues; when chemical, the products of stagnant food injure the epithelial surface, and thus expose the deeper tissues to infection.*
>
> *2. The bone lesion is a progressive rarefying aesthetes (sic) commencing at the margin of the bone, and there is no evidence to support the claim, made by some writers, that the initial bone changes are of an atrophy character.*
>
> *3. The disease is caused by an alteration in the character of the diet of the animal either of a physical or chemical nature—in other words, by a departure from natural diet and conditions.*
>
> *Expressed in biological terms, the disease is due to an alteration in the environment of the mouth.*"

By mid 1979, we had clearly come to respect the name "Colyer."

Subsequently, another extensive literature search was undertaken to learn more about Dr.

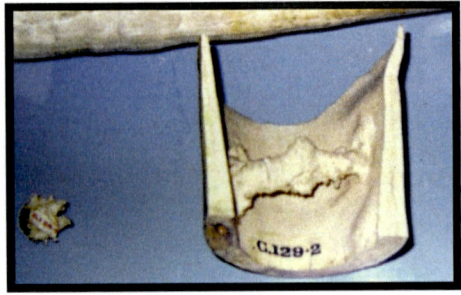

From the files of David A. Fagan

I photographed the object on the right above in the display cabinet at the end of the room seen in the room view on the left. It is an opened cross-section of the internal repair process within the ivory tusk of an elephant. The small round/irregular object to its left of the photo is actually a musket ball found within the pulp chamber of an elephant's tusk, and encapsulated in bone. Both the ball and the mineralized trajectory path through the tusk are covered in what appears to be secondary dentin, thus displaying very dramatically the remarkable healing potential of elephant dental pulp tissue, as we recently confirmed in our Vus Musi partial pulpotomy investigation discussed near the end of Chapter Twelve. This tusk repair specimen is just one example of an array of very interesting artifacts to be found in the Colyer section of the Hunterian Collection at the Royal College of Surgeons' museum.

Colyer's work and contributions. We learned he had published several other books, including a major textbook in 1910 with a Morton Smale, titled *Dental Surgery and Pathology of Humans* comprising 1024 pages with numerous illustrations. Then in 1912 he published another, titled *The Extraction of Teeth*. This one was a treatise involving the techniques and instruments necessary to master the art and practice of removing teeth. Both of these publications represent some of the earliest, most authoritative texts on the subject concerning human oral surgery.

Our search further revealed that Sir Frank Colyer's brother Stanley was a radiologist. In 1926, Stanley published a book titled *The Chronic Infection of the Jaws, a Short Radiographic and Clinical Study.* Dr. Stanley Colyer also published a series of photographic books featuring a variety of footpaths and road bridges in the surrounding English countryside.

Both of the Colyer brothers were active clinicians, competent researchers and prolific writers. Their scientific works were often published in a journal known as *The Dental Record*—a respected scientific journal published before and around the turn of the last century in London. Frank Colyer systematically compiled many of his smaller articles into book format, which eventually became the foundation for his classic textbook on dental disease in animals.

Frank was born in 1866, and died in 1954. Just as Colyer seemed to follow in the footsteps of the famous Scottish surgeon/anatomist John Hunter, who was born nearly a century earlier in 1728, we've spent the past thirty-plus years forging a similar path to Sir Frank Colyer's nearly a century after him.

John Hunter is considered one of the greatest anatomists of all time, and the founder of experimental pathology in England. Hunter put the practice of surgery on to a solid scientific foundation, and laid the framework for many twentieth-century developments. His saying "Don't think, try the experiment!" has inspired generations of modern surgeons—including Sir Frank Colyer. The story of Hunter's life was published in a book titled *The Knife Man: Blood, Body Snatching, and the Birth of Modern Surgery* by Wendy Moore. Colyer's classic 1936 textbook was edited and re-published in 1971 as *Colyer's Variations and Diseases of the Teeth of Animals* by A. E. W. Miles (editor), Caroline Grigson (editor).

Jim Oosterhuis, Alan Roocroft, and the author pose in front of this gate of Hagenbeck Tierpark in 2003, the year the Euopean Elephant Management School began. Alan, who initially conceived the idea for the school, was taking Jim and me on a personal tour of his old stomping grounds. Alan was an elephant keeper at Tierpark Hagenbeck in his early days.

Hagenbeck's Tierpark, founded in 1848, housed Asian elephants of all age groups with a high hands-on training standard. Important elephant management procedures are taught, and with the help of these animals (e.g. foot trimming, transportation, habitat management, etc.) The school is held annually in a nine-day-session. The course is meant for professional elephant keepers, elephant curators, zoo veterinarians and zoo directors only.

From the files of David A. Fagan

Hagenbeck's 160-year-old zoo is home to countless species of animals, a beautiful new tropical aquarium, several restaurants, a magnificent recreation garden park, and in 2009 a new destination hotel. The animals live in specially designed rocky environments, historically famous, spacious, watering holes and panoramic vistas.

More than 100 years ago, Hagenbeck's zoo design team worked on and influenced the design of the zoos in Detroit, Chicago, San Diego, Rome, Paris, Dehli, Colombo and elsewhere. Today, the G-B Hagenbeck Zooquarium Consulting Architekten Gruppe is still quite active offering their unique professional expertise to the international zoo community.

In September of 1980, with his usual direct and focused observations, Dr. Kurt Benirschke, then director of research at the Center Reproduction of Endangered Species at the world-ramous Zoological Society of San Diego, observed that the American scientific community would benefit from an organization that would specifically encourage, assemble, focus and coordinate further study and research of the various oral-related medical issues we had been identifying and treating in numerous exotic animals in various captive maintained collections. It was decided that the most productive way to achieve these objectives was a nonprofit organization dedicated to, and named to recognize the memory of the work of Sir Frank Colyer and his brother.

So, established in early 1982, The Colyer Institute became that non-profit organization, with three primary objectives:

• Provide clinical care in selected situations where local facilities lack the funds and/or the means to provide appropriate solutions.

• Conduct continuing research in the area of oral medicine and nutrition across the entire spectrum of animal species.

• Establish a solid education program for the veterinary medical community, the wildlife administrative community, and for the public at large via all the usual and customary venues.

In order to realize these mission statement objectives for the past thirty-two years, The Colyer Institute has methodically assembled a diverse network of experienced clinicians and manufacturers with specialized equipment, experience and expertise in the disciplines of zoo and wildlife medicine and dentistry. Then we established solid working relationships with numerous off-exhibit or privately held animal collections, zoological and natural history facilities around the world. Individually and collectively, this fluid, collaborative networking group has managed to stay focused on our mission statement objectives, treat a great deal of oral disease, and generate a fair amount of educational material. As the previous chapters have demonstrated, we've extended our reach to the global community by maintaining a philosophy of working only with established, reputable individuals in harmony with their institution's objectives.

The Road Ahead...

If I've learned anything during the past thirty-plus years, it is that the quality of our lives is inextricably interwoven with the quality of our environment, and the general health and welfare of the various life forms and creatures with whom we share life on this unique planet. Currently, the true number of species on the planet Earth is unknown, but knowledgeable estimates vary from two million to one hundred million species, with only about 1.4 million having actually been named.

We are told there are now approximately 5000 known species of mammals sharing this space with us. When I was in college there were only 4226. Various circumstances are driving some of them to extinction, a few at an astonishing rate, while others are adapting very well to humankind's footprint. At the same time, and almost as fast as the extinctions, expanding field research is finding a surprisingly large number of new species in the most unexpected places. Hard archeological evidence also tells us that of all of the species that have evolved on this planet, ninety-nine percent are long extinct. With this many life forms on hand, and many new ones showing up each day, it seems fairly clear that our little planet is well adapted to accept and accommodate changes of all sorts.

There are numerous successful, as well as many very poorly planned and badly executed attempts to preserve many of these species and spaces. One way or another, all are ultimately dependent upon common sense, good science, natural parks and preserves, modern zoological facilities, and various educational and research institutions for their success. One of the most fundamental clinical health problems common to all of these animals, whether in captivity or not, is nutrition and oral disease. Both of these issues directly impact the systemic health and reproductive capacity of these animals—including humans. These clinical issues remain our focus.

My good friend Dr. Benirschke sees the issue as a continual state of warfare with a varied, rapidly evolving, disease-making, microbial population. We may win our share of the battles, but the war will never be over. Ours is a journey through this battlefield, and science-based medicine and technologies are our primary weapons.

I have thoroughly enjoyed my journey of discovery and adventure for the past thirty-plus years. With the clarity of hindsight, I've attempted to recall a small assortment of the memorable battlefield milestones marking a few of the paths I've traveled. I hope I've been able to share a little bit of it with you in as interesting and understandable manner as it has been for me to live through it.

The Colyer Institute offers just another arrow in the quiver of those of us who have come together in the quest to preserve, and improve the quality of life for many species. For more information concerning the work of The Colyer Institute, see our website at:

www.colyerinstitute.org

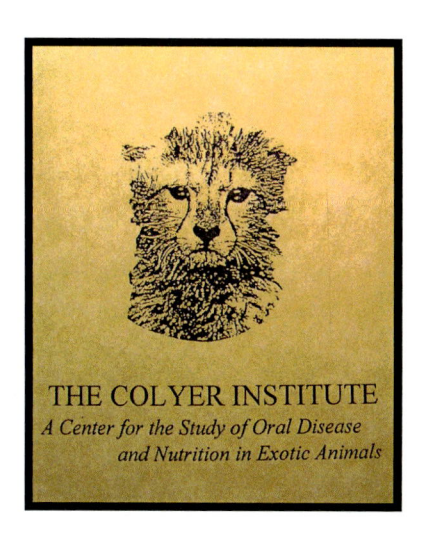

Much of the institute's early clinical and research work was focused on the oral problems of large carnivores—especially the cheetah, as discussed in Chapter Ten. Consequently, the institute's staff elected to incorporate an image of a cheetah cub as our official logo. The image to the left is the result, and was created for us by P.J. Falconbridge. The Colyer website has a special section devoted to the cheetah, which interestingly enough shares a common ancestor with North America's mountain lion or puma.

Acknowledgements

Kurt Benirschke, Jim Oosterhuis, and Alan Roocroft have all been true mentors, teachers, co-authors, friends, and a big help with my book writing. My father, Major Charles H. "Hal" Fagan, was the oldest of ten kids. He learned how to be the world's best father, helping to raise his nine siblings during the Great Depression years between the two big wars. So, by the time he got around to me—essentially his twelfth kid—he really knew how to guide and help prepare someone to thirst for an education in order to cope with all of the commotion life has in store for them. I also owe a great deal to my mother Edith, who in spite of the turmoil in her life and times, managed to mold a hyperactive mass of protoplasm into a fairly functional human being, as only a real mother knows how.

Growing up as a WWII army brat certainly provided an exceptionally interesting educational element to my life. And, then there was Frau Hanna Voit, who in the middle of all the post-conflict turmoil in her country, managed to provide a little American kid with a solid education in classical German equestrian dressage, and in the process, taught me how to listen for the words to be found in an animal's eyes. My dear friend and mentor Dick Lynch spent another twenty-five years adding polish, and hopefully putting a little finish on the process.

I utilized the Internet extensively to access a wealth of material in the free on-line Wikipedia encyclopedia, Roget's Thesaurus, various Google and clone search engines, assorted volunteer and informational blogs, etc. to help find and provide a few additional or interesting factoids to add depth and a little more color as I fleshed out various details or images.

The "Ode to the Elephant" illustrations were done by John Whalen. Except as cited, all of the other material is mine.

All in all, there've been hundreds who've helped me along the way, too many to acknowledge them all individually. But I'd like the record to reflect my profound appreciation, and thanks to all for their help.

DENTIST GOES ANIMAL 152

Appendix A

These are my logbook entries for the seventy-four cases treated in 1980. This degree of diverse patient population has been representative from year to year ever since. Most of the cases required multiple visits to complete treatment.

African Lion / oral surg
Spider monkey / scurvy suspect
Black Rhino / tx herpetic lesion on lip
Brown Hyena / extensive tx
Wombat, coarse-haired / tx malocclusion
Cockatoo female / trim beak
Spotted Hyena / extensive tx
Black/white lemur / exam n clean teeth
Lion Tail Macaque / exam
Hamlyn's Guenon / gingivectomy
Spotted Hyena / extensive tx & oral surgery
Sumatran Orang 01 / exam
Sumatran Orang 01 / sinus surgery
Spotted Hyena / extensive tx & oral surg
Lowland Gorilla 01 / extensive oral surg broken k9
Lowland Gorilla 02 / remove incisor
Black and White Lemur / clean incisors
African Lion 01 Whitfield / oral surg endo
African Lion 02 Whitfield / oral surg endo
Sumatran Orang 02 / sinus surgery
So African Cheetah 02 / extensive tx
So African Cheetah 03 / exam
So African Cheetah 04 / exam
So African Cheetah 05 / exam
So African Cheetah 06 / exam
So African Cheetah 07 / exam
So African Leopard / exam
Lion tailed Macaque / oral surg
Palm Cockatoo / trim beak
Lowland Gorilla 03 / oral surg
Black handed Spider Monkey / tx scurvy
So Asian Black Eagle / repair broken beak
Tiger 01 / extensive work / S&R Las Vegas
Lion / extensive work / S&R Las Vegas
Tiger 02 / extensive work / S&R Las Vegas
Tiger 03 / extensive work / S&R Las Vegas

Lion tailed Macaque / endo n perio
Lion / Endo / Ron Whitfield SFO
Tiger / K9 endo / Wayne Reagan SFO
Lion tailed Macaque 03 / endo
Humboldt's Woolly Monkey / endo
So. African Cheetah 08 / oral surg
Clouded Leopard / multiple endo
Lesser Panda / oral surg
Pigmy Chimp / extractions
Domestic Dog Shepard / heart murmur
Domestic Dog Doberman / repair fx k9
Domestic Dog Rottweiler / oral surg endo
Palm Cockatoo / correct deformed beak
Parma Wallaby / tx lumpy jaw infection
Aardwolf / exam – clean teeth
Capybara / fx incisors w extensive tx
Small Clawed Otter / tx facial abscess
Lowland Gorilla 04 / remove primary teeth
Lowland Gorilla 05 / remove primary teeth
Agile Wallibie / tx facial laceration
Spotted Hyena 03 / extensive tx
Françoise Monkey / endo
Kikuyu Colobus Monkey 01 / oral surg
Black and White Ruff Lemur / endo
Hamlyn's Guenon / exam
Prong Horn Antelope / fx mandible
Ringtail Lemur / tx k9 abscess
California Sea Lion / exam
Colobus Monkey 02 / remove sialolithiasis
Agile Wallaby / oral surg
Hamlyn's Guenon 02 / exam
Reeve's Muntjac / tx of fx k9
Zulu Suni / tx fx jaw
Domestic Goat / remove incisor float teeth
Pigmy chimp / exam
Spotted Hyena 04 / perio tx
Black Lemur / partial pulpotomy

Appendix B

Bibliography

David Fagan was sole or co-author of each of the following publications, as indicated.

1. Fagan, David A., **"Equine Dental Recommendations,"** *Stud Managers Handbook (1973)*, Vol. 9, pgs. 109-114 @ University of California at Davis Veterinary Medical Teaching Hospital.

2. With P.T. Robinson, DVM, "Veterinary Dentistry in the Zoo: New Insights," San Diego Zoo's *ZoonooZ* (Jan. 1978).

3. With P.T. Robinson, DVM, **"Endodontic Surgery for Treatment of a Fistulated Molar Abscess in an Orangutan,"** *Journal of the American Association of Zoo Veterinarians* (1978), Vol 173 @ San Diego Zoo

4. With P.T. Robinson, DVM; and J.P. Roffinella, DDS, **"Surgical Removal of Impacted Molar Teeth in an Orangutan,"** *Journal of the American Veterinary Medical Association*, (Nov. 1, 1979), 175(9) :1000-1 @ San Diego Zoo

5. Fagan, David A., **"Dental Equipment & Instrumentation and Its Relationship to Veterinary Dental Care,"** *Collected Proceedings of the American Association of Zoo Veterinarians* (Oct. 1979) Denver, Colorado @ San Diego Zoo and Wild Animal Park.

6. Fagan, David A., **"A Discussion of Endodontic Techniques in Carnivores,"** *Collected Proceedings of the American Association of Zoo Veterinarians* (Oct. 1979), Denver, Colorado @ San Diego Zoo and Wild Animal Park.

7. With J.E. Oosterhuis, DVM, **"Gingival Hyperplasia Induced by Diphenylhydantion in a Gorilla,"** *Journal of the American Veterinary Medical Association* (1979), Vol.175, No. 9, pgs. 960-961 @ San Diego Wild Animal Park

8. Fagan, David A., **"Diet Consistency and Periodontal Disease in Exotic Carnivores,"** *Collected Proceedings of the American Association of Zoo Veterinarians* (1980), Washington D.C.; and proceedings of the first annual Dr. Scholl Nutrition Conference - a conference on the nutrition of captive wild animals, Dec. 5 and 6 at Lincoln Park Zoological Gardens, Chicago, Illinois (with Q & As) @ San Diego Zoo

9. Fagan, David A., **"The Pathogenesis of Dental Disease In Carnivores,"** *Collected Proceedings of the American Association of Zoo Veterinarians* (1980), Washington D.C. @ San Diego Zoo.

10. Fagan, David A., **"Oral Disease in Avian Species,"** *Collected Proceedings of the American Association of Zoo Veterinarians* (1981), Seattle, Washington @ San Diego Zoo.

11. With K. Ensley, DVM; and Tim Reichard, DVM, **"Sialolithiasis In A Colobus Monkey,"** *Journal of the American Veterinary Medical Association* (1981) Vol. 179 @ San Diego Zoo.

12. Fagan, David A., **"Extraction of Elephant's Tooth Requires 4-hour Procedure,"** *Norden News* (1981) 56(3):36-37 @ San Diego Zoo.

13. Fagan, David A., **"Focal Palatine Erosion Associated with Dental Malocclusion in Captive Cheetahs,"** *Journal of Zoo Biology,*1:295-310, with H.M. Fitch (1982) @ San Diego Zoo.

14. Fagan, David A., **"Veterinary Dentistry: Preserving Exotic Animals through Clini-**

cal Care, Research, Education and Teamwork," *Journal of the American Dental Students Association, Dentistry 83*, (Oct. 1983) @ Marine World-Africa, USA Redwood City, California

15. With G.W. Ellison, DVM; T.W. Mulligan, DVM; and R.K. Tugend, DVM, "**A Double Reposition Flap Technique for the Repair of Recurrent Oronasal Fistulas in Dogs,**" Journal of American Hospital Association (1986) 22 (6), pgs 803-808, @ Main Street Animal Hospital, San Diego.

16. Fagan, David A. "**Diagnosis and Treatment Planning, Veterinary Clinics of North America, Small Animal Practice,**" (Sep. 16, 1986) (5):pgs 785-99 @ San Diego Zoo and Wild Animal Park.

17. With Christine V. Fiorello, MS; James E. Oosterhuis, DVM; Helena Fitch-Snyder, and Janet E. Fagan, "**Use of CT Imaging and Three-dimensional Color Reconstruction for Comparison of Cranial Anatomy and Density in Captive and Wild Cheetahs (*Acinonyx jubatus*),**" *Collected Proceedings of the American Association of Zoo Veterinarians* (1997) @ San Diego Zoo and Wild Animal Park.

18. With J.E. Kirkman and J.E. Oosterhuis, "**A 25-year Review of the Expanding Field of Exotic Animal Oral Health Care - Veterinary Dentistry,**" *Journal of Veterinary Dentistry* (Sep. 1998), Vol. 15, No.3, pgs. 117-128.

19. With J.E. Oosterhuis, DVM, "**A One-Step Procedure to Repair a Class III Fracture (Exposed Pulpal Tissue) of Any Continuously Growing Tooth or Tusk,**" *Proceedings of the American Association of Zoo Veterinarians* (1998) @ San Diego Wild Animal Park.

20. With J.E. Oosterhuis, and A. Roocroft, "**Significant Dental Disease in Elephants,**" *Proceedings of the 39th International Symposium on Diseases of Zoo and Wild Animals*, (May1999), Vienna, Austria.

20. With K. May, DVM; and J.H.S. Simon, DDS, "**Understanding Pathologic Equine Dental Resorption Associated with Trauma,**" *Proceedings of the Veterinary Dental Forum* (Nov. 1999) Baltimore, Maryland.

21. With J.E. Oosterhuis, DVM, "**A Dental Extraction Site Management Protocol Utilizing a Synthetic Bone Graft Particulate Technique,**" *Proceedings of the American Association of Zoo Veterinarians* (Oct. 1999), Columbus, Ohio.

22. With J.H.S. Simon, DDS; K.Benirschke, MD; and A. Roocroft, "**Elephant Dental Pulp Tissue: Where Are the Nerves?**" *Journal of Veterinary Dentistry* (Dec. 1999), Vol. 16 No. 4 @ San Diego Wild Animal Park.

23. With M.S. Edwards,Ph.D.; and J.E. Oosterhuis, D.V.M, "**Oral Disease and Its Impact upon Systemic Health in Spite of the Diet Consumed,**" *Proceedings of the Comparative Nutrition Society Biennial Symposium* (Aug. 2000) @ Asilomar Conference Center, Pacific Grove, California.

24. Fagan, David A., "**Focal Palatine Erosion - A Historical Review and the Implications of Current Research,**" *Proceedings of the FELID Taxon Advisory Group (TAG) & S.S.P. Meeting (2000)* @ Riverbanks Zoo, Columbia, South Carolina.

25. With M.S. Edwards, Ph.D., "**Influence of Diet Consistency on Periodontal Disease in Captive Carnivores,**" *Proceedings of The 6th International Small Felid Workshop* (May 2001) @ San Juan, Costa Rica.

26. With J.E. Oosterhuis, DVM; and A. Roocroft, "**Gefangenschaftskrankheiten - Captivity Disorders In Elephants - Impacted Molars and Broken Tusks,**" Der Zoologische Garten, 71 (2001) 5, S. 281-303 @ Vienna.

27. Fagan, David A., "**The Relationship of Oral Disease to The Systemic Health of Felids,**" *Proceedings of the 1st Wild Cats Technical Meeting and Workshop*, Centro Brasileiro para Conservacao de Felinos Neotropicals (2001) @ Sao Paulo, Brazil.

28. With A. E. Bicknese, "**Low Dose Doxycycline Treatment to Control Periodontal Disease in Multiple Primate Species - A Preliminary Report,**" *Collected Proceedings of the American Association of Zoo Veterinarians* (Oct. 2002 Dental Symposium, Milwaukee, Wisconsin).

29. With J.E. Oosterhuis, DVM, "**A Dental Extraction Site Management Protocol Utilizing a Synthetic Bone Graft Particulate Technique,**" *Proceedings of the American Association of Zoo Veterinarians* (Oct. 2002 Dental Symposium, Milwaukee, Wisconsin). Presented to dental consultants working with the zoo veterinarians.

30. With J.E. Oosterhuis, DVM, "**Lumpy Jaw - Another Perspective,**" *Collected Proceedings of the American Association of Zoo Veterinarians* (Oct. 2002 Dental Symposium, Milwaukee, Wisconsin) @ San Diego Wild Animal Park.

31. With Rose Borkowski, DVM; Paul Wollenman, DVM; Jan Bellows, DVM, Dipl ACVD, Dipl ABVP; "**Health Assessment, Medical and Dental Interventions for a Group of 33 Chimpanzees (*Pan troglodytes*),**" *Collected Proceedings of the American Association of Zoo Veterinarians* (2004) @ Lion Country Safari, Loxahatchee, FL.

32. With J.E. Oosterhuis, DVM; and K.Benirschke, MD; "**Lumpy Jaw in Exotic Hoof Stock - a Histopathological Analysis,**" *Journal of Zoo and Wildlife Medicine* (2005), 36(1): 36-43, @ San Diego Wild Animal Park.

33. With B. Bicknese, DVM, "**Chronic Low Dose Doxycycline as a Treatment for Periodontal Disease in Primates,**" *Collected Proceedings of the American Association of Zoo Veterinarians* (Oct. 2005), Omaha, Nebraska @ San Diego Zoo.

34. With Nancy C. Boedeker, DVM; David Hager, DVM, MD, Dipl ACVR; Allan P. Pessier, DVM, Dipl ACVP; and Patrick J. Morris, DVM, Dipl ACZM, "**Management of Severe Dental Disease in an Indochinese Tiger,**" *Collected Proceedings of the American Association of Zoo Veterinarians* (2005), Omaha, Nebraska @ San Diego Zoo.

35. With Wm. Kirk Suedmeyer, DVM, Dipl ACZM; Jim Oosterhuis, DVM; George Kollias, DVM, PhD, Dipl ACZM; Bill Hornoff, DVM; John Dodam, DVM; PhD, Dipl ACVA; and Heidi Shafford, DVM, "**Elephant Restraint Device Assisted Anesthesia in an African Elephant (*Loxodonta africana*),**" *Collected Proceedings of the American Association of Zoo Veterinarians* (2005) @Kansas City Zoological Park.

36. With K. Benirschke, MD, "**Predator Eaten By Its Prey – An interesting Case Report,**" *Journal of Natural History* (2006) @ San Diego.

37. With Duane E. Ullrey, PhD, "**Understanding the Relationships Between Species-Specific Dietary Requirements, Oral Disease, and the Systemic Health of Animals Held in Captive Environs,**" begun in 2003 @ San Diego Zoo, finally published. Dec. 2008 as "**Dental Malocclusion in a Course-haired Wombat (*Vombatus ursinus*),**" *Journal of Veterinary Dentistry*, Vol. 25, No. 4, pg. 240-44.

38. With Suedmeyer, Wm. Kirk, DVM, Dipl ACZM; Jim Oosterhuis, DVM; and others, "**Surgical Correction (Apicoectomy) of Molar Dental Plate Sequestrum in an African Elephant (*Loxodonta africana*),**" *Collected Proceedings of the American Association of Zoo Veterinarians* (2007) @ Kansas City Zoo.

39. With Elizabeth J. Bicknese, DVM, MPVM; and Nadine Lamberski, DVM, Dipl.

ACZM, **"A 'Cyclic' Regiment of Low-dose Doxycycline to Treat Periodontal Disease in a Chacoan Peccary (*Catagonus wagneri*), Red Pandas (*Ailurus fulgens*), and Bat-Eared Foxes (*Otocyon megalotis megalotis*),"** *Collected Proceedings of the American Association of Zoo Veterinarians* (Oct. 2008), @ San Diego Zoo.

40. With Shawn Johnson, DVM, MPVM; James Oosterhuis, DVM; Eric Jensen, DVM, **"Advanced Technologies and Methodologies in Diagnosis and Treatment of Endodontic Disease in California Sea Lions,"** *Proceedings of the American Association of Zoo Veterinarians* (Oct. 2008), @ U.S.Navy Marine Mammal Program, Pt. Loma.

Appendix C
List of protocol development cases

Following is a partial list of species treated by the author with Dr. Jim Oosterhuis at the Wild Animal Park, and Dr. Beth Bicknese at the San Diego Zoo for a period of five-plus years, while developing a more effective clinical protocol for the treatment of "lumpy jaw" infections. The protocol is know as the "Beta-Infusion Technique with Compound Apicoectomy." In 2013 / 2014 the protocol was further refined with the addition of the 810nm Diode LASER to help facilitate the decontamination of the osteomyelitis and provide biostimulation of the tissues to promote more rapid wound resolution and healing.

Camelus dromedarius - Dromedary, Arabian camel
Elaphodus cephalophus - Western tufted deer
Muntiacus muntjak - Indian muntjac
Mazama americana - Mexican red brocket
Pudu mephistophiles - Northern pudu
Antilocapra americana - Pronghorn
Aepyceros melampus - Black faced impala
Connochaetes gnou - White-tailed gnu, and back wildebeest
Damaliscus pygargus - Bontebok
Antidorcas marsupialis - Springbok
Gazella dama ruficollis - Addra gazelle
Gazella dorcas - Dorcas gazelle
Gazella leptoceros - Slender-horned gazelle
Gazella rufifrons - Red-fronted gazelle
Gazella soemmerringi – Soemmerring's gazelle
Gazella thomsonii – Thomson's gazelle
Neotragus moschatus - Zulu Suni
Tragelaphus eurycerus - Bongo
Tragelaphus spekei - Sitatunga
Ammotragus lervia - Aoudad, Barbary sheep
Capra caucasica - West Caucasian tur
Capra ibex - Alpine ibex
Equus caballus - Oldenburger black stallion.
Hemitragus jemlahicus - Himalayan tahr
Ovis aries - Mouflon
Ovis canadensis - Bighorn sheep
Oryx dammah - Scimitar-horned oryx
Loxodonta africana – African elephant

Additional general background information concerning some of these species is found on the Ultimate Ungulate website at www.ultimateungulate.com.

Appendix D
Some interesting readings

Veterinary Dentistry Text Books

Small Animal Dentistry, by Colin E. Harvey and Peter P. Emily
Veterinary Dentistry: Principles and Practice, by Robert Wiggs and Heidi Lobprise

All four of these authors are original officers and founders of the American Association of Veterinary Dentistry. All are recognized as leaders in the field. Colin Harvey is a veterinarian and was editor of the *Journal of Veterinary Dentistry*. Pete Emily is another dentist.

Books by Individuals who work with animals

Vanishing Animals, by Andy Warhol and Kurt Benirschke
My Wild World, by Joan Embery with Denise Demong
Appointment at the Ends of the World: Memoirs of a Wildlife Vet, by William B. Karesh, DVM
Monkeys on the Interstate, by Jack Hanna, director of The Columbus Zoo
The Best of Friends, by John Aspinall, gambler and owner of Port Lympne Zoo
A Bevy of Beasts, by Gerald Durrell, naturalist and founder of the Jersey Zoo
Blanca and Arusha: Tales of Two Big Cats, by Georgeanne Irvine
(George is an old friend, and Arusha is the same cat discussed in Chapter 10. Hers is a children's book.)

Miscellaneous Interesting Animal Books

Zoo 2000: A Look Beyond the Bars, by Jeremy Cherfas
The Animal Smugglers and Other Wildlife Traders, by John Nichol
Sex in Nature, by Chris Catton and Jim Gray
Hard Green: Saving the Environment from the Environmentalists, by Peter Huber
Keepers of the Kingdom: The New American Zoo, by Michael Nichols
Shadow of the Salmon: A Fly Fisherman's Quest for the Vanishing Wild Salmon, by C. Barr Taylor
In a Dark Wood: The Fight Over Forests and the Rising Tyranny of Ecology, by Alston Chase

Made in the USA
San Bernardino, CA
30 March 2015